D1024896

Reading, Writing, and the Hickory Stick

The Appalling Story
of Physical and Psychological Abuse
in American Schools

IRWIN A. HYMAN

Foreword by Phil Donahue

Lexington Books

D.C. Heath and Company • Lexington, Massachusetts • Toronto

Library of Congress Cataloging-in-Publication Data

Hyman, Irwin A.
Reading, writing, and the hickory stick: the appalling story of
physical and psychological abuse in American schools / Irwin A.
Hyman.
p.   cm.
ISBN 0-669-21990-8 (alk. paper)
1. School discipline—United States.   2. Corporal punishment—
United States.   3. Child abuse—United States—Prevention.
4. Rewards and punishments in education.   I. Title.
LB3012.2.H96   1990
371.5'42'0973—dc20
89-48071
CIP

Published simultaneously in Canada
Printed in the United States of America
Casebound International Standard Book Number: 0-669-21990-8
Library of Congress Catalog Card Number: 89-48071

The paper used in this publication meets the minimum requirements of American
National Standard for Information Sciences—Permanence of Paper for Printed
Library Materials, ANSI Z39.48-1984. ∞™

The first and last numbers below indicate year and number of printing.

90 91 92 10 9 8 7 6 5 4 3 2 1

*To Susan, Rachel,
and Adah*

Contents

Foreword

Phil Donahue

H IAM Ginott, the late, highly respected child psychologist, often told the story of a six-foot father bending over to strike his five-year-old son so that "you will learn to pick on someone your own size!" What is not so funny is that millions of American adults refuse to recognize not only the hypocrisy of corporal punishment of children but also the brutalizing results of this medieval practice. Our nation is still inhabited by adults who use a folded newspaper to train a pet animal but exercise no such forethought when they physically discipline a young child.

In this well-researched book, Irwin Hyman details the inefficiency and pain of this anachronistic child-rearing strategy. Although increasing numbers of Americans are refusing to sanction this practice on a local level, it may also be true that if we promoted a national referendum on whether teachers should be allowed to take recalcitrant students to the woodshed, we might win.

Our parents spanked us, so many of us quite naturally spank our children. It is a legacy passed from generation to generation and serves as the rationale for investing local school boards with this obscene power. We use the Bible to justify our behavior, which may bespeak an insecurity and guilt on the part of those who practice it. Something, inside even the most enthusiastic corporal punishers must be saying, "This is wrong." Dr. Hyman believes that the subtle voice of conscience is right, and he offers more than a little grim evidence to support his enlightened position.

Although it is true that countless young people grew up surrounded by parents and teachers who did not spare the rod and "turned out" just fine, the evidence offered in this book demonstrates that sanctioned classroom use of corporal punishment makes it much easier for adults with short fuses to move far beyond "prudent paddling" (whatever that means) and into punitive behavior that is often mean and out of control.

Exorcising this widespread feature from our culture is a long and difficult process. This book makes a powerful contribution toward that end and also addresses the equally serious problem of psychological maltreatment of American school children. Helping Dr. Hyman and others achieve the goal of nurturing all students is no less than an act of love for our young, who should never be subjected to the humiliation, the loss of self-esteem, and the bewilderment of being physically and mentally abused by older and presumably wiser human beings who appear to be less respectful of children than they are of the family dog.

Acknowledgments

I WANT to acknowledge the courage of the Gaspersohn family in their fight against corporal punishment in North Carolina schools. Shelly is the first survivor of school abuse to be evaluated by me. My feelings for her and her family resulted in the transformation of an academic interest in corporal punishment to my emotional commitment to the cause.

This book was made possible by my students of school psychology. Their dedication to improve school discipline and understand why parents and teachers maltreat children resulted in much of the research quoted in this book. I am especially indebted to Eileen McDowell, who helped establish the National Center for the Study of Corporal Punishment and Alternatives in the Schools. Her tragic and premature death ended the career of a true child advocate. I am also indebted to many other devoted students including Loretta Alderman, Dave Bogacki, Jacqueline Clarke, John D'Allesandro, Andrea Fina, Arnold Farley, Elizabeth Gasiewski, Angela Jones, Barbara Keane, Dolores Lally, Chuck Lambert, Naomi Lennox, Amy Mishkin, Peggy O'-Grady, Maryann Pokalo, Bill Russell, Beth Sofer, Andrea Stern, Bobbi Witkowski, and Wendy Zelikoff. They spent many hours conducting research and volunteering time at the Center.

I wish to express appreciation to my wife, Susan, who spent long hours proofreading and suggesting changes. She gave up many days of summer vacation so I could complete this book, sacrificing much of her own precious time to relieve me of many pressures so that I could continue to write and work at my regular employment.

I wish to thank Bob Pressman, David Clauss, Renny Deese, Dan Hedges, John Roessler, and all of the other dedicated attorneys who have litigated to eliminate corporal punishment in the schools. Special thanks to Judge Charles Brown for giving up part of his summer vacation to read the manuscript and offer helpful suggestions about the legal discussions presented herein. Special thanks also go to Charles Woodford for his support and encouragement and for editing the initial drafts of this book.

Last, but certainly not least, I want to thank Adah Maurer and Alan Reitman, who helped establish the National Center and encouraged and supported my efforts for over a decade. Without them this book would not have been possible. Thanks are also due to James Wallerstein, whose financial support and advice were crucial in the first five years of the Center's functioning.

Introduction

I T WAS a gloomy, overcast December day in rural North Carolina as I sat looking into the blue eyes of a young woman who seemed to be a person of compassion and warmth. Of all the twelve faces I had scrutinized on this particular jury, this was the face of a person who would understand. Here was a woman, perhaps a young mother, who could appreciate the pain and suffering of a seventeen year old who had been severely bruised by a high school coach twice her size and strength. Here was someone who would be sympathetic to the plight of a teenager crying out in pain and pleading for an end to a vicious paddling. Surely she would have a powerful reaction to the descriptions of humiliation, pain, and fear that were identical to the descriptions I have heard rape victims give as they talk about the violation of their bodies and the withering of their spirits.

I was wrong. That woman and eleven other citizens of Harnett County, North Carolina, decided that it was not unreasonable force for an adult male educator to beat severely a teenaged honor student for the single disciplinary infraction of her school days: Shelly Gaspersohn had cut school for a day. Corporal punishment, the infamous last resort of educators, was hardly the last resort that an enlightened educator in the 1980s could think of to punish a student with an exemplary background.

Was Shelly such a hard-core case that extreme measures were necessary to "teach" her never to cut school again? Did the jury, under state law, have to decide that it was reasonable for a grown man to smack a fully mature teenaged girl's behind so badly as to produce bruises?

Some would argue that what happened to Shelly Gaspersohn could happen only in a place such as Harnett County, a stronghold of archconservative Jessie Helms. Is this a backwater of the American judicial system—a dirt-poor rural area where people do not know any better, a place where child abuse by educators is tolerated because they believe that God commands that sparing the rod is a sin? Or is Harnett County, as represented by the jury, a place where tradition rules over common sense and contemporary knowledge about education and learning?

Although North Carolina shared a unique status with Ohio and Florida at the time of the trial on December 12, 1983, by 1989 it stood alone. It is the only state that does not allow local school boards to stop their own employees from hitting students. Belief in spanking was further supported when, in September of 1989, the North Carolina Day Care Commission rescinded the ban on spanking in day care centers across the state. The citizens of Harnett County; reflecting state tradition as represented by their courts, their educators, and their media, had spoken. Their reasoning convinced jurists up through the appeal system all the way to the Supreme Court of North Carolina.

Although many citizens of North Carolina defend hitting with more vigor than others, they are little different from millions of other Americans who believe that spanking, smacking, swatting, and demeaning children are necessary for good discipline. For many, a flick of the hand against a child's bottom is an automatic reaction to misbehavior. They are no different from the hundreds of millions of people who state, "I was hit when I was a kid, and it didn't do me any harm." Also, they are not much different from citizens in Texas, Florida, and Arkansas who support the highest rates of corporal punishment in American schools.

It seems almost bizarre that in an advanced and supposedly civilized nation, there should be a need to write this book about child abuse in schools. Yet as of September 1989, thirty-one state legislatures and the U.S. Supreme Court have refused to stop teachers from inflicting physical pain on school children. No states have taken active measures to alleviate the far more pervasive crime of psychological abuse in the schools.

For me, this book serves several purposes. It is the story of the millions of Shelly Gaspersohns who each year are exposed to primitive pedagogy. They are victims of deeply rooted traditions stemming from Calvinistic and Puritan beliefs that children are "imps of darkness" (Radbill 1974). It is about what Philip

Greven in his fascinating book *The Protestant Temperament* (1977) calls the evangelical ambivalence whether children are "embryo-angels or infant fiends."

This book is written within the context of an unnecessary climate of psychological and physical violence that pervades the lives of American children and adolescents. It is estimated that over 1.5 million are abused and neglected each year by their primary caretakers. Every day on television many children view repeated murders, rapes, karate chops, and cartoon mayhem. Despite convincing evidence about the detrimental effects of violence on commercial television specifically aimed at child audiences, the attempts by child advocates to bring about change have been largely futile.

This book is my attempt to talk to people interested in the facts about the history, practice, and alternatives to physical and verbal assaults of American students. It is for people who want to know what to do about the problem.

Why I Wrote This Book

Frequently after giving a speech or workshop, I have the opportunity to talk informally with sponsors and participants. They often ask why I have spent over thirteen years in intensive research, scholarship, and advocacy about corporal punishment and psychological maltreatment of school children. Their questions have helped me to focus on two major reasons. The first lies in an experience common to many Americans.

My earliest memory of school is of a traumatic event. I was a very active first grader. In fact, using contemporary terminology, I would probably have been described as hyperactive. But in 1941 active kids were judged as just bad. My teacher (I long ago forgot her name) had her own method for making "bad" kids sit still. Whenever I got antsy, she stood behind my chair, grabbed the desk with both hands, and attempted to join the chair with the desk. This task would have been easier if I had not been sitting in the chair, thereby preventing its amalgamation with the desk. To me, the apparent purpose was to see how much she could compress my body before I cried "uncle."

The outcome of this punishment was predictable, even by

enlightened opinion in the early 1940s: I hated the teacher, I hated school, I avoided school as much as possible, and I was left back in the first grade.

Fortunately, my parents moved to a better school the following year. My new first-grade teacher realized, among other possible causes of my hyperactive behavior, that I could not see the blackboard because I was nearsighted. Glasses corrected the problem. Nevertheless, because of that early experience, I developed a deep and abiding anger toward punitive, authoritarian, mean-spirited teachers.

As a former discipline problem myself, as an elementary school teacher, and a school psychologist, I continued to be fascinated with teachers' use and overuse of punishments that were obviously ineffective. There is little question that my own experiences working with students and teachers contributed to the development of this book.

One might ask if this book is written objectively or whether it is a one-sided, unfair diatribe against our educational system. The answer is yes and no. Yes, this book brings together objective, scientific, data-based facts about punitive approaches to education. Yes, it is one-sided because the amount of research favoring positive techniques of discipline is one-sided. But no, this book is not unfair in the light of reason. Although I have confessed my own motivations to pursue a lifetime career as a student of child and adolescent discipline, I promise to avoid ranting in most of the text.

Besides my personal history, there are other factors important to the development of this book. In the early 1970s, when I was editor of *The School Psychologist*, I received a pleading letter from a woman in San Francisco. For many years, Adah Maurer, a retired school psychologist, had been waging a one-person war against corporal punishment in American schools. Not many people were paying attention, and she pleaded with me to publish some of her writings. This was just the type of child advocacy material I was looking for, and I was happy to help her. Like most other professionals in the country, however, I saw many more pressing issues. Child poverty and malnutrition, students' First Amendment rights, and child abuse in the home were issues around which the growing child advocacy movement was coalescing. But Ms. Maurer persisted.

I knew that Alan Reitman of the American Civil Liberties Union, Ms. Maurer, and others had established a national committee seeking to eliminate corporal punishment in the schools. I knew they had held a national conference and figured that in a few years they would accomplish their goals. After all, the 1970s were a time of great change. In those times of expanded programs for children, why should it be difficult to convince teachers to stop beating children. How wrong I was.

I did what all other good academics do in response to the problem of corporal punishment: I wrote an article—or, more correctly, a student and I wrote an article on the role of school psychologists as child advocates. We described how natural it would be for school psychologists to work against corporal punishment. Little did I know that that article would eventually shape over a third of my professional career.

In 1975, Adah Maurer and Alan Reitman asked if I would be willing to take over the role of the somewhat moribund National Committee to Abolish Corporal Punishment in the Schools. About a year later, with significant help from the American Psychological Association, several small grants, and participation by a number of professionals, laypeople, and organizations, the National Center for the Study of Corporal Punishment and Alternatives in the Schools (NCSCPAS) was founded at Temple University. Not including specific research grants or projects, the operating budget of the center has never exceeded $4,000 per year.

National Center for the Study of Corporal Punishment and Alternatives in the Schools

In many ways, this book is the story of the work of NCSCPAS. Almost all of the case studies, the research, the litigation, and personal anecdotes flow from the activities of those who work at or with the center.

The NCSCPAS is the only center of its kind in the world; it is unique as a center for research, scholarship, clinical investigation, the advocacy concerning corporal punishment and, more recently, psychological maltreatment in the schools. It is not unique in terms of being underfunded and sparsely staffed. We may have a record of some sort for almost totally failing to attract the interest and support of foundations. Just when we began to elicit some interest and grant monies from the government, President Reagan was elected. The conservative, right-wing minions who descended upon the federal bureaucracy in the Reagan administration were hardly sympathetic to our efforts, especially since the president called for a return to "good old-fashioned discipline."

The NCSCPAS exists because of the largesse of the School Psychology Program and the College of Education at Temple University. Temple provides space, telephones, scholarships, and assistantships for student staff. The center has six basic functions.

As a *repository* of information about corporal punishment, the center serves as a unique function. Since its inception, it has maintained an indexed file of press clippings on corporal punishment; copies of all state legislation and progress toward eliminating it; letters, activities, and opinions; and papers related to important legal issues and cases. A rather large collection of alternatives to corporal punishment is an important part of the holdings of the center.

Scholarship is a valued activity at the center. Besides aiding scholars needing historical and legal information, staff frequently write, publish, and present on a wide variety of issues related to discipline. The center has hosted visiting scholars from all over the United States and a number of foreign countries.

Research is probably the most important activity of the staff at the center. Although initial efforts focused only on school-related corporal punishment, studies have expanded to include issues of child, institutional, sexual, and psychological abuse. Staff research and integration of the work of others has been the major source of social science data used in most movements to abolish corporal punishment in local school districts and state legislatures.

Consciousness raising has been an important activity in helping to change public attitudes. Center activities have been reported extensively in the media.

Workshops and speeches have been offered all over America to organizations, schools, mental-health centers, institutions, and other groups. Most workshops help parents and professionals to learn positive methods of preventing misbehavior and effective methods of punishment that are not abusive and counterproductive.

Social policy changes have been sought through direct contact with politicians. This has included testimony before state legislatures and Congress. In addition, ten years of expert testimony in litigation has resulted in legal strategies that have brought about an increasing number of wins for abused children who sue schools.

New frontiers of punitiveness in schools and other institutions, including the home, are constantly explored. As a result, center staff have pioneered research and approaches to the prevention of psychological abuse in the schools.

Almost everything written in this book flows from the work of the center. Everything that is factual in nature is documented there. Let us now turn to the young girl mentioned at the beginning of this book.

The Story of Shelly Gaspersohn

No single story can reflect the true magnitude of punitiveness in our schools. Facts and figures will be discussed and are available from the NCSCPAS, but we need to hear from the victims. Although I refer to them as victims, many are survivors who have managed to overcome their victimization. Others continue to suffer symptoms resulting from their punishment throughout their lives.

I began by describing my feelings as I sat in the witness stand for the first time in a case involving corporal punishment. I failed to convince the jury of the damage that six vicious swats caused, but I came to know a courageous family that wanted only to protect their children and others from abuse in schools. As the story unfolds in succeeding chapters, it describes the travails and triumphs of the Gaspersohn family. It may shock you. I also hope it, and the others presented throughout this book, will move you to action in your community and your state.

If you or your children have never experienced corporal punishment in schools, count your blessings. If you or your children have never experienced psychological abuse, you share that blessing with fewer than half of your fellow citizens. Just because it happened to you or because you or your children seem to survive these practices, it does not mean they are all right.

The long-term effects of these practices take a terrible toll on both victims and survivors and on society. These practices do harm to our collective psyche as we become more indifferent to pain and suffering. If we cannot prevent educators, major caregivers in our society, from psychologically and physically battering children, how can we as a nation stop the unacceptably high rates of child abuse? What you will read in this book reflects the reality that we accept a climate that promotes and extols the use of force and aggression to solve problems.

On Behalf of Good Teachers

Some who read this book will see it as pure "teacher bashing." I have already admitted that the book is one-sided and is an attack on the use of corporal punishment and psychological maltreatment in education. In the sense that I attack educators who practice and/or support these approaches, I am guilty of bashing.

Some might consider this a downbeat book because it focuses on a depressing topic. The book's message would be hopelessly diluted, however, if I balanced every horrifying story with a narrative of great teaching. But for every educator I attack, there are hundreds of hard-working, dedicated, humane ones who will never receive the recognition and rewards that are due.

Most of my near relatives have spent their lives as educators. Following graduation from college, I taught elementary school for four years and have been associated with schools ever since. My wife, my sister, and my brother-in-law were teachers. My parents and their families had high regard for most educators, as I still do. In reading this book, keep in mind that it is not an indictment of a profession but a plea for change.

1

Good Old-Fashioned Discipline

W HACK! Smack! The long, arcing swing of the paddle ended abruptly against her behind. Her legs were spread as she leaned over with both hands tightly gripping the edge of the counter. Her thin blue pants offered little protection from the earnest efforts of the man with broad shoulders and powerful arms. Her blue eyes filled with tears as she cried out in anger and rage.

In her seventeen years she had never experienced such excruciating pain. In reaction to the trauma, and unknown to her, her uterus began to contract with increasing force as the blows struck her buttocks. The paddling occurred during normal menstruation, and she would later need medication to stem the heavy menstrual hemorrhaging.

The short break since the last two swats offered little relief from the mounting pain. The cries of the other girls and the stone-faced demeanor of the powerful disciplinarian increased her feelings of outrage. The situation was hardly relieved by what seemed like gallows humor from the other man who entered the scene. Through her tears she heard him say, "save one for me," and then giggled at what appeared to be his self-appreciated cleverness. He later denied this, but then, it is easier to believe the master than the victim, whose perceptions were distorted by pain. But it was clear that he did not object to what was happening.

Although she was a physically and emotionally mature seventeen year old, she could only think, "I want my mother." She ruefully remembered that her parents had warned her not to allow herself to be degraded. Her later descriptions of the incident were similar to those of rape victims: "I felt humiliated and violated. That and the pain caused me to start to cry. I never thought anything could hurt so much."

This description is not from a pornographic novel. Nor is it a description of the experiences of the punishment of a young woman in a boarding school in Victorian England or of the torture of a young, attractive political prisoner by sadistic jailers whose final goal is rape. It is, instead, a true account of discipline in a contemporary high school in North Carolina. The paddler was coach Glenn Varney, disciplinarian at Dunn High School. The witness was vice-principal Roger Lee McKoy. The victim was Shelly Gaspersohn, a student who, like all other students in American schools, should not be beaten in the name of education.

Not everyone agrees with me. Twelve jurors in Harnett County, North Carolina, acquitted Coach Varney. Like many other Americans, they probably felt that since they had been hit as children and they turned out "all right," spanking cannot be so bad. If you can't take a little humiliation, how can you deal with the real world? How many times have I heard this rationalization? But even if they had been against the beating of a mature young woman, they may have felt constrained by North Carolina law in determining what is reasonable when a grown man hits a woman with a wooden paddle.

The Survivors

The Gaspersohns are warm, loving parents who moved from Michigan to rural North Carolina, where they bought a small factory. Both parents might be described as politically moderate, deeply religious, and devoted to their four children.

The Gaspersohns are not permissive parents or radicals in any sense. On some few occasions, they had spanked their children, including Shelly. But their discipline was based on love, patience, mutual respect, and persuasion. Their child-rearing practices were based on New Testament concepts of forgiveness and love rather than the single Old Testament concept of "spare the rod," which seemed to pervade the community where they lived.

Shelly, the youngest of four daughters, was an honor student in her senior year. She had no record of disciplinary infractions. Rather, she was a considerate, well-behaved, deeply religious young woman. She was an accomplished flutist and a member of the all-state band. She enjoyed school and wanted to be a music teacher. She was hardly someone who would require the infamous "last resort."

Shelly committed one indiscretion, common to seniors: she and Renee Bynum skipped school for a day. Not being an accomplished truant, she was caught. How was it that Shelly, a girl who never broke school rules, committed a sin worthy of a flogging? Here is what she said under oath during courtroom testimony in response to Renny Deese, her attorney:

> Q. Have you ever skipped school before, prior to December 1st?
> A. No, sir.
> Q. . . . Why is it that you skipped school . . .
> A. Well, I rode to school every morning with Renee. [That day] . . . she asked that I go with her to find her boyfriend . . . and we rode around [all day] looking for her boyfriend.

The girls were offered the alternative of corporal punishment or a five-day in-school suspension. In-school suspension at Dunn High School meant sitting with other punishees all day in a monitored room. Theoretically teachers from all classes provide assignments for each day, but teacher cooperation in providing schoolwork is inconsistent. Often students are left with long periods of time in which there are no work assignments. Shelly and Renee accepted the suspension, partly because of the reputation of the disciplinarian, Glenn Varney, the strapping, paddle-swinging assistant principal and football coach.

After several days of in-school suspension, Shelly became worried about keeping up with her precalculus class because she was not being supplied with assignments. School policy allows suspended students to volunteer for three licks with the paddle for each day of parole from suspension. Shelly, Renee, and some other students in suspension volunteered to take their licks from Varney in order to return to regular class. (The defense, the judge in the case, and the North Carolina Supreme Court pointed out that Shelly "asked" for the beating. It is clear that she had no way of knowing how severely she would be hit, but it is clear that other punishments were available by the school's own rules. Her motivation for the request was to get back to her schoolwork, not to receive swift punishment so she could return to a life of crime.)

When Shelly arrived home after the beating, her mother was horrified by the large welts on Shelly's buttocks. An examining physician became so enraged that he filed child abuse charges against Coach Varney. But in North Carolina and many other states, teachers were (and still are) immune to child abuse charges, so the child abuse authorities had no recourse. (Ironically, if Shelly's parents had administered the beating, they would have been liable to charges.)

The Gaspersohns' complaints to the principal, superintendent, and school board fell on deaf—and hostile—ears despite the fact that the beating left bruises that lasted three weeks and caused menstrual hemorrhaging and long-lasting emotional trauma. Finally the Gaspersohns hired Renny Deese, a lawyer devoted to civil rights issues, and filed suit against the school and Varney. They made two claims. The first was that "Glenn Varney's violent and forceful striking of the plaintiff . . . required . . . [her] . . . to undergo medical treatment, limit her activities and general enjoyment of life." Compensatory damages of $5,000 were requested. The second was that Varney willfully and maliciously struck Shelly, with the approval of the Harnett County School Board. Here $50,000 in punitive damages was claimed.

The Setting and the Judge

The trial took place on December 12, 1983, before Judge James Pou Bailey. I was there because I had conducted an extensive psychological evaluation of Shelly and was to serve as an expert witness.

Judge Bailey was a rather rotund gentleman with a distinct southern drawl and manner that suggested, despite the robes, he was really just a good old boy. His familiarity and humor seemed to be expressed for the benefit of the defendants. He was more stern with and certainly indicated some distaste for the legal objections and strategies of the plaintiff. He seemed unwilling or unable to understand my credentials as a licensed psychologist trained in school and child psychology at a major university.

My feelings of dismay were intensified by his charge to the jury. He discounted my expertise by ignoring my clinical training, research, and practice by indicating I had "a number of courses in educational psychology." And although he indicated that the defendant's expert witness was licensed to practice psychiatry, he neglected to mention that I was licensed to practice psychology.

The problems we faced seem typical of what is wrong with the justice system in many rural areas. In my experience, I have observed a typical scenario: a de facto ruling oligarchy in which the community leaders are associated by family and social and religious ties. The local officials—including judges, lawyers, superintendents, law enforcement officers, and prosecutors—because of their close ties, are able to influence policy to a greater extent than they might where there are strong coalitions of opposition. Generally these officials back a conservative agenda that, I believe, is resistant to the rights of children.

The Helms Connection

At the time of the trial, I did not know much about the leadership in the community of Dunn. I was more concerned with accurately presenting the clinical information than attending to conversation about the community. I remember the Gaspersohns talking about connections between the judge and an unsympathetic editor of the local newspaper. They also commented on the editor's relationship to Senator Jesse Helms, well known for his support of far right religious ideology.

The connections became clear when I read *Hard Right: The Rise of Jesse Helms* by Ernest Furgurson, the chief of the *Baltimore Sun's* Washington bureau and a syndicated columnist. Furgurson describes the relationship between Pou Bailey and other members of the right-wing leadership of North Carolina, including Hoover Adams, publisher of the avowedly right-wing *Dunn Daily Record*; Thomas Ellis, a wealthy right-wing scion; and Helms.

In his first column as a writer for the *Tarheel Banker*, the house organ of the North Carolina Banker's Association, Helms touted his friend Pou Bailey. This was back in the 1950s when Bailey was counsel to the Banker's Association and hosted a poker club. In those early days, the members of the poker club were already beginning to become involved in right-wing political agendas.

Bailey, Ellis, Adams, and Helms became good friends when they worked together to defeat incumbent U.S. senator Frank Porter Graham in 1950. Graham, a former president of the University of North Carolina, presided over that institution's rise as one of the premier southern universities. His support of academic freedom, liberal education, and high-level research gnawed at the hearts of the truly conservative. His support for due process, intellectualism, and liberal thought angered those who represented the small town antielitism element in North Carolina. He represented the beginning of the national wave of liberal thought, the empowerment of trade unionism, and "the first threats to the old system of social and political segregation."

Helms and company supported Willis Smith against Graham in what has been described as the meanest Senate fight in North Carolina. (This was before Helms's recent battle with former governor Jim Hunt in 1984, which pitted the enlightened liberal element of North Carolina against the religious and political right.) The Helms quartet painted Graham as a communist menace who threatened to desegregate the workplace. He was pictured as a supporter of fair employment practices and a harbinger of racial strife. They appealed to the worst racial fears of the Deep South.

This is the background from which Judge Bailey emerged. His old friend, Hoover Adams, has been judged by other journalists as promoting a right wing and biased newspaper. Roy Parker, editor of the *Fayetteville Times,* said that Adams "made a career of being biased in favor of things he wants." Parker claims that Adams has "this wonderful attitude that 'everybody else is biased and I'm not.'"

Following the trial, one of Shelly's married sisters, in an unrelated event, complained about religious classes that were taught in the Dunn public schools. While the school's own attorney ruled that the classes were unconstitutional, Hoover Adam's paper led a campaign against cancelling the religion classes. Allegations against the Gaspersohns surely encouraged the threats they received against their personal safety. The Gaspersohns finally gave up their business and left Dunn.

Limiting the Testimony

During the trial, the examining physician was not allowed to testify that he had filed child abuse charges; moreover, the judge restricted other testimony in his charge to the jury. After a year and a half of careful preparation and research for the trial and three days of testimony, twelve men and women of Harnett County, North Carolina, rendered a verdict of "not guilty" after fifteen minutes of deliberation. They decided that Coach Varney had not used unreasonable force. Their decision supports the erroneous belief that educators cannot commit child abuse as long as they call it corporal punishment.

The Gaspersohns were radicalized by this experience. Unlike most other parents of children severely abused by educators, they had the financial and emotional resources to continue the fight in the courts. They appealed the case to the Supreme Court of North Carolina, where it was rejected.

Why was it rejected? The law in North Carolina states that "principals, teachers, substitute teachers, voluntary teachers, teachers' aides and assistants and student teachers may use *reasonable* [emphasis added] force in the exercise of" discipline. North Carolina is now the only state that has a statute forbidding local control of corporal punishment. Based on rulings from 1837 and 1904, North Carolina law holds that "no local board of education or district committee shall promulgate or continue in effect a rule, regulation or bylaw which prohibits the use of [corporal punishment]."

In 1837, in the case of *State v. Pendergast*, the state supreme court ruled that the whipping of a six- or seven-year-old girl can leave bruises and can be severe up to the point of causing "long lasting mischief." Therefore, any such beating must be inflicted "honestly in the performance of duty."

In their rejection of the appeal of the Gaspersohn jury decision, the contemporary Supreme Court of North Carolina was apparently loathe to base its decision solely on a nineteenth-century ruling and reached forward to the 1904 case of *Drum v. Miller* in which a child received serious injury as a result of his teacher's throwing a pencil that struck the child's eye. The court exonerated the teacher since the act was "not prompted by malice." Ignoring research, the current North Carolina Supreme Court agreed with the belief that corporal punishment furthers educational goals.

Could the jury or the judge be expected to challenge a legal interpretation of "reasonable force" based on knowledge and beliefs about children and education that were over a century old? These are issues we will explore in this book.

The Gaspersohns' views about children's rights were considered so radical that they were ostracized in their community. They moved to Greensboro, a city known for enlightened attitudes. Ms. Gaspersohn devotes a significant part of her time to eliminating corporal punishment in North Carolina schools. Shelly gave up any thought of teaching and studied electrical engineering instead. The injustice of the system and the associated psychological trauma had obliterated her desire to become part of the educational establishment. Meanwhile, cases of abuse of children in North Carolina, and many other states, continue. The response in most cases is the same as in Dunn.

What's the Problem?

- "All some kids need is a good swift kick in the pants!"
- "Sometimes you need to hit kids to get their attention."
- "If we don't have corporal punishment as a 'last resort' in the classroom, kids won't have anything to fear; they won't behave."
- "I was spanked when I was a kid, and it didn't do me any harm."
- "The Bible says, 'If you spare the rod you will spoil the child.'"
- "If parents use spanking at home, it's the only thing the kids understand in school. Teachers who don't do it are just too soft."

- "If you want a winning team, you have to instill fear of losing. It's necessary to humiliate kids when they get too cocky."

If you have never heard anyone make these statements, you probably did not grow up in America. In fact, if you were never spanked by your parents or swatted in school, you were either a perfect angel or one of the lucky ones. Spanking kids and psychologically assaulting them is as American as apple pie. But is it necessary?

Washington Irving's "Legend of Sleepy Hollow" relates the fictional story of Ichabod Crane, the skinny schoolmaster who wielded a birch switch. Although the story is fiction and meant to be funny, it reflects the reality of violence in colonial education. There was a constant struggle for power between teachers and students, and the rod of correction was often the equalizer. It worked until the students were big enough to overpower the teacher (which did happen on occasion). The stories of these struggles have become part of tradition and American humor concerning the punishment of errant children.

How many children first learned about school from the song that tells about

> *Reading and writing and arithmetic*
> *Learned to the tune of the hickory stick?*

Most middle-aged adults still remember the meaning of "taking a walk behind the woodshed with dad." If you are too young to know about woodsheds, you might have heard Bill Cosby's barn story, which he related on *The Donahue Show* and wrote about in his book *Fatherhood* (Cosby 1986). Cosby has humorously recounted using a stick in the family barn to teach his son never to tell a fib again. After several swats, Cosby told his son he would not hit him again. But after turning around to leave, he surprised his son with a final hit, demonstrating what it feels like when someone lies. Audiences typically find this an amusing anecdote. They and Cosby are not the only ones who think there is something funny about hitting children.

You may have noticed that many cartoons about mischievous children feature some type of physical punishment. Despite the fact that spanking, swatting, and hitting, otherwise known as corporal punishment, are meant to inflict pain, we somehow think it is jolly fun. And spare us the old "this hurts me more than you" routine. I have yet to talk to a child who believes that one.

While you may not see any humor in spanking children, if you are like the majority of Americans, you probably see no harm in a loving pat on your child's behind. But how do you feel about a teacher or principal who applies a wooden paddle three-quarters of an inch thick to little Jimmy's derrière? How would you feel if the school principal informed you that, whether you liked it or not, Jimmy would be paddled when "he deserved it"? And to complete the picture, how would you feel if your child were paddled so severely that an examining physician filed child abuse charges—only to discover that the beating was legal because it was defined as a form of school discipline protected by state law? You would then learn that children in public schools are the only people in America who have no constitutional protection from beatings by authorities. In fact, you might feel quite like Marlene and Arnold Gaspersohn.

Defining Corporal Punishment

I am frequently asked to give an official definition of corporal punishment. The definition that I developed started with a dictionary and has since evolved from over a decade of studying some educators' ingenuity in finding new ways to inflict pain. It is this: *Corporal punishment in the schools is the infliction of pain or confinement as a penalty for an offense committed by a student.*

The use of a wooden paddle is the most frequent method of administration. Often these are manufactured by potential victims in school woodworking shops. Some school boards even decree official specifications as to thickness, width, and length. There are other methods. Children in a class for the learning disabled claimed that their teacher and her aide banged their heads into their desks, twisted their arms, and even tried strangulation. Another teacher shook hot Tabasco sauce in the mouths of the errant students and smeared it on their faces (Butterfield 1983). The parents were outraged; local, county, and state officials saw nothing wrong with forcing kids to eat something they did not like.

The list of weapons teachers employ is long: rubber hoses, leather straps and belts, switches, sticks, rods, ropes, straight pins, plastic baseball bats, and arrows. But teachers are not powerless without weapons. Punching, slapping, kicking, and shaking are popular forms of "getting children's attention." So is ramming students up against lockers or a wall.

One of the arguments for corporal punishment is that its abolition would leave teachers powerless to control students, especially those who might otherwise threaten teachers. Despite this claim, most corporal punishment is inflicted against relatively defenseless students. It is hardly likely that an attacking student will respond to a request that he bend over so the teacher can paddle him. Corporal punishment, by definition, is not self-defense by teachers against attacks by students. In fact, most corporal punishment is against students too small or weak to strike back. Therefore, in states where corporal punishment is forbidden, the use of force is allowed in specific situations (with the incidental and unintentional infliction of pain): to quell a disturbance or to protect oneself, property, or another person. Teachers may use force to protect a student from self-injury. All states and all school districts that forbid corporal punishment recognize teachers' rights to protect themselves against student assaults.

Time-Out

Corporal punishment can be carried out in ways other than direct assaults upon children's bodies. It may also be inflicted by the use of electrical shock, confinement in closed spaces, or forcing students to assume painful bodily postures or engage in excessive exercise drills as punishment. Confinement for long periods has become increasingly popular, especially with handicapped children. Too frequently, this approach to discipline is a distortion of a legitimate punishment procedure, time-out.

Time-out is a procedure developed by behavioral psychologists as punishment for misbehavior. It is based on the concept that removing a child from a positive experience (classroom) to a negative experience (a situation removed from the classroom) will cause the child to want to return to the positive situation. A general rule of thumb has been to "time children out" for one minute less than their age.

Some educators have developed unreasonable and irrational variations on the theme of time-out. Time-out has caused anguish for many children who have experienced virtually the equivalent of solitary confinement in jails. They have been locked in school safes, buried in boxes, left in unventilated, stifling storerooms, and confined in all manner of uncomfortable boxes for periods lasting from days to weeks (Hyman et al. 1987). In a case in the Northwest, the teacher not only confined the children in a specially built box as punishment; she tied them to their chairs with nylon ropes that caused rope burns when the children struggled to get free.

The following is a case example of a particularly brutal example of the misuse of time-out. I have changed the names at the mother's request, although much of what I report here was in the local press where the incident occurred.

In the mid-1980s, Shirley was a high-achieving, happy, outgoing first grader in elementary school. During the last few weeks of school, Shirley learned, through overhearing her parents' conversations, that several couples who were close family friends were having intense marital discord. Divorces seemed imminent, and her parents, Mr. and Mrs. Jones, were quite upset. The Jones were having no marital problems, but Shirley came to believe that they too were considering divorce. She became convinced of this when her father went on a business trip. As a result, for no apparent reason to her teacher, she began crying in school. For three straight days, Mrs. Jones was called to come to school to calm her daughter. On the first two days, she took her home. When Mrs. Jones arrived on the third day, she was dismayed and angered to hear what had been done to stop Shirley's crying.

Shirley's teacher had taken her to the principal, who came up with a solution. "Bend over and touch your toes," said the principal. "I have a perfect way to stop your crying." When Shirley responded as requested, the principal paddled her. Mrs. Jones blew up at the principal, excoriating him with admittedly somewhat obscene language. After letting the principal know how she felt, Mrs. Jones calmed her daughter and decided to leave her in school.

What happened next was worse than anything Mrs. Jones could have imagined. Worse, she did not find out for two years, when Shirley was finally able to talk about it. When Shirley came home after the day of the paddling, her mother discovered Shirley's fears of divorce. Surely mother's reassurances would end the crying.

During the summer following first grade, Shirley started to have intense headaches and nosebleeds when under stress. Her mother, who suffered from stress-triggered migraines, assumed that her child was having similar problems. Aspirin relieved the headaches, but the stress-induced nosebleeds did not appear to be treatable. In second grade the child had a warm-hearted, supportive teacher. However, Shirley began to exhibit a new and disturbing set of behaviors. Her self-image plummeted whenever she received a poor grade. When anything negative happened, she repeatedly reproached herself: "I can't do anything right" or "I'm no good." Perceived failures were followed by periods of silence and withdrawal.

The situation improved dramatically when the family moved to Texas and Shirley enrolled in third grade. About halfway through the year, Shirley finally revealed to her parents the tragic sequence of events that had occurred that day, two years earlier, after she had been paddled and her mother had left her in school.

Shirley reported to her mother that she was escorted to a clothes closet across from the nurse's office. The principal and the nurse sat Shirley, still crying, on a stool in the closet, turned off the light, and closed the closet door. When Shirley continued to cry, the nurse stuck a sock in Shirley's mouth to muffle the noise. When the child did not cease sobbing, they enlisted the help of one of Shirley's chums, who was requested to enter the closet and told to try to calm Shirley. This did not work either. Eventually the tears did stop, but obviously the combined traumas became a source of long-standing stress.

While enrolled in third grade in Texas, Shirley's headaches and nosebleeds subsided, and fourth grade was a good year for her. However, when Shirley discovered that the family was going to return to her old home town, she began again to have problems with headaches and nosebleeds. The problems worsened in fifth grade, and the parents sought psychological help. Psychotherapy was begun, and the symptoms subsided.

Defining Psychological Abuse

When a child is physically abused or neglected, removal from the traumatizing caretakers results in relatively quick healing of the physical wounds; however, the emotional scars can last a lifetime. Experts now recognize that emotional reactions are at the core of all abuse. Yet most of our national efforts and financial resources are still focused on the identification and treatment of physical abuse.

In August 1983 an international group of distinguished scholars, researchers, and practitioners met to define psychological abuse and maltreatment and discuss its extent and impact on children. By their definition, psychological maltreatment occurs (Brassard et al. 1987):

- As a result of acts of both commission and omission.
- When acts against children violate community standards and professional estimates of psychological damage.
- When the acts are committed by caretakers or others whose power renders the child vulnerable.
- When the acts committed result in immediate or long-term psychological, intellectual, or social damage.

Follow-up studies have suggested that abuse be subsumed under the rubric of the more encompassing term *maltreatment.* Some prefer a two-level definition: emotional neglect occurs as a result of subtle or outright neglect of the child's psychological needs, and abuse usually implies active, overt, and verbally assaultive actions against the child.

James Garbarino, director of the Erikson Institute, prefers to bypass the dichotomy and refer to both abuse and neglect as maltreatment (Garbarino et al. 1986). He is right, but I feel that the word *abuse* is more emotionally charged, more familiar to the public, and of greater use in conveying the issue to the public. Therefore, throughout this book, I use the terms interchangeably despite the fact that I recognize the technical reasons for the definitions proposed by my colleagues.

Psychological abuse takes many forms: mental cruelty, sexual exploitation, causing children to live in dangerous or unstable environments, encouraging or allowing children to use destructive drugs, providing negative and destructive role models, exposing children to systematic bias and prejudice, emotional neglect, and exposing children to institutional practices that are clearly demonstrated to deny the opportunity for the maintenance of basic human needs. The last occurs when children in institutions do not receive appropriate human contact and attention because they are unattractive or because personnel are too overburdened. Some feel that *emotional maltreatment* is a better term than *abuse* because the former indicates that damage can occur by acts of commission.

Stuart Hart, director of the Office for the Study of the Psychological Rights of Children at Indiana-Purdue University, has provided an inclusive definition of psychological maltreatment in schools (Hart 1987). He associates five conditions with psychological maltreatment:

1. Discipline and control techniques based on fear and intimidation.
2. Low quantity and quality of human interaction in which teachers communicate a lack of interest, caring, and affection for students.
3. Limited opportunities for students to develop competencies and feelings of self-worth, especially for children who lack ability or motivation for high-level academic work.
4. Encouragement to be dependent and subservient, especially in areas where students are capable of making independent judgments.
5. Denial of opportunities for healthy risk taking such as exploring ideas that are not conventional and approved by the teacher.

While an all-inclusive definition of psychological abuse is of academic interest, it may not be particularly useful to parents who are wondering why Jane is always sad, why Johnny is instantly ready to fight, and why Alice has changed so much lately.

More immediate questions have to do with identifying psychologically abused students and doing something about the problem.

The case of Jimmy is a good example of how psychological abuse resulted in clear and devastating consequences.

Jimmy was a rather shy sixth grader in a northeastern state that forbids corporal punishment. He was a nice-looking boy who could best be described as average. He had a few friends, played soccer, and attended church regularly with his parents and five siblings. The next to the youngest of six children, he was overshadowed by several very bright older brothers and a six-year-old sister whom his parents described as "a real delight." Jimmy's mother was active in the PTA, and his father belonged to several civic groups. The parents were practicing Catholics who were somewhat conservative. All in all, theirs was a typical, community-minded middle-class family—hardly malcontents who would sue a teacher.

As a student, Jimmy frequently functioned below his potential, but since he was never a behavioral problem, his busy parents and teachers were never seriously concerned. Because his family was close knit and very earnest about studies, his parents and older siblings frequently helped him with homework. They sometimes became impatient with his awkward writing and periodic inability to remember material from one day to the next. Despite these sporadic deficiencies, he received passing grades and seemed happy. Then almost overnight, he changed.

Although never outgoing, Jimmy began to withdraw. He lost interest in soccer, rarely played with friends, complained about nightmares and insomnia, and began to spend a great deal of time in his room. He complained about stomachaches, especially on Monday mornings. His stomachaches and headaches resulted in increasing visits to the school nurse's office. His grades began to deteriorate and were accompanied by immature behavior and refusal to do schoolwork. As a result, his parents became impatient and demanding. Escalating punishments led to more oppositional behavior and physical complaints. Finally, when he developed stomachaches daily, his parents scheduled an appointment with the family physician. Following a series of exams, the physician determined that Jimmy was becoming a likely candidate for an ulcer.

An experienced teacher or parent reading this case carefully might recognize a familiar pattern. Perhaps Jimmy had a learning disability and was being pushed beyond his ability by demanding parents. Maybe teachers who had taught his extremely bright older siblings openly compared him with them. Perhaps he was having peer problems, or maybe jealousy toward his adorable younger sister was at the root of the problem. Experienced teachers know that all of these can cause the symptoms described. But the psychologist found that Jimmy's problems, while perhaps related to some of these factors, were directly caused by a teacher. Here is the story that Jimmy finally told.

During art class Jimmy was requested to make some sketches. He complained about his poor copying and drawing skills and begged for help. His teacher became increasingly impatient with Jimmy's whining and his refusal to complete the assignment, which he was required to do independently.

Finally, Jimmy's teacher said, "If you want to act like a baby, you can sit with the babies." She took him next door to the first-grade class and made arrangements for Jimmy to sit there for class sessions during the following three weeks until he completed his assignment. Anger at his teachers, fear of his parents' finding out what happened, and growing ridicule from peers resulted in the stress-related symptoms described.

Psychological evaluation revealed that Jimmy was suffering from posttraumatic stress disorder, a diagnosis usually reserved for victims of unusual and overwhelming disasters such as wars, earthquakes, and physical assaults. Although Jimmy had not been physically assaulted, the psychological symptoms observed were in many ways identical to those of physically abused children. It appeared that his problem was precipitated by the art teacher and complicated by the events described.

Jimmy's parents were shocked when they learned the cause of his problems. They were beset by guilt for having punished him for apparent "laziness." They were angry that he had been humiliated and became infuriated when the school authorities stonewalled and refused to admit that a mistake had been made. They sued the art teacher and the school. After several years, the litigation was settled out of court for a sum that included the cost of two years of psychotherapy for Jimmy.

This case is startling on several counts. Surely the art teacher was not a sadist or child abuser who anticipated the psychological damage she was causing. Should teachers be expected to know the psychological profile of every child before using any punishment? How is one to know how much to punish each child? Are teachers legally liable under child abuse laws when punishments result in severe psychological stress? Let us examine some of the issues.

The major effect of psychological abuse is the disintegration of self-esteem and confidence. Research with school-aged children suggests six sets of symptoms. Some may be directly observed by parents and teachers, and others can be discovered only by talking to the child or obtaining reliable information from the home.

Personality Change. Any sudden and dramatic change in a child's behavior is usually related to extreme stress. Psychological abuse often results in sudden withdrawal from previously enjoyed activities. Some children become extremely aggressive and contentious; older children often become very angry and dream of revenge against verbally abusive teachers. Loss of confidence and self-esteem may be exhibited by self-deprecating statements and voiced fears about failure: "I am no good." "I always fail." "Nobody likes me." A previously well-adjusted child may develop mood swings and appear to be anxious or evidence inappropriate behavior. Some children develop facial tics, begin to bite their nails, or twitch.

Avoidance Behavior. Children who are psychologically traumatized will begin to avoid the person responsible. Quite frequently the fear generalizes to avoidance of people who look like the offender, to the place where the maltreatment occurred, or to activities related to the setting in which the child felt abused. The child, unable to avoid the feared situation, may experience intense physical symptoms such as nausea, trembling, muscle spasms, or faintness. If the offender is a teacher, the child may develop school phobia.

Academic Deficiency. Children who are psychologically abused frequently begin to function poorly in school. The child may suddenly stop completing homework assignments or begin to do poorly on tests. A child who previously paid attention in class may start daydreaming.

Sleep Disturbances. Psychological abuse may cause sleep disturbance, especially with younger children. These include the reappearance of bedwetting, nightmares, sleepwalking, and fear of falling asleep in a darkened room. Children may have repeated nightmares in which they are chased and harassed by either the offender or a symbolic representation, such as a monster.

Somatic Symptoms. The most common physical symptoms in school-aged children are stomachaches, headaches, fatigue, and bowel disturbances. These often accompany refusal to go to school.

Unwanted Recollections. While children who are abused rarely have the type of startling flashbacks experienced by traumatized adults, they may have unwanted memories of the traumatic event popping into their consciousness. Young children often have repeated nightmares that may replay the events or may be disguised versions of what actually happened.

The symptoms of psychological maltreatment are identical to those that occur from physical abuse. A severe paddling leaves bruises that usually last no more than three weeks. The psychological scars of both physical and verbal assault are identical, however.

Observant parents who have good communication with their children are usually able to diagnose the behavioral symptoms of physical and verbal abuse. Behavioral changes are often dramatic. But some children are able to "cover up" because they do not want to remember the traumatic incidents. And too often children are afraid to tell their parents from fear of further punishment or humiliation at home.

Parents who discover that their child has been physically or verbally abused in school may find that doing something about it is not easy. This brings us to the question of why the United States is one of the last of the developed countries to cherish the belief that the infliction of physical and psychological pain is a useful pedagogical tool.

American Myths

An outsider examining the treatment of American school children and schools might wonder what is going on in one of the richest and most advanced societies ever to exist. By many measures, it appears that our children have more opportunities than any others in history. As one of the first countries ever devoted to universal mandatory education, surely Americans care about and value education. The undergirdings of democracy are built on the assumption of an educated populace.

If children were highly valued as torchbearers of democracy, education would be the nation's highest priority. Schools would be modern and air-conditioned; teachers would be well paid and have the highest academic credentials; administrators would match their successful counterparts in corporations in terms of intelligence, creativity, flexibility, and leadership. Perhaps as a result of some collective unconscious, Americans still believe that children are the "imps of darkness" described in earlier times. Maybe at some level many Americans still subscribe to admonitions to beat the devil out of children. Why else would American schoolchildren be among the minority of students in the industrialized world who are still corporally punished?

A review of surveys in popular magazines reveals that 60 percent to 95 percent of respondents spank their children and believe that corporal punishment is sometimes necessary in raising children (Mishkin 1987). Many parents recognize the contradictions between their feelings about violence as an inappropriate solution to problems yet still spank their children as if it is not basically an aggressive act. Yet at some level most parents understand that these practices have negative psychological consequences and are related to high rates of child abuse. This is demonstrated in a number of studies when parents recognize that hitting is an expression of parental hostility and is not usually effective. As long as any level of brutalization of schoolchildren in the name of discipline is acceptable to educators, parents, or policymakers, change will be slow, painful, and expensive. Meanwhile, the verbal and physical assaults inflicted on American schoolchildren each year teach them that force, violence, and humiliation are legitimate ways to change another person's behavior. These beliefs are reinforced on television by the portrayal of violent solutions to personal and social problems. It is no wonder that violence is ingrained in our national psyche.

If we want to lessen violence in the lives of children, we must end the legally sanctioned infliction of physical and psychological pain by educators. Is it too much to ask that we join all of continental Europe, the communist countries, and others such as Japan, England, Ireland, and Israel and stop beating children in school? We will never eliminate psychological maltreatment in the schools if we cannot stop teachers and principals from swatting students in the name of education.

Schoolchildren as Political Victims

School abuses reflect wider issues about our concerns for children and political realities. While many politicians speak enthusiastically about their concerns for children's welfare, it is obvious that they also attend to social, political, and economic factors that mitigate against children's welfare.

According to studies completed at the NCSCPAS, the schoolchildren who receive the most corporal punishment are poor, live in rural areas, and are boys. Blacks are more likely than others to get swatted. The greatest amount of reported corporal punishment occurs in rural areas, especially in the South and Southwest (Hyman 1988c). Areas with high illiteracy, high poverty rates, and low per pupil expenditures on education have the highest rates of corporal punishment.

Children in public schools have historically been victims of struggles between the political right and left. Regardless of who is in political power, the value of children in schools can be gauged by low teacher salaries, lack of resources, and a dearth of administrative talent. We are moving toward a fragmented society as private schools grow almost exponentially, leaving large numbers of poor and minority students attending meagerly supported public schools. Millions of inner-city children attend school in decaying buildings housing burned-out teachers who struggle to teach with inadequate materials.

The dearth of adequate support for children might be

understood historically if one were to examine the periodic portrayal of "the evil child" in the media. Do we share a view similar
to some Victorian fundamentalists who considered children "a
swarm of little vipers" (Collins 1963, p. 187)? Many of their descendants still consciously believe that it is necessary to "beat the
devil" out of children in order to instill appropriate character
development.

Certainly in many areas we have done well. Medical advances
in the twentieth century have been phenomenal. We have reduced the devastating number of infant deaths resulting from
childhood diseases. Education is universal, the ubiquitous use of
flogging has been reduced, and the economic exploitation of
children bears little resemblance to what occurred during the
Industrial Revolution. Unfortunately, however, contemporary
analysis yields disturbing similarities to the past. For instance,
the hunger Charles Dickens documented seems to have a modern sequel—perhaps not as dramatic but just as real to hungry
children. While Nancy Reagan was publishing her second book,
To Love a Child, " . . . a tearful tribute to the joys of intergenerational affection, her husband's administration was pocketing
the lunch money of three million American children and depriv-
ing millions more of subsidized snacks, dinners and breakfasts"
(Ehrenreich and Nasaw 1983, p. 597). Denying proper nutrition
to poor children became public policy. With problems like this,
many child advocates find their energies expended on issues that
seem more pressing than spankings in school. There are other
issues that reflect the problems of helping children in America.

Dickens's *Nicholas Nickleby* described a world of childhood in
which dirt and disorder caused much disease. Modern hygiene
has reduced filth, yet chemical pollutants in the environment
currently affect the lives of too many children "who are substan-
tially more sensitive than adults to the toxic effects of many pollutants" (Freeman and Weir 1983). There is evidence that many
childhood cancers are related to environmental pollutants.
These formerly rare conditions now appear at rates of more
than 6,000 per year, and yet funding for research on the effects
of environmental pollutants on the young was discontinued.
Again, public policy became disastrous for children. The prob-

lem of teachers' calling students names seems to pale before these kinds of issues.

Child labor laws, while well meaning, set the stage for another type of abuse by disenfranchising children as economic assets for families. Most Americans at some level view children as economic liabilities. The American business establishment exacerbates the problem through manipulation of the youth market. Television provides a perfect medium for catching young children and turning them into uncritical consumers. Television executives contribute to psychological abuse as they continue to program excessive amounts of violence. The passive acceptance of violence adds to a climate where children readily accept the use of force to solve problems. Hundreds of thousands of children are constantly exposed to violence on television and learn to accept it as a way of life.

This view may be overly pessimistic, but it emphasizes the paradoxes of our views about children. The examples suggest that the efforts of child advocates have historically been drained by issues that seem more severe than a few million children being paddled or verbally assaulted in schools. You should be aware of the myths of our society and the politics of pain.

2

Punitiveness in American Education:

Why We Can't Stop

"I cannot begin to elaborate on the personal trauma and anguish my husband and I have felt as parents not being able to protect our daughter." So began the testimony of Marlene Gaspersohn before the cameras, press, audience, and members of the Subcommittee on Juvenile Justice of the Committee on the Judiciary of the U.S. Senate. Chaired by Senator Arlen Specter (R–Pennsylvania), the subcommittee met to hear testimony about corporal punishment. It was October 17, 1984, and Marlene, despite her nervousness, spoke clearly and emphatically.

> In recent times, we have all become aware that there are child abusers in every walk of life. However, not only has their existence in the field of education not been acknowledged, but a haven for such people is provided by law in most states.
>
> I can speak from my own experience only of North Carolina; but I have read about and been in contact with other parents from North Carolina and other states who have had similar exasperating tales of unjust and brutal treatment of their children at the hands of their "educators."
>
> There is a professional unwillingness on the part of educators to admit that such incidents occur. I know this to be true from our own experience. The best way to deny they happen

is not to acknowledge the incident, play down its significance when the news media does hear of it, cover up with lies and insults and try to turn public opinion against the child victim and his or her family by branding them as "trouble makers."

1. Shelly was corporally punished for her first offense *ever* in 13 years of public school, so it was the primary means of discipline (even though the school discipline guide indicated that corporal punishment should not be the first punishment tried).

2. In the student handbook there is no reference to what specific offenses can result in corporal punishment.

3. No notices are posted anywhere in the school appraising students of what infractions may result in corporal punishment.

4. No adult witness was present in the room. (School policy required that a witness be present during the paddling. The witness who testified during the trial said most of the time he was standing outside the door talking to a student, yet no one saw him).

5. Since no witness was present, he was not informed in the presence of Shelly the reasons for the corporal punishment.

6. The written report that must be filed with the principal was neither signed nor dated the morning after her beating.

7. The principal would not provide us personally or our attorney with a copy of the report until a few days before the trial, which was two years later, even though it had been requested in writing.

8. An alternative discipline to corporal punishment of raking leaves would have been offered to Shelly had she been a boy. Therefore, we charge that there was sex discrimination as well.

Painfully Marlene recalled the suffering she felt for her daughter:

The day after her corporal punishment, I took Shelly to Dr. John Smith, Medical Examiner of nearby Sampson County. Not only was Shelly badly bruised, the beating had caused her menstrual flow to turn into hemorrhaging.

After examining her, Dr. Smith called Harnett County Social Services and reported Glenn Varney as a child abuser. He was informed that there is no agency in North Carolina that has the authority to investigate the charge of child abuse against a public schoolteacher. It is classified as a "school matter" and must be dealt with by the local Board of Education.

The Board of Education had already met for their once a month December meeting, so we could not bring a grievance before the board until January, we were told. In January there was not enough time to prepare since they said we must make the request in writing two weeks prior to the meeting.

By February we were ready to present our grievance to the board, but were told that they couldn't hear us that month because of a reception after the meeting for a retiring teacher which meant that they would have no executive session after the regular board meeting.

Marlene's story was beginning to sound like an account of stonewalling: if you can keep the parents at bay long enough, they will eventually give up. It works most of the time when parents have limited resources and fear retribution from the school or people in the community. She continued:

So it was March 1982 before our attorney, Renny Deese, was allowed to make our presentation. . . . Up to that time no reference had been made of the other three girls [who were paddled at the same time as Shelly] . . . and I realized it would be all covered up if I did not inform the local press. That is how the notoriety began.

After the school board heard the complaints, they said nothing until just before graduation, and then they claimed that Varney had done nothing wrong. Marlene reasoned that the board decided that with graduation behind her, Shelly and her family would drop the issue. Instead they had created a family of angry people who would not give up. A cruel act by a local school administrator and a stonewalling school board propelled a compassionate, loving parent all the way to a congressional hearing.

Opposition to
Marlene Gaspersohn's View

Contrast the congressional testimony of Marlene with that of Paul Armstrong, who at the time he testified at the same hearing as Marlene, was president-elect of the West Virginia Association of Elementary School Principals.

Armstrong, somewhat indignant, noted that "the West Virginia Supreme Court ruled in June 1982 that corporal punishment by use of any device other than the open hand violated the West Virginia code dealing with child abuse." Armstrong recounted how the education association and other paddlers in West Virginia responded: "Several bills were introduced into the West Virginia Legislature [in the following year]. . . . Of these bills, one was passed that would permit corporal punishment under certain conditions, procedures and regulations." But he then complained about the bill's provisions, which he claimed were unnecessary, designed to reduce the incidence of corporal punishment in West Virginia. (Armstrong's objections provide insight into the mind of the paddling pedagogues, who generally know little about discipline but consider themselves experts in punishment. A study of elementary school principals in West Virginia, conducted by Elizabeth Dennison (1984), found that the more they supported corporal punishment, the less they knew about the research literature on it. Although the strongest supporters of corporal punishment had not read the research, they considered it inconclusive.)

Armstrong enumerated four provisions he predicted would have ominous results. He claimed the first problem was that the bill required that corporal punishment be used "only as a last resort: This statement almost kills implementation due to the possible literal interpretation of last resort." Interestingly, however, defenders of corporal punishment invariably claim that it should be allowed since it is used only as a last resort. Is it possible that the West Virginia principals' association feared that if that were written into law, they might have to prove that swatting is used only as a last resort. This certainly makes them more vulnerable to successful litigation by angry parents.

Armstrong's next objection hinted at a basic but incomplete knowledge of the research on punishment. The bill required at least twelve hours' notice before a paddling. Armstrong claimed that "any correction of behavior should be done as close to the misbehavior as possible." Research on punishment does indicate that short-term behavior change occurs best when the punishment immediately follows the undesired behavior; however, there are many other conditions for the punishment to be effective. For instance, the intensity and duration must be carefully controlled; it must increase in intensity each time it is used; it must be used each time the misbehavior occurs (that is, the child must be caught each time he or she misbehaves); it cannot be reinforcing (that is, some children feel that they must be punished in order to get any attention from adults); and there must be no possibility for escape (Bongiovanni 1979). These and other conditions for the effective use of punishment cannot be met in the school setting without turning the classroom into a carefully controlled environment focusing on the infliction of pain and the imposition of a climate of fear.

Third, the bill forbade the use of corporal punishment with pupils "identified as handicapped, learning, hearing, mentally or behaviorally disabled." Of all school children, these are the most vulnerable to abuse. Many, especially the emotionally disturbed, have histories of emotional, physical, and sexual abuse. The infliction of pain caused their problems; it hardly ranks as a cure. Armstrong claimed that this provision "creates a double standard for application of disciplinary procedures. Any time you have a double standard you create several other problems."

Without any research to back him, this principal proffered arguments long refuted by data. When challenged, he resorted to personal experience. He claimed that without the use of corporal punishment, "I have witnessed an increase in students talking back to teachers, making the remark, 'you can't touch me,' and even, 'I don't want to, what are you going to do about it?'" From the last statement, it seems that fear and "strong-arming" are Armstrong's recommendations for discipline. After all, if children are not terrified of teachers and principals, how could they be expected to learn?

It would be unfair to blame Mr. Armstrong for the plight of

children who are abused daily in schools. Education, maybe
more than any other field of study, is affected by social and religious tradition and political ideology more than by research
findings. In fact, much of what one might observe in a classroom
is as much shaped by local religious and political ideology as by
the findings available in the massive body of research on human
learning, personality, and teaching. In order to understand why
so much corporal punishment occurs in America, especially in
the Bible Belt, we must start with the historical and religious context of that old saw "Spare the rod and spoil the child."

Historical Roots

The use of corporal punishment in child rearing and education
appears early in the recorded history of Western cultures. Its
roots in the Old Testament trace to Proverbs (13:24), where Solomon urges that "he that spareth the rod hateth his son, he that
loveth him, chasteneth him." Also from Proverbs come two other
admonitions: "Withold not correction from the child: for if thou
beatest him with the rod, he shall not die. Thou shalt beat him
with the rod, and shall deliver him from hell" (23:13–14) and
"Foolishness is bound in the heart of a child; but the rod of correction shall drive it from him" (22:15).

Ian Gibson (1978) points out that the Victorians attributed
the expression "spare the rod and spoil the child" to Solomon,
the supposed author of Proverbs. This well-known defense of
corporal punishment is, in fact, not in the Bible. It was first used
by the English author Samuel Butler in a satirical poem, "Hudibras," published in 1664. Of further interest, Gibson points
out that the much-quoted phrase is about an amorous lady:
"[She] urges Sir Hudibras to undergo a whipping on her account—as a fitting and tradition hallowed proof of nightly love
and also, perhaps, as a parody on the practices of the religious
flagellants" (p. 49). In the poem the lady speaks as follows:

> *But since our sex's modesty*
> *Will not allow I should be by,*
> *Bring me, on oath, a fair account,*
> *And honour too, when you have done it;*

And I'll admit you to the place
You claim as due in my good grace.
If matrimony and hanging go
By dest'ny, why not whipping too?
What medicine else can cure the fits
Of lovers, when they lose their wits?
Love is a boy, by poets styled,
They spare the rod and spoil the child.
(Butler 1885, pp. 113–114)

A critic, Henry Salt, in 1916 pointed to an obvious irony in the poem: "It is significant that a witty writer, who frankly treats the subject of whipping for what it is—an indecent subject—should have provided many generations with a supposed precept from the Bible" (p. 49).

The Devil Made Me Do It

In Christian theology, the use of corporal punishment is historically related to concepts of original sin and the need to combat Satan by "beating the devil" out of children. This belief was, and still is, an important element of evangelical and fundamental Protestant belief (Greven 1977). The concept of possession by some sort of evil spirit is a common explanation of deviant behavior in ancient and primitive cultures. The ancient Hebrews used this explanation to account for mental illness, misbehavior, and even hereditary diseases. The demon theory of deviance was carried from Catholic theology to Protestantism by, among others, Martin Luther, who in "sixteenth-century Europe ordered mentally defective children drowned because he was convinced they were instruments of the devil" (Radbill 1974).

Contemporary concern with the devil's effect on children remains an important part of fundamentalist theology. Like their sixteenth-century forebears, educators in so-called Christian schools that preach fundamentalist doctrine believe that corporal punishment instills character, obedience, and humility—traits needed to ward off the devil (Hyman and Wise 1979).

There is some evidence that belief in the devil may underlie the lack of services to children in the United States as compared to other developed countries if one were to believe that "beating the devil out of them" is the answer to building good character and creating upstanding citizens. A Gallup poll reported in the December 1988 issue of *Psychology Today* reveals some startling information. People in fourteen countries were asked if they believed in the devil. The results of percentages of respondents who said "I believe in the devil" were as follows: United States, 66 percent; Northern Ireland, 66 percent; Republic of Ireland, 57 percent; Spain, 33 percent; Italy, 30 percent, Great Britain, 30 percent; Finland, 29 percent; Norway, 28 percent; Belgium, 20 percent; Netherlands, 20 percent; West Germany, 18 percent; France, 17 percent; Denmark, 12 percent; and Sweden, 12 percent.

If those 66 percent of Americans who believe in the devil also believe, as did the Puritans, that pleasure is the work of the devil and that good character can be forged only in the crucible of pain and humility, it is no wonder that we are having such problems convincing Americans to stop hitting and denigrating school children. Studies by experts on family violence—among them Murray Straus, Richard Gelles, David Gill, and James Garbarino—have documented the American belief in the value of physical force and psychological denigration in raising and educating children.

It is unfortunate that Fundamentalist and Evangelical Christian theologians and their many followers depend on a few passages attributed in *Proverbs* as the basis for child rearing. Worse, they are frequently misquoted.

The "devil theory" provides a convenient argument for parents who do not wish to take responsibility for the "sins" of their children. This theory is also helpful for those who do not want to accept responsibility for their own transgressions. Transferring blame for children's misbehavior from faulty parenting to supernatural intervention is as simplistic as trying to change their behavior by spanking.

The devil offers a convenient excuse not only for parents but for some of the preachers and televangelists who are most supportive of the spare the rod dictum. For instance, when caught in sexual imbroglios, they can claim, "The devil made me do it." (Perhaps "fallen" fundamentalists and evangelicals who so vociferously promote corporal punishment should follow their own advice for misbehavior. Or, rather than receiving the rod of correction recommended for children, they should be punished as recommended in the Old Testament for adults. Deuteronomy 25:2,3 recommends forty stripes for "he who is worthy to be beaten.")

There are many passages in the Bible to turn to for wisdom in child rearing. We no longer use execution for rebellious children as is recommended in Deuteronomy: "And all the men of his city shall stone him with stones, that he die" (21:18–21). Some believe that Solomon's recommendations were actually meant as a reform for the more odious punishment of stoning. Others believe that the "rod" Solomon referred to was the rod of guidance as in the Twenty-third Psalm.

Nowhere in the New Testament does Jesus Christ suggest the use of violence against children or adults. In fact, it seems clear that he was against the use of violence as a solution to problems in almost all situations. When the elders wanted to stone an adulterous woman, he said "Let whoever is without sin cast the first stone" (John 8:7).

Reverend Theodore Lorah of the Maple Grove United Methodist Church in Hunlock Creek, Pennsylvania, sent me his response to the theological support for corporal punishment:

> A better passage in raising children is found in Ephesians 6: 1–4. Children are told to obey their parents, for it is right. But parents (fathers, specifically) are told not to provoke their children to anger, but to bring them up in the 'discipleship' and instruction of the Lord. Even the use of the word 'discipline' in place of 'punishment' is more to the point. Jesus took our punishment on the cross. We teach people to be disciples, followers; we don't punish. Disciplining is not accomplished by beatings.

THE ANGLO-SAXON TRADITION

The more recent history of brutal floggings and denigration of children in seventeenth-century English schools and in colonial America is well documented (Hyman and Wise 1979). One only has to read the novels of Dickens to understand the relationship between education and child abuse as part of the historical English mind-set.

In 1669 and in 1698, children in England were unsuccessfully represented in petitions to Parliament for redress from beatings and sadism (Freeman 1979). The petition was not only a plea for relief against corporal punishment but against the sadistic schoolmasters who sought "punishment for its own sake." The petition was written on behalf of "the children of the land" and complained that knowledge of Latin and Greek should not automatically qualify one to be a teacher. The petitioners asked for teachers to have some knowledge of children and childhood. (This was a precursor to contemporary requirements that certified teachers must have training in child development, psychology, and teaching methods—requirements that many back-to-basics advocates deem unnecessary.) The petitioners prescribed methods of discipline based on rational approaches rather than the infliction of pain and terror. Yet today we still have many advocates of the "get tough" approach that did not work in 1669 and will not work now.

Contemporary efforts by the petitioners' descendants were finally successful. In the summer of 1987, English law banned corporal punishment in the schools. The majority of the original English-speaking colonies have not, however.

CORPORAL PUNISHMENT: AN AMERICAN TRADITION

Corporal punishment of school children had firm roots in colonial America. The spirit of the times was exemplified in a schoolhouse in Sunderland, Massachusetts, in 1793. Built into the floor was a sturdy whipping post to which miscreant children were tied. This method ensured no escape from the vigorous birchings of the schoolmaster.

In those days teachers like Master Todd, described in the *Annals of Philadelphia and Pennsylvania* (1870), reigned supreme, as long as they were stronger than their students. Master Todd did not need a whipping post, as this account attests (Manning 1979, p. 50):

Wanting elbow room, the chair would be quickly thrust on one side, and master John Todd was to be seen dragging his struggling suppliant to the flogging ground in the center of the room. Having placed his left foot upon the end of the bench, with a patent jerk peculiar to himself, he would have the boy completely horsed across his knee, with his left elbow on the back of his neck to keep him securely on. . . . having his victim thus completely at his command. . . . Once more to the staring crew would be exhibited the dexterity of the master and strap. . . . Moving in quick time, the fifteen inches of bridal rein would be seen . . . leaving on the "place beneath" a fiery streak at every slash.

"Does it hurt?"

"Oh yes, Master! Oh don't, Master!"

"Then I'll make it hurt thee more. . . .

Thou shan't want a warming pan tonight."

This is one of the many memoirs and stories of floggings, beatings, humiliations, and sadism in colonial American education. Is this what contemporary self-styled educational reformers mean when they plead for a return to "good old-fashioned discipline" (Hyman and D'Allesandro 1984)?

Even as late as 1850, reports from Boston indicated that it took "sixty-five beatings a day to operate a school of four hundred" (Hyman and Wise 1979). In the school year ending in 1876, before the New Jersey ban on flogging had been fully implemented, Newark, New Jersey, recorded 9,408 beatings in a system of 10,000 students. The birch rod was synonymous with education until secular philosophies proposed by people like Jean-Jacques Rousseau, Johann Pestalozzi, and Horace Mann began to effect reforms.

Not all of society thought whippings were needed for education. In 1853 the Indiana Supreme Court suggested:

The public seems to cling to the despotism in the government of schools [that] has been discarded everywhere else. . . . The husband can no longer moderately chastise his wife: nor . . . the master his servant or his apprentice. Even the degrading cruelties of the naval service have been arrested. Why the person of the schoolboy . . . should be less sacred in the eyes of the

law than that of the apprentice or the sailor, is not easily explained. (Hyman and Wise 1979 p. xi)

The first major change occurred in 1867 when the New Jersey legislature banned the use of corporal punishment in
schools. Local control prevailed, however, and it was not until
the twentieth century that the ban was honored.

Determinants of Punitiveness
MODELING THEORY

Throughout history, sages have offered many theories about human behavior. Until recent times, it was believed that most behavior was caused by supernatural forces or heredity. These approaches were used to explain misbehavior in children and aggression in adults. In contemporary times, scientists have
developed a number of theories to account for aggressive behavior between children and by adults toward children. Many of
these theories may be used to describe attitudes and behaviors
of parents toward children who misbehave. In almost thirty
years of experience, I have come to believe that modeling theory
can best explain the way parents react to misbehavior in their
children.

Modeling theory is based on the belief that almost all behavior is learned by watching others. The old saying that the apple
does not fall far from the tree is true in that children learn to
imitate the behavior of the parents. A great deal of research evidence supports this belief.

Albert Bandura, one of the major proponents of modeling
theory, attempted to understand how children learn aggression.
He and his associates acknowledged that inherited predisposi-
tions and temperament certainly account for some of personality
formation, but most of personality is learned. In 1961, Bandura
and his associates exposed nursery school children to aggressive
and nonaggressive behavior using adults as models. Children observed situations in which adults hit an inflatable plastic "Bobo"
doll with a mallet. In addition to hitting it, the adult model yelled
at the doll, sat on it, punched it, kicked it, and tossed it in the

air. Another group of children watched nonaggressive play with the doll, and a third group did not view play with the doll at all. When the three groups were placed in playrooms with the Bobo dolls, only those who had viewed the aggression against the doll became aggressive themselves.

Bandura conducted other similar studies, as have other researchers. Most interesting in the context of corporal punishment is a series of studies done by Owens, Strauss, Gelles, and Gil demonstrating that parents who use excessive corporal punishment to the point of abuse were themselves abused. Aggression toward misbehaving children is learned in childhood through adult models. Actual abuse may be triggered by a variety of factors, such as parental stress, isolation, and alcoholism. However, because society sanctions hitting children, the mechanism for abuse is in place early in life when children are hit themselves or observe their siblings being hit.

Leonard Eron, a research psychologist at the University of Illinois, studied 870 eight year olds in rural New York to see how severely punished they were. His indicators ranged from no physical punishment at all to slaps and spankings. He then asked other children to judge how aggressive the children in his sample were. The more aggressively children were punished, the more aggressive they were with other children. Twenty years later, Eron again studied the aggressive children as adults. It was no surprise that they had become aggressive adults with aggressive children.

In the late 1970s when the NCSCPAS was organized, we conducted a series of studies that asked the same question: "Why do teachers assault children, physically and psychologically?" Since our major mandate was to investigate corporal punishment, we began with studies of hitting. Although we found a great deal of research on parent-child discipline, there was very little about teachers.

Naomi Lennox (1982) conducted the first study to determine why teachers used corporal punishment. She devised a questionnaire, which was administered to teachers in Pennsylvania, New York, Florida, Tennessee, and Mississippi. Teachers were asked a variety of questions about their training, their years of experience, and their own childhood. Other significant questions were asked, including how often they paddled their students.

The study clearly showed that the most significant predictor of whether teachers paddled was how often they had been spanked as children and/or paddled in school. Teachers who had been spanked rarely or never in their own childhoods almost never paddled children. Most of those who had been paddled or spanked did the same as teachers. A small group of those who had been paddled or spanked (which has appeared in all of our studies) did not use punitive techniques as teachers. The reasons that modeling theory did not hold with this group will be explained later.

Following the study by Lennox, we studied other groups of professionals who work with teachers and children. Beth Sofer (1983) developed a questionnaire for psychologists. We reasoned that if the education and training of teachers did not significantly influence their use of corporal punishment, then it could be because they lacked specific in-depth training in the use of positive methods of discipline. Surely psychologists, who are highly trained regarding the use of rewards and punishments, would reflect that training in their recommendations about the use of corporal punishment. The questionnaire sent to psychologists throughout the country was similar to the one Lennox developed but with additional items. Sofer asked the respondents to indicate what research or theory they would use to support whether they would recommend the use of corporal punishment. The results were surprising. Although 49 percent of the respondents said they would never recommend the use of corporal punishment and accurately cited the research and theory supporting that belief, 51 percent said that in certain instances— perhaps situations that were dangerous to the child or where the misbehavior was severe and occurred repeatedly—they might recommend its use. Thirty percent said they would recommend its use in schools.

We were surprised that so many psychologists considered corporal punishment appropriate. We were even more surprised at the explanations they gave for recommending it. The largest group of psychologists who would recommend its use cited the research of B.F. Skinner, which falls under the general category of behaviorism. Their rationale was absolutely incorrect. Skinner himself has repeatedly spoken and published articles about the ineffectiveness and inadvisability of the use of corporal punishment with children (Hyman and Wise 1979).

The reason that the psychologists recommended corporal punishment was that they had been physically punished themselves as children. Also, regional differences were important predictors; psychologists in the Northeast were much less likely to recommend the use of corporal punishment.

The research conducted at the center is clearly convincing about modeling theory. One question not addressed in our early research or most of our studies, however, was the role that religion played in the use of corporal punishment.

RELIGION AND CORPORAL PUNISHMENT

The historical evidence suggests that religious attitudes affect how parents punish their children. In order to study this issue, Mariann Pokalo (1986) developed a questionnaire designed to determine if modeling theory and religious orientation might affect the level of punitiveness of child care workers in institutions for mentally retarded children. She asked how severely the respondents would punish a variety of misbehaviors.

The frequency of punishment in their own childhoods was the best predictor of how severely respondents would punish the retarded children in their care. Those who described themselves as Baptists with a fundamentalist orientation were by far the most punitive group; that is, they would use much more severe punishments for almost all misbehaviors than would Catholics, Jews, and other Protestants who said they were Methodists, Lutherans, or Presbyterians. Those who said they were evangelical in orientation were the second most punitive but were closer to the other groups.

A study by Vernon Wiehe (1989) at the University of Kentucky focused on religion and attitudes toward corporal punishment. In his research, he found that respondents who belonged to church groups that claimed literal belief in the Bible valued the use of hitting as a disciplinary tool more than those whose religious beliefs were not based on literalism.

Literalists, fundamentalists, and conservative Catholics have historically supported the use of corporal punishment in schools.

Church-related schools have always enjoyed constitutional protection and freedom from standards that are applied to public schools. As a result, although state and local districts move toward the elimination of abuse in schools children in church-related education remain vulnerable. Students in literalist-oriented Christian schools are most at risk. It appears that Catholic schools are moving away from the use of punitive techniques. It also appears that the courts and state legislatures are becoming more reluctant to excuse abuse of school children in the name of God.

Conservative Catholic and Protestant educators are often obsessed with the concept of original sin and its relation to teaching. Their preoccupation with saving children from the devil results in sanctimonious adherence to a "spare the rod" mandate. In the past, the Catholic church maintained the vast majority of church-related schools. Nuns had a formidable reputation for their unrelenting battles with the forces of evil that emanated from the secular world. No restraint was considered prudent in the vigorous application of the yardstick on open hands, across knuckles, and to derriers in an effort to save the souls of errant youth. Now, however, increasing numbers of dioceses are forbidding the use of corporal punishment.

Children in conservative Christian schools are still at risk. Although these schools are generally immune from public control, there is increasing awareness among policymakers that abuse in the name of God is still abuse. A case resolved in September 1989 reveals that church-related schools, at least in some areas of the country, may need to show some restraint in physically punishing school children.

A jury in Dauphin County, Pennsylvania, found David Douglass, the principal of a Christian school, guilty of simple assault in the paddling of a seven-year-old student. An article in the *Hershey Chronicle* (Rounds 1989) indicated that Douglass faced two years in prison and a $5,000 fine.

Doctor Eric Krieg, the physician who examined the bruises on the boy's buttocks seven hours after the incident, testified that the pain after each swat "was like a lighted cigarette being pressed against the flesh."

Douglass told Deputy District Attorney Todd Narvol, who

vigorously prosecuted the case, that if Narvol found offense with the paddling he was "arguing with God, not me."

Douglass's attorney invoked the usual appeal in defense of his client when he stated to the jury, "The day a man's religious beliefs are held up to ridicule in the courtroom, we are all in trouble." His attempts to justify child abuse in the name of religious freedom did not work, even in a basically conservative area of rural Pennsylvania.

Unfortunately, the above case is the exception to the rule; however, it does offer hope. The case was successful because the district attorney made a politically dangerous decision in a rural, conservative area by prosecuting an educator who claimed that God was on his side when he stated, "the blueness of a wound cleanseth away evil."

All of these studies tell us that if we want to eliminate punitiveness, especially corporal punishment, in society, we need to convince parents and teachers of one generation to use other techniques to shape and change children's behavior. Yet despite modeling theory, some people in each of our studies who did experience significant corporal punishment or general punitiveness as children refused to act punitively toward children. Why? We decided to develop a study designed to answer that crucial question. We started with parents.

THE WERE-HIT-BUT-DON'T-HIT PARENTS

Amy Mishkin (1987) developed a questionnaire similar to the others described; however, she asked more detailed questions relating to experiences that might convince that hitting is a bad idea. As with the other studies, modeling theory explained most of the adults' (in this case, parents) disciplining of children.

We were most interested in the group who were hit as children but who rarely or never hit their own children. These parents tended to have their children later in life; thus, they were more mature when they became parents. In addition, on a general scale of temperament and anger level, they tended to become frustrated less readily.

In general these parents had a much higher education level than the general population. As a group they had gone to graduate and professional schools. Many reported that courses in child development and psychology had made them think about alternatives to spanking. Many had taken workshops in parenting.

Another important factor was who hit them as children. Many in the group said that they were hit only by their mothers. Apparently being hit by one's father or by both parents increases the chances that one will become a swatting parent.

Finally, these parents said that a major factor in their conversions to not hitting was the experience of seeing the bad effects of hitting on other children. They tend to view a swatting parent as more out of control than the misbehaving child. This group had developed empathy for children; they could put themselves in the shoes of the child experiencing the pain, frustration, and anger of being hit.

SOCIETAL FACTORS AND MODELING THEORY

Societal traditions and individual modeling are factors that account for regional differences in punitiveness in the United States. Leopold Bellak and Maxine Antell (1979) were interested in national characteristics that might result in differences in punitiveness toward children. They studied differences in aggression toward children in three European countries generally portrayed as quite dissimilar: Germany, Denmark, and Italy.

Germany is often thought of as one of the most aggressive European countries. (Interestingly, Britain, with its long history of school floggings, has engaged in more wars than any other modern nation.) Moreover, German children are taught reflexive obedience. They live in a society where order and conformity are highly valued. Germans believe that their culture is *kinderfeindlich*, or hostile to children. In fact, a West German poll Bellak and Antell reported showed that "up to 60 percent of parents believed in beating, not slapping or spanking, but beating their children."

Denmark, like other Scandinavian countries, is generally considered a peaceful country that places high regard on cooperation and children's welfare. (Sweden, with a somewhat similar culture, has even passed legislation prohibiting parents from hitting their own children. This national legislation was prompted by publicity about a few child abuse cases.)

Bellak and Antell made an interesting comparison between Germany and Denmark based on assumptions about the after-effects of excessive punitiveness against children. The rates of auto accidents, all other accidents, suicide, self-inflicted injuries, and homicide are much higher in Frankfurt than in Copenhagen, perhaps suggesting that Germans may have a much higher need to discharge aggression.

Italy offered the possibility of a country somewhere between Germany and Denmark in terms of aggression toward children.

To conduct the studies, trained observers in playgrounds in the three countries observed aggressive acts between adults and children and between children. The types of aggression were verbal, physical coercion, assault that could not cause severe injury, and assault that had the potential for causing severe injury or death.

In Italy and Denmark, the observers recorded no acts of aggression against children and relatively little child-to-child aggression. In Germany they observed high rates of both types of aggression. German playgrounds were characterized by pushing, kicking, fighting over toys, beatings, and aggressive pursuits. In the other playgrounds children played cooperatively and nonaggressively. This research showed the powerful effects of tradition and modeling.

PSYCHOHISTORY, CORPORAL PUNISHMENT, AND CULTURE

Another way of examining the issue of harshness toward children is through psychohistory in which history is examined by looking at the personal traits of leaders and how their backgrounds affected their political and leadership decisions.

Alice Miller (1980), a psychoanalyst, analyzed the effect of punitiveness on individuals and the societies in "lands with the kind of hidden cruelty that is so often rationalized in the time honored phrase, 'this is for your own good'" (Montague 1983). She described the frequent association of corporal punishment with the demand for reflexive, unquestioning obedience as a major contributor to the development of character in Adolf Hitler. In discussing Hitler, Miller explains how a child who was once persecuted became a persecutor. She describes the dynamics of Hitler's family and concludes it could well be characterized as "the prototype of a totalitarian regime" (Montague 1981, 1983). The connection between institutionalized mental and physical cruelty is clear. Miller also disclosed how "poisonous pedagogy" in the home and at school contributed to a self-destructive adolescence and the development of a child murderer. She demonstrated through clinical evidence and case study what happens to children who are physically punished, humiliated, and demeaned by parents "who are expected, indeed commanded, to respect and love those who have abused them."

Miller's case is extreme but highly instructive. Reflexive obedience to authority enables the continuing existence of systems that depend on a combination of physical and psychological abuse. In American schools, classes in social studies teach the concepts of democracy. But there is a palpable reluctance to institute developmentally appropriate democratic processes in school. There is a reluctance to teach the importance of and need for legitimate debate, dissent, and opposition to unjust practices and laws. The process of schooling in the United States stresses the need for conformity and obedience. Administrative procedures in schools too often exemplify a lack of due process that is endemic to the most authoritarian political systems (Hyman 1970).

It is peculiar that Americans, who take pride in the freedoms they say citizens enjoy, still use traditional methods of inflicting pain on school children. Yet, a cross-cultural study of the demographics of pain reveals that, among the technologically advanced countries of the world, it is the English-speaking ones that are more reluctant to give up flogging, switching, and swatting.

England, a country with a history of international aggression and successful conquests of other nations, finally outlawed corporal punishment in their equivalent of U.S. public schools in the summer of 1987. Children in private and religious schools were not protected, however.

The Anglo-Saxon tradition of paddling is most dramatically

revealed in a study conducted by Jean Hewitt (1981) in London, Ontario. As part of her study of the efforts to eliminate corporal punishment in London, she reported the results of various polls. Over a twenty-year period between the 1950s and the late 1970s, public opinion supporting teacher use of corporal punishment remained stable. Hewitt's survey conducted in the late 1970s agreed with the findings of Johnson in 1952.

On the question, "Do you agree with teachers being allowed to inflict corporal punishment?" overall 48 percent of a national sample agreed and 44 percent disagreed. A breakdown by ethnic background revealed that 60 percent of respondents in Ontario agreed compared to only 28 percent in Quebec.

Although communist countries forbid the use of corporal punishment, they nevertheless have effective methods to inflict pain. Principally they rely on shaming by publicly humiliating children who do not conform. Mao's cultural revolution provided the Chinese with the ultimate use of this technique. Landowners, scholars, artists, and anyone else disapproved of by the Red Guards were forced into lengthy sessions of self-confession and public ridicule.

In his account of teaching in Russian schools, Cassie (1979) reports on an observation by Downey: "As a corrective disciplinary measure in one school, an unruly student was not permitted to wear the uniform as a punishment and was so disgraced in the eyes of his classmates that day" (Downey 1972 p. 30). Group approval is a major technique used to obtain conformity.

Pearl Oliner (1988) studied those who rescued Jews during the Holocaust. She states that the "rescuers often talked of being close to their parents while growing up, yet they emphasized that their parents had not insisted on mindless obedience. Discipline in their family of origin was based more on reasoning than on physical punishment."

Babcock (1977) studied the use of pain on children in sixty cultures. He found that the nature of religious beliefs was a major determinant of the amount of pain inflicted on children. Cultures whose religions centered on warlike, angry, or vengeful gods were more likely to promote anxiety and pain in order to socialize their children.

Yet cultures can emphasize bravery and warrior heroes without depending on hitting children, as is illustrated by native American cultures. An anecdote illustrates this point. A great Nez Perce chief was once on a peace mission to a white general. While riding through the whites' camp, he saw a soldier hitting a child. He reined in his horse and said to his companions, "There is no point in talking peace with a barbarian. What could you say to a man who would strike a child?" (Hyman and Wise 1979).

How the Media Perpetuate Punitiveness and Psychological Maltreatment

The media play an important role in perpetuating punitiveness toward American school children. This is exemplified in the portrayal of Joe Clark, one of the few educators ever to appear on the cover of *Time* magazine. Clark's philosophy seems to represent an attempt to prove that everything research says about psychological maltreatment is wrong. My investigations of Joe Clark (Hyman 1989) indicate that his school is a case study of what not to do to build self-esteem.

Most Americans who watch Clark in action are likely to love him or hate him. His carefully orchestrated public persona is the embattled, tough guy, no-nonsense principal who took over Paterson, New Jersey's Eastside High in 1982. He is the educator made famous by wielding a bullhorn and baseball bat. Clark is the embodiment of Ronald Reagan's "good old-fashioned discipline" and the buddy of William Bennett, who succinctly defined Clark's role in education: "Sometimes you need Mr. Chips and sometimes you need *Dirty Harry*." Clark is assured his place in folklore with the release of the movie *Lean on Me* in 1989, which became a nationwide box office earner.

The movie is an inspiring and exciting docudrama. It is also a perfect example of how badly the public can be misled by offering simplistic, wrong solutions to their fears of teenagers, blacks, Hispanics, drugs, crime, and the inner cities. *Lean on Me* is education's version of the Charles Bronson Death Wish genre of vigilante cinema.

Middle-class teenagers, who would be horrified if their own principal humiliated, denigrated, manhandled, or suspended them, as Joe Clark does to his own students, cheer during the film and rave about their new hero as they leave the theater. Black parents who applaud Clark's methods on screen would not be happy if their own children were his victims. But what a great movie. The most inspiring part is the ending. There, between the Grecian columns of Paterson's city hall, stands the triumphant Joe Clark, cheered by hundreds of loyal students. His enemies, portrayed as devious politicians and scheming school authorities, had just freed him from jail in order to stave off a riot by his student minions. He had been jailed for illegally chaining the fire doors in his building, allegedly to keep out drug dealers. Joe Clark, the hero of law and order, had broken the law for a higher purpose—his own purpose.

Film critic Carrie Ricky in the March 3, 1989 issue of the *Philadelphia Inquirer* said *Lean on Me* reminded her of the portrayals of Hitler in *Triumph of Will*. Leni Riefenstahl (the German movie director who glorified the Third Reich) made brilliant use of cinema by exalting another "charismatic figure who argued that a state of emergency precluded democracy."

Clark's actions such as suspending students for not knowing the school song, and his public support demonstrate the fragility of democracy and citizens' willingness to forgo constitutional rights, especially those of poor minority students. According to the media and professional forums, few administrators, including those in inner cities, support Clark's educational pronouncements (Hyman 1989b). His posturing stretches the limits of tolerance of educators who have even the slightest appreciation for democracy, due process, and mental health in the schools.

I have been fascinated—and horrified—by Joe Clark's public acclaim ever since he suggested that he ought to wring my neck. This incident followed our debate on the "Donahue Show" in which he claimed I made him sound like Hitler. Clark was particularly enraged when, with support from the few educators in the audience, I suggested that he was not truthful in reporting that he had doubled the test scores of Eastside High in less than a year. Yet in the make-believe world of *Lean on Me,* he had a powerful medium to further the myth that he could raise test scores by denigrating, humiliating, and rejecting students and faculty who refused to submit to the reflexive obedience he demanded. He was saying that psychological maltreatment is good for students. In fact, all of the research on school discipline, educational leadership, and the actual scores in Clark's Eastside High School belie his claims to success (Hyman 1989b).

Bending the truth does not seem to bother Joe Clark. For instance, when he was publicly exposed for lying about his illegal actions in an attempt to fire Eastside's highly regarded basketball coach, Dominick Pelosi, he responded by stating, "I plead the Fifth" (Rossi 1987). How is it that this exemplar of authoritarianism, this breaker of laws, this claimer of the unclaimable strikes such a resonant chord with the American public? How is he able to manipulate the media to promote a philosophy that most Americans would consider repugnant in any setting other than in schools or prisons?

To me, Clark typifies the demagoguery of charismatic authoritarians who offer themselves as the answer to social crises. They identify a common enemy as being responsible for complex problems and offer draconian methods of controlling the enemy. Few will complain of the suspension of a few civil liberties of obviously undeserving groups. The future czar must convince people that only he can carry out the solutions. In order to do this, he rationalizes that the end justifies the means. This excuses the wholesale use of half-truths and outright lies. Finally, the potential potentate must manipulate a willing media in order to accomplish his goals.

Historically adolescents have been suspect in American society. Ever since the economic emancipation of juveniles, the advent of child labor laws, and legislation requiring universal education, the adolescent has changed from a contributor to family and society to a liability. Further, every generation of puritans, right-wing authoritarians, fundamentalists, and fellow travelers has carped about the immoral excesses of adolescents and the need for ever stricter punishments. Their constant calls for stricter and harsher punishment blur the historical and factual evidence of repeated failures of their past policies.

The successful exhortations of politicians to a periodically conservative population, accompanied by the cacophony of tel-evangelists who reach many Americans each week, further extol the virtues of punitiveness, control, and strict discipline for sin-ful, hormonally driven adolescents. It is no coincidence that the United States is the only Western country in which juveniles may be subject to the death penalty.

Minority adolescents are truly feared. The common stereo-type is that most black teenagers are muggers, drug users, and pushers. Violence and the drug culture in inner cities strike ter-ror in the hearts of many Americans. Their answer is to coun-terstrike with the use of force. Yet I believe that the drug culture would be relatively impotent were it not for suburban white teen-agers and adults who drive into the city for their supplies of il-legal drugs. These buyers, however, play a relatively small role in the public's perception of the problem of inner-city youth. Nor do we want to marshal the long-term economic resources or make the complex social policy changes necessary to address the real causes of drug use in a poverty culture. It is cheaper to tell kids to "just say no" to drugs.

Lean on Me clearly identifies the enemy. In the tradition of John Wayne westerns, when Joe Clark arrives in town, we im-mediately recognize the good guys and the bad guys. Clark had little trouble mobilizing positive public opinion when he illegally expelled three hundred minority students and the school staff who did not show him the respect and obedience he demanded. He claimed that all of the students expelled were educationally hopeless overaged underachievers, parasites, hoodlums, and/or drug pushers, all code words for black youth. Teachers who did not agree with him committed the crime of disloyalty. The movie audience cheered his actions against punks and inner-city teach-ers. Many citizens view the latter as burned-out, malingering wimps who do not care about students.

The educators I have interviewed and others who know Clark agree that the movie honestly portrays Clark's egomania-cal personality as he summarily dismissed, humiliated, and ver-bally assaulted students and staff alike (Logan 1989). Clark, when asked about his dictatorial style, said, "I am a dictator and they love it" (Rossi 1987). In truth, followers and adoring public, who later flocked to his movie, do love him. In the movie he quickly identified the enemy and wasted little time on what he called "fruitless egalitarianism."

Clark, a black proponent of conservative ideology, was the ultimate political tool of the Reagan administration's simplistic and cost-cutting attempts to deal with school crime. Reagan installed his right-wing sycophants in the educational bureaucracy in order to promote punitiveness. They buried the results of the massive Safe Schools Study, which demonstrated that Clark is actually the antithesis of the effective inner-city secondary school principal identified by massive research. Crime and violence are reduced by principals who are fair, firm, and consistent (Hyman and D'Alesandro 1984).

Rather than revive the Educational Equity Group, which had recognized expertise in school violence, President Reagan appointed Gary Bauer to head the Working Group on School Violence/Discipline to construct a policy on discipline consistent with conservative ideology. The so-called Bauer Report, presented to Congress in 1984 and viewed as hopelessly flawed by almost all experts on school crime, was used to create a climate of fear in which the Reagan administration began a campaign to attack the constitutional rights of students (Hyman and D'Alesandro 1984). Elimination of due process in discipline cases was a major goal, since they claimed that due process procedures were tying the hands of school administrators.

Bauer and the rest of his group completely ignored a study that refuted their contention. The survey of secondary school principals by the National Center for Educational Statistics revealed that administrators did not perceive due process requirements as an impediment to good school discipline (Hyman and D'Allesandro 1984). The data did not fit into the scheme of making heroes out of people like Joe Clark. *Lean on Me* demonstrated the need for a shoot-from-the-hip, law-and-order solution to misbehaving students.

There is no evidence that Clark was part of President Reagan's early planning to return to "good old-fashioned discipline," but it is no wonder that his tactics deserved congratulatory telephone calls from the president and deification by Secretary of Education William Bennett. Clark, a black, could get away with making outrageous statements about poor, alienated, inner-city minority students that would be considered overtly racist if made by whites. Part of his rhetoric, reported by Dan Morris in *Zeta* magazine, includes familiar "right wing denounciations against welfare, affirmative action and other social programs."

The writer and director of *Lean on Me* did not sort fact from fancy in glorifying a punitive disciplinarian rather than an educator, especially in regard to the central theme of the movie: raising test scores to save the school from state takeover. There is no evidence that Clark was able to double the scores on the New Jersey minimum basic skills tests during his first year as principal (Hyman 1989b). Nor was it possible that the state could come in and take over the school if a minimum score were not achieved. What is the reality of Clark as an educator rather than "kick-out artist"?

The scores of Clark's students on the New Jersey High School Proficiency Test (HSPT) were the lowest in the state for 1986, 1987, and 1988 (Hyman 1989b). Over this three-year period, only an average of 24.1 percent of Eastside students passed all three sections of this basic skills test. Compared to all other urban schools in the state, Eastside's average student passing rate over the three years is 24.1 percent lower than comparable inner-city schools. While some of the differences of pass rates with equivalent schools may be small, Eastside is hardly a model of good education, let alone good discipline.

Clark's former principal at a Patterson elementary school, Wendell Williams, a respected black educator, was "fascinated and appalled" by him. He wrote in a local paper, the *Paterson Greater News,* in 1983 that "Mr. Clark had a knack to keep unrest brewing . . . his brand of trouble was invariably aimed at disorganizing whatever was established. . . . He talked like a revolutionary and dressed like a fop. His language was filled with street talk and vulgarities, yet his speeches were a series of stiff, archaic phrases and infrequently used, melodramatic, stagelike expressions. . . . I am not surprised that he has attracted so much attention in the media by his methods and antics."

Why was *Lean on Me,* a film about a punitive, psychologically abusive disciplinarian, a box office smash? Because it is an escape that fulfills the fondest dreams of a public that yearns for the good old days of education—days that never existed except in the fantasies of all who would like a simpler, safer world, the kind promised by the solutions offered by the *Dirty Harry* of education, Crazy Joe Clark.

The Demographics of Abuse

Over ten years of research on corporal punishment and psychological abuse clearly indicates the demographics of pain. Certain regions of the United States and specific traditions determine who the majority of victims will be. Staff at the NCSCPAS first looked at this issue in 1977 following the *Ingraham v. Wright* case.

Events leading to the decision in the Ingraham case began on October 6, 1970 in Dade County, Florida. James Ingraham was a fourteen-year-old eighth grader in Drew Junior High School. James and other students were requested by a teacher to leave the stage of the school auditorium. They moved too slowly. The school principal, Willie Wright Jr., took James and the other students to his office to be paddled. James protested that he had not disobeyed the teacher and did not deserve a paddling. Because of his resistance, Wright called in Lemmi Deliford, the assistant principal, and Solomon Barnes, an assistant to the principal. The following is James Ingraham's account of what happened.

> Q: Do you remember if he [Wright] told you how many times he was going to beat you?
>
> A: [He] started off at five, then went up to twenty.
>
> Q: How did he paddle you, if you resisted it?
>
> A: They took off their coats when they came in . . .
>
> Q: Who were "they"?
>
> A: Mr. Deliford, Mr. Barnes, and Mr. Wright.
>
> Q: They took off their coats?
>
> A: Yes, and their watches.

Q: Then what did they do?

A: [They] told me to take stuff out of my pockets and take off my coat.

Q: Then what did they do?

A: [They said], "Stoop over and get your licks."

Q: Did you do what they told you?

A: No.

Q: What did you do?

A: I stand up.

Q: Then what happened?

A: Then they grabbed me, [and] took me across the table.

Q: Who were "they"?

A: Mr. Deliford, Mr. Barnes, and Mr. Wright.

Q: You say Mr. Barnes and Mr. Deliford did what?

A: Put me across the table.

Q: Show me how they did that.

The court record indicated that James lay prone, face down, and feet off the floor across a table.

Q: Who held you there?

A: Mr. Barnes and Mr. Deliford.

Q: Who held what?

A: Mr. Barnes held my legs, and Mr. Deliford held my arms.

Q: Who paddled you?

A: Mr. Wright.

Q: You said he was going to give you how many licks?

A: Twenty.

Q: How many did he give you?

A: More than twenty.

Q: Did it hurt?

A: Yes, it hurt.

Q: Did you cry?

A: Yeah.

James went home despite threats from the principal that he would bust him on the side of the head if he left the school. When he got home, his mother saw how badly beaten he was and took him to the hospital. The examining physician diagnosed hematomas and prescribed ice packs, pain killers, a laxative, and a sedative to help James sleep. Eight days later, a six-inch hematoma was observed on his buttocks, swollen, tender, and oozing. Other students at Drew Junior High had been severely beaten (one coughed up blood after several severe beatings). The parents of the abused students banded together with a suit that eventually reached the Supreme Court.

The severe beatings administered by Wright and company were not considered assault and battery because no prosecutor in Florida would seriously have pressed charges. The defendants maintained that what they did was merely to administer corporal punishment, which is a protected disciplinary procedure under Florida law. The student plaintiffs claimed that the beatings were cruel and unusual and did not allow proper due process under the Constitution.

On April 17, 1977, the Supreme Court denied the students constitutional protection under the cruel and unusual punishment clause of the Eighth Amendment and the procedural due-process clause of the Fourteenth Amendment. This particular ruling has invariably been invoked by defendant educators who have beaten, punched, kicked, and bruised students. Ironically, in every other setting but the schoolhouse damage similar to that inflicted by Willie Wright would require prosecution by the state.

When one considers the demographics of abuse, it is not surprising that the most infamous case of legally sanctioned maltreatment of school children occurred in Florida. Florida has consistently been one of the top three "swatting" states in the country. However, at the time Ingraham reached the Supreme Court there were no data to show just how bad the situation was throughout the country, especially in the South.

Because there were no national studies on the incidence of corporal punishment in schools, we turned to a source not usually used in research: newspaper editorials. Although editorials hardly rank as an accurate reflection of public opinion, as would scientific public-opinion polls, it is generally true that the majority of editorial policies do not vary greatly from traditional sentiment in a particular region of the country. Therefore NCSCPAS researchers gathered a sample of editorials on corporal punishment from around the country, divided them by geographical region, and then separated the opinions as to whether they were positive, negative, or neutral on the subject. A statistical analysis of them showed that New England and the mid-Atlantic states were unfavorable toward the Supreme Court decision; that is, it could be assumed that the editors did not favor corporal punishment. The majority of opinions favorable to corporal punishment were in the East-South-Central states (Kentucky, Tennessee, Alabama, and Mississippi), the South Atlantic states (Delaware, Maryland, Washington, D.C., Virginia, West Virginia, North Carolina, South Carolina, Georgia, and Florida), and the West-South-Central states (Arkansas, Louisiana, Oklahoma, Texas). These states, according to the biannual Office of Civil Rights (OCR) surveys of education, are among the top swatters of school children in the United States.

The researchers then obtained census data and correlated demographic information with the findings in the nine geographic regions. The results showed that the regions most favorable to corporal punishment also had the lowest educational expenditures per capita, the highest dropout rates, and the highest illiteracy rates, and they were among the lowest in terms of the amount of money spent on psychological staff as a percentage of the school budgets. Stated another way, this study showed an association indicating that as editorial opinion in a region becomes more favorable to corporal punishment, the people in that region are poorer, less educated, and spend less on school mental health services.

What Does the Public Think?

The results of a 1989 Harris poll of a random, representative sample of 1,250 Americans showed that Americans are slowly moving away from support for corporal punishment in the home (Hyman 1989a). This is an important finding since support in the home is a base for support in school, and support for paddling in school has declined dramatically. Murray Straus, an eminent researcher on family violence, indicates that until recently, 90 to 95 percent of Americans approved parental spanking, yet the new Harris poll demonstrated that 86 percent of the respondents supported this practice (Hyman 1989a). A recent Gallup poll of teachers showed that only 38 percent disapprove of school paddlings; the Harris poll showed that 54 percent of parents were against it.

The most resistance to corporal punishment in the schools is in the East; 66 percent of respondents are against it. Only 33 percent of the respondents from the South are against it.

Among those with family incomes over $50,000, 58 percent say hitting children in school is never right. In comparison, 52 percent of those with family incomes of $7,500 or less think it is never right. Of those in the upper income bracket, 31 percent say it is never right for parents to hit children, as compared to 13 percent of the respondents with family incomes below $7,500. These findings suggest that approximately 37 percent of upper-income people who do not think that parents should hit their children think it is right for teachers to hit children. Approximately 24 percent of parents responding said that their children were hit in school. The greatest percentage were hit in the South (31 percent).

These data support previous NCSCPAS research showing that people who were hit least as children, who come from families with higher levels of education, who are more affluent, and who are in more professional levels of employment tend to hit their children less and do not approve of other parents' hitting their children.

About 72 percent of males and 28 percent of females report having been hit often or very often as children. Of these, 71 percent of the females and 30 percent of the males report they spank their children very often or often.

Race was a factor in determining how frequently respondents were hit as children. Of those reporting that they had been hit "very often" as children, 7 percent were white, 11 percent were Hispanic, and 25 percent were black. The data suggest to me that poor and minority persons suffer harsher discipline in childhood. Historically blacks have felt that strong discipline is needed to protect their children from making fatal mistakes in the white world (Hyman 1989a).

Office of Civil Rights Surveys

In the 1970s the OCR began to collect data about various issues related to possible discrimination against school children. They requested that schools, among other things, indicate the number of corporal punishments by race. The first such survey was conducted in 1975–1976. NCSCPAS staff obtained the results of it and looked at data on Pennsylvania, Maryland, West Virginia, and Delaware.

According to the survey, 14 percent of the black male students, 12 percent of the Hispanic or other minority male students, and 8 percent of the white students received corporal punishment. Four percent of black females and less than 2 percent of other females received corporal punishment. These results suggest racial and sexual biases in terms of who was getting hit. Other data (Rose 1984; Hyman 1988b), suggest that the combination of race and poverty most affects the rate of black children being hit.

OCR has collected similar data every other year since then. Its methods of data collection and types of reporting procedures have varied over the years, however, making longitudinal comparisons difficult. Policy changes determined by political considerations of changing federal administrations complicate the issue. Therefore the NCSCPAS decided to do its own analysis of the data.

Bill Russell, NCSCPAS staff member, has found that the OCR data grossly underestimate the actual numbers and percentages of children who are hit each year. (For a full discussion of the reasons for this discrepancy, see Russell 1989.) The most recent data available are those from 1986 (table 2–1). (Data for previous years are shown in appendix B. Data from the 1978, 1980, and 1982 surveys are not included. During these years the sampling procedures were flawed in terms of validity of the sample.) The table provides information on the number of students sampled in each state, the number of students who were paddled at least once, the percentage of students sampled who were paddled at least once, and OCR projections for each state's school population.

The OCR figures are problematic because they represent only the number of students hit, not how many times each student may have been hit. The percentages given in the table are considered underestimates in most cases for a variety of reasons. For instance, in Pennsylvania during 1986, the sample included Philadelphia and Pittsburgh, school districts that enroll approximately 50 percent of the state's students. Because these two systems ban corporal punishment, the percentages estimated for the state are gross underestimates.

Other problems with the survey are that some schools never respond, some included in the samples no longer exist because of redistricting changes, and some respond to the rest of the survey but do not report corporal punishment, even though it is practiced in their schools. Finally, there is no assurance that teachers record all cases of corporal punishment. Moreover, records may be kept, but they may not reach the office from which they would be reported to OCR.

Even where corporal punishment is illegal, it still occurs. Note from the table that New Jersey, which banned corporal punishment over one hundred years ago, reported eleven cases. Kreutter (1982) did a survey of junior high school students in Trenton, New Jersey, to determine how they were usually disciplined. Almost 2 percent of the students reported being hit by their teachers. The eleven cases in New Jersey in table 2–1 are

Table 2–1
INCIDENCE OF CORPORAL PUNISHMENT IN SCHOOLS
(1986)

State	Projected Total No. of Students	Total No. of Students Sampled	No. of Students in Sample Who Received Corporal Punishment	Percentage of Total Sample
Alabama	755824	445708	42770	10
Alaska	98608	88078	233	*
Arizona	586583	286883	5911	2
Arkansas	470224	207965	23013	11
California	5028304	2825200	5103	*
Colorado	622285	413703	683	*
Connecticut	492025	262453	89	*
Delaware	86755	85009	1204	1
Washington D.C.	86125	84630	152	*
Florida	1576212	1318229	87218	7
Georgia	1191158	728704	49186	7
Hawaii	80305	178947	0	0
Idaho	206143	141416	534	*
Illinois	1713625	783709	957	*
Indiana	1144490	499159	15975	3
Iowa	482448	210146	269	*
Kansas	459107	222066	1167	1
Kentucky	632985	353415	14733	4
Louisiana	786442	569399	23476	4
Maine	199191	102608	0	0
Maryland	606441	550694	552	*
Massachusetts	763174	382122	0	0
Michigan	1626732	703700	4322	1

Table 2–1 continued

State	Projected Total No. of Students	Total No. of Students Sampled	No. of Students in Sample Who Received Corporal Punishment	Percentage of Total Sample
Minnesota	738500	400640	21	*
Mississippi	539174	313211	33463	11
Missouri	900172	431065	5589	1
Montana	180461	91588	158	*
Nebraska	307106	143389	173	*
Nevada	160439	146490	917	1
New Hampshire	157002	92326	0	0
New Jersey	1234431	607768	11	*
New Mexico	286055	214574	6787	3
New York	3138207	1660453	23	*
North Carolina	1043809	634966	18300	3
North Dakota	120080	69901	5	*
Ohio	1597848	606304	19747	3
Oklahoma	645918	392931	26493	7
Oregon	493929	264046	631	*
Pennsylvania	1586882	588584	2424	*
Rhode Island	145399	108306	1	*
South Carolina	560533	412683	21051	5
South Dakota	133800	78854	67	*
Tennessee	745538	448275	42769	10
Texas	3342108	1945398	121862	6
Utah	336484	293797	55	*
Vermont	76497	41063	0	0

Table 2–1 continued

State	Projected Total No. of Students	Total No. of Students Sampled	No. of Students in Sample Who Received Corporal Punishment	Percentage of Total Sample
Virginia	993976	959760	3059	*
Washington	783722	473414	2021	*
West Virginia	340379	229751	2597	1
Wisconsin	676248	310461	101	*
Wyoming	96153	71422	189	*

*Incident rate of less than 1 percent.

indications of illegal activities, indicating that the teachers were probably disciplined by the school district or were prosecuted.

The No Hitters and the Top Hitters

By the summer of 1989, nineteen states had outlawed corporal punishment in the schools: New Jersey, Massachusetts, Maine, Rhode Island, Vermont, New Hampshire, New York, California, Hawaii, Nebraska, Wisconsin, Michigan, Oregon, Connecticut, Virginia, North Dakota, Iowa, Minnesota, and Alaska. Puerto Rico also forbids the use of corporal punishment in schools. (Appendix A cites dates of enactment.) In addition, most large cities, such as Chicago, Washington, D.C., Baltimore, Philadelphia, and New Orleans, have banned it. Many affluent suburbs do not allow corporal punishment either.

Nevertheless, based on the evidence gathered over the years at the NCSCPAS and the OCR, it is likely that at least 2 million to 3 million incidents occur each year. The states with the highest proportion of hitting are Arkansas and Mississippi (table 2–1).

based on actual reported incidents of corporal punishment from the samples; it does not include those on the samples who were not tallied.

The data from 1985–1986 indicate that the twelve southern states accounted for at least 80 percent of the reported 1,099,731 paddlings during 1986. Texas had the most whacks, but Arkansas had the greatest per pupil ratio. Outside the South, Ohio and Indiana were the leaders in number of whacks. Arkansas had the top percentage spot in 1982 and 1984, but Florida and Texas have shared top billing over the years. The top ten swatting states have also included Mississippi, Tennessee, Alabama, Oklahoma, Georgia, Missouri, and Kentucky.

Special education students seem to be particularly vulnerable to excessive paddlings. According to a report in the December 28, 1987 issue of *Nashville Tennessean,* when the number of reported incidents was divided by the number of students the results suggested that 215 percent of the students were paddled in 1986–1987. The rate for blind and crippled children was 176 percent. These figures indicate only each incident. Therefore, we do not know if ten incidents reflect ten students being hit once or one student being hit ten times.

Abusing Schools, Abusing Teachers

There are many conflicting studies about which teachers do the most paddling. But if there is a clear finding, it is that as students get older and bigger, their teachers seem less likely to hit them. Perhaps the teachers are afraid they will be hit back; perhaps the students who were most hit drop out of school; or perhaps high school teachers are more compassionate as a group than their elementary school colleagues (this last one is the least likely explanation based on my own observations). Nevertheless, although there are fewer paddlings in high school, high school teachers are not unfavorable to hitting. In the 1988 Gallup poll of teachers' attitudes, 56 percent of elementary school teachers and 55 percent of high school teachers approved of corporal punishment in the lower grades.

There have been few studies of the types of teachers who paddle most frequently. One study in Tennessee found that teachers who paddled the most were more rigid in their views and had more emotional problems (Rust and Kinnard 1983). It also indicated that they tended to be less experienced and more impulsive than their peers. These findings are similar to those of Bogacki (1981), who concluded that teachers who are more punitive and authoritarian have more favorable attitudes toward corporal punishment and are more likely to hit children.

A study by Reardon and Renolds (Hyman and Wise 1979) conducted in Pennsylvania surveyed attitudes of different groups toward corporal punishment. School board presidents were most favorable (81 percent), followed by principals (78 percent), administrators (68 percent), teachers (74 percent), parents (71 percent), and students (25 percent).

What Happens When Corporal Punishment Is Stopped?

A national survey conducted by Arnold Farley (1983) at the NCSCPAS offers some detailed information about regional differences. The survey, based on results from 400 junior high schools across the United States, was designed to describe the characteristics associated with the use and nonuse of corporal punishment. A nineteen-item questionnaire on student, school, and respondent characteristics was sent to the principal of each school, asking that the person responsible for discipline respond. Analyses were completed on 219 questionnaires (58 percent return); 67 percent of the respondents were principals, 26 percent were vice-principals, and 7 percent had other titles. The schools reporting high use of corporal punishment had the poorest student populations, the largest average class size, and the most severe disciplinary practices. They were concentrated in the Southeast (38 percent). Schools that did not use corporal punishment had larger student enrollments and more white students and were concentrated in the Northeast (48 percent). No significant differences were found for perceived effectiveness in maintaining a climate suitable for learning. The decision to use corporal punishment appeared to be based in part on an orientation toward physical punishment by school personnel, which may have been supported by local values and/or traditional beliefs.

Significantly, respondents from schools that had abolished corporal punishment reflected less severe disciplinary practices than those from schools using corporal punishment. Their perception of their ability to maintain a climate suitable for learning was no different from the respondents who utilized corporal punishment frequently.

One of the purposes of this study was to investigate respondents' attitude toward the U.S. Supreme Court's position that corporal punishment is necessary to maintain discipline and to allow for the proper education of children (*Ingraham v. Wright,* 1977). The study clearly indicated that responding school administrators most directly concerned with discipline functioned effectively without inflicting pain. Further, eliminating corporal punishment did not result in increased disciplinary problems. In fact, according to respondents, schools with reported high use tended to be generally more punitive in all disciplinary situations, regardless of the rationale that corporal punishment is needed as a last resort to control students.

Characteristics of School Abuse

Another series of studies looked at the actual characteristics of corporal punishment. The sample consisted of cases from newspaper reports of public, religious, and private school children, aged five to twenty years. (Cases involving preschool, vocational, and/or higher education were not analyzed.) In all cases, the aggressor was an employee of the school district—typically teachers or principals but also bus drivers, janitors, and even a school board member.

The infractions resulting in severe corporal punishment were divided into two categories: violent and nonviolent. Violent acts were those that caused harm to other persons or damage to property, such as fighting at school and/or on the school bus, pulling a chair out from under another student, and kicking rocks against the school building. Nonviolent acts included truancy and/or class cutting, possessing cigarettes, getting poor grades, staying in the bathroom too long, and incorrectly pronouncing words in a kindergarten phonics class (Clarke et al.

1982). The study showed that most of the offenses committed by students were nonviolent (80.3 percent).

The severity of the punishment was subdivided into three categories: cases that required medical attention, cases that resulted in some type of physical injury not considered severe enough to require medical treatment (such as blistering, bruises, and welts), and punishments that parent(s) thought were improperly administered, unnecessary, and/or excessive but did not result in any observable physical injury.

As we found in other studies, the highest proportion of victims are males, who are most often punished by males. Also, males were three times more likely to inflict severe corporal punishment than females. Remember that this study examined extreme cases that reached the press. The vast majority of teachers are females, especially at the elementary level. Much of the corporal punishment they inflict probably is not severe enough to cause parental concern or to result in press reports. However, over 80 percent of administrators are male (*Statistical Abstracts of the United States* 1982). In many districts, physical punishment is inflicted only by administrators. Therefore, the data suggest that the greatest likelihood of damage may occur when a male student is sent to an administrator for punishment.

Males also were twice as likely to require medical attention. Since males were more frequent recipients of corporal punishment and more frequently hit by men in this sample, it is possible that the "macho myth" was operating; that is, boys have to be tough and "take it" when physical punishment is administered. Anecdotal records suggest that girls are more likely to cry when pain becomes severe. Since boys are less likely to cry and more likely to be defiant, this may increase the anger of the punisher.

The study found a low frequency of primary grade students who were severely punished. As students' age increased, the frequency rose sharply; it peaked in the junior high school years and then dropped off dramatically for older students. The major contribution to this trend was the participation of males. The curve for the male staff mirrored the overall results. In the cases studied, a greater proportion of corporal punishment in the primary grades was administered by females than by males. The frequency of female staff involved in corporal punishment declined as student age increased. No student aged fourteen or older was physically punished by a female teacher.

These patterns reflect everyday observations: a higher percentage of primary grade teachers are female (*Statistical Abstracts in the United States* 1982); female staff who strike young children are less likely to have a student retaliate in kind; as the student age (and size) increases, the chances of a female teacher being at risk in a corporal punishment situation becomes greater (Eyre 1984).

The high incidence of corporal punishment cases among junior high school students may be related to the relative frequency of their misbehavior: "Junior high schools are more violent than senior high schools because junior high schools have a high proportion of students who would rather not be there" (Cordes 1984). Several reasons appear to explain the low incidence of use of corporal punishment of older students (ages fourteen to twenty). First, using physical punishment with this age group makes the educator more vulnerable to a hostile student's reaction ("School Shooting," 1978; "Student Hits," 1979). Second, the student dropout rate and school policies that push out disruptive students tend to distort that portion of the overall curve. And even proponents of corporal punishment may feel that it is inappropriate with this age group.

Actual punishments might vary in length and intensity but nevertheless result in extreme consequences. For example, an eighteen-year-old football player died after completing a series of forced exercises, including running and drills ("Player's Punishment," 1978). Similarly, a seven-year-old girl required to run 170 yards during gym collapsed and died (Richardson 1981).

Evaluations of traumatized children have focused on the emotional after-effects of the infliction of physical pain in schools, the same types of symptoms observed in victims of psychological maltreatment. It is difficult to imagine that the two do not occur simultaneously. It is evident that emotional trauma is at the core of all abuse of children and that the psychological after-effects should be of critical concern. This is discussed in chapter 4, which focuses on educator-induced posttraumatic stress disorder (EIPTSD).

Often when physical or psychological maltreatment, or witnessing of abuse, occurs in school, children begin to complain at home. Young children frequently develop a fear of going to school. Yet forcing children back to school may prevent the development of school phobia.

Most experts agree that phobias generally develop as a result of a traumatizing situation. A child who is hit by a schoolteacher cannot protect himself or herself and thus develops hyperalertness to fear of being hurt. Fear reactions, often betrayed by frequent startle responses, automatically trigger a host of hormonal responses in the body. One of these is an increased flow of adrenaline, which prepares the child for flight. But a child in school and under the authority of the teacher cannot flee. The unused adrenaline results in feelings of anxiety and tension.

A phobia may result as the child's brain links physiological fear responses with the appearance of the teacher, the classroom, and eventually the school. Hence, approaching the school, class, or teacher may cause an automatic physical fear reaction that the child cannot control. Since the school building or the classroom cannot hit the child, the fear response generalizes from the teacher to the surroundings associated with her. I have observed this response in many cases of EIPTSD.

If the child receives immediate support from other teachers, school psychologists, counselors, or other school staff, there may be no generalization of anxiety to the rest of the school. In those cases the anxiety remains focused on the teacher. Sometimes the anxiety shifts to anger when the child returns to the classroom. This response is more likely among older children and adolescents. And sometimes the constant exposure without further hitting may desensitize the child to the teacher.

Corporal Punishment, Crime, and War

Victor Streib of Cleveland–Marshall Law School examined the OCR corporal punishment data and drew some interesting conclusions. Reasoning that violence begets violence, he investigated whether states that were the most punitive toward school children would also be characterized by parental punitiveness. He thought that a general atmosphere of aggression toward children would show aggression by children and youth against others. He concluded that the top ten swatting states produced the greatest number of convicted youths on death row. Florida, Georgia, and Texas were the leaders in absolute numbers of convicted sixteen- and seventeen-year-old murderers in 1986.

In order to examine the possible relationship between corporal punishment and the prevalence of other types of violence, Strauss (1989) used an innovative approach. He weighted states in four categories based on an analysis by Friedman and Hyman (Hyman and Wise 1979); the higher the weight, the greater the legal authorization for the use of corporal punishment. He thereby created a Corporal Punishment Permission Index. Using the index, he analyzed states on two dimensions. He correlated it with the within-school assault rate and the homicide rate by children in each state. His analysis was used to study what he calls "cultural spillover theory." This theory suggests that legitimized violence in one sphere of society spills over into other spheres. As a result, it is difficult to determine the boundaries between legitimate and illegitimate violence; if parents can hit children, why shouldn't teachers? Even if others who are not supposed to hit children are charged with assault, it is more difficult for a jury to separate their thinking about the legitimacy of parental hitting from the illegitimacy of children's peers or police committing the act.

The data gathered by Straus demonstrate that states with high rates of homicide committed by children tend to have high rates of corporal punishment in schools (Straus 1989). This conclusion is admittedly tentative since relatively few children commit homicide. However, the actual homicide rate by adults does correlate with the amount of corporal punishment in schools. This study goes on to show higher rates of violence by students against other students in states that have high rates of striking by teachers. Instead of reducing student-to-student violence, the use of corporal punishment only provides a model that suggests violence is a way to solve problems. Straus also found, as have others, that "significantly more children who were physically punished at home committed both violent and property crimes."

Babock (Hyman and Wise 1979) studied the amount of violence in primitive cultures. A major finding was that the more warlike the gods of a culture, the more likely the people were to abuse children and the greater the infant homicide rate. Also, such a society was more likely to use war to resolve problems with other groups.

Summary

Attitudes of punitiveness toward children are developed in our own childhood. These attitudes are shaped by our own parents' practices, our religious beliefs, national identity, and even the region in which we live. Despite the powerful effects of modeling, it is clear, especially from the research by Mishkin, that teachers and parents can break old habits.

If we relied in all areas of life on the kinds of nonsensical assumptions used to support corporal punishment, we would still be using leeches to cure all types of diseases and burning witches at the stake.

I have had two interesting experiences that reflect on this problem. The first occurred on a radio talk show in Detroit. After giving my usual pitch about why hitting children is a bad idea, one of the callers disputed my statements. She claimed to have a doctoral degree and to teach education courses in college. After making her argument, I asked her, "How can you teach college students and yet ignore all of the research that is against the use of corporal punishment? Can you point to one research study that says it is beneficial for teachers to hit children?" Her reply, considering her education and position, was surprising: "Research is one thing, and teaching is another. I just believe that some kids need to be hit."

The other experience was quite positive. I was conducting a two-day workshop on psychological and physical abuse in the schools and effective disciplinary alternatives to punishment. The workshop in Panama City, Florida, was in a region noted for its high rate of paddling. During the first day of the workshop, which was attended by over 150 educators, I presented all of the research against the use of verbal and physical assaults, and I also answered practical questions and talked about alternatives. The next day, one of the participants, a guidance counselor, reported to the audience: "Last night, I sat in bed talking to my five-year-old daughter. I told her that I had been at a workshop during the day, and I learned that you don't have to hit little children to make them behave, and that I would not spank her anymore. My daughter replied, 'I'm really glad, Mommy. Now I don't have to spank my children when I grow up.'"

3

Reactions to Abuse
in Schools

"**M** RS. Gaspersohn, you probably already suspect that you
are not going to get, necessarily, all kinds of enthusiastic
understanding from this audience, or very possibly any audience
in this country," television talk show host Phil Donahue stated.
The audience included about 300 people in the studio and millions watching on television. Marlene Gaspersohn and her
daughter, Shelly, had just described Shelly's brutal beating at
Dunn High School and related how the trial judge would not
allow the examining physician to report that he had tried to file
child abuse charges against her abuser, Glenn Varney.

Phil Donahue, a man dedicated to eliminating corporal punishment, was playing the devil's advocate. The topic of the show
was school violence. The audience and two of the panelists were
lamenting about student violence against teachers and other students. Their concern was not violence by teachers against students. But that was very much on the minds of the few who
understood how violence begets violence. The Gaspersohns
were there to tell that side of the story.

During the first half-hour of the program, which was aired
in April 1984, the panelists were locked in angry debate and po-
lemic. A principal from El Paso, Texas, and I were set against
Joe Clark, principal of Eastside High in Paterson, New Jersey,
and Gary Bauer, under secretary of education who later became
President Reagan's chief domestic affairs adviser. Bauer had
been the principal author of a government report alleging that

the nation's schools were in chaos and the solution was "old-fashioned discipline."

As I tried to present the data that clearly negated Clark's clever phrases and hatemongering statements and Bauer's fallacious reasoning, it was clear that the audience was not sympathetic. Clark and Bauer had struck a responsive chord. Fear of inner-city black and Hispanic youths provides fertile ground for any vigilante approach to school discipline. Clark represented to many the great black hope for taming the uncivilized blackboard jungle. Without even touching on the problems of class and race, he could easily arouse deep-seated transgenerational fears of the takeover of society by rebellious, out-of-control adolescents. The audience responded to the climate of punitiveness that results in physical and psychological abuse of school children.

Responding to the audience's obvious sympathies, Donahue went on to say, "We appear to be a nation which is fed up with what we perceive to be kids on the loose who have no discipline. You also set yourself up, [Mrs. Gaspersohn], I might say with a good deal of courage, for being accused of cry babiness here." His voice began to take on a mocking quality: "'Oh, your baby was hit. So what! She will live. Maybe it was good for her.' How do you respond to that attitude?"

Unhesitatingly Ms. Gaspersohn emphatically replied, "It makes me mad to think that anyone would even think that. That anyone has the right to do something to my child. If I beat her that way, social services could have come in and taken her away from the home. But in North Carolina, there is no agency that can even investigate a charge of child abuse against a teacher. Almost anyone in the school system can do anything they want to." Ms. Gaspersohn, like so many other parents of abused school children, had studied the education laws concerning school discipline. She went on, "Teachers, assistant teachers, volunteers, teacher aids, student teachers can beat a child!"

Marlene Gaspersohn, a gentle soul, a housewife and mother, a devoted helper to her husband, and a person active in the Lutheran church, could hardly be called a radical. But her experiences with the ruling oligarchy of Harnett County had made her angry, as she stated before millions of people. The insensitivity, stonewalling, and absolute ignorance of school authorities had created an activist.

Ms. Gaspersohn, like many other parents of child victims, became a victim herself. She remained a victim until she became empowered by knowledge, anger, and the desire to protect all school children and parents in North Carolina from the excesses Shelly and her family had suffered. Many parents of school-abused children with whom I have talked say the same thing: their protectiveness toward their own children quickly extends to the children of others. Parents from as disparate places as Afton, Wyoming, and Clearwater, Florida, say almost the same words: "We don't want other children and parents to have to put up with what we suffered."

Marlene and Arnold Gaspersohn expected a rational response from school officials when confronted with evidence of the physical damage caused by the beating. At the most, they expected an apology from and an appropriate reprimand of Glenn Varney. They knew that corporal punishment was legal and that school officials might stick together and defend Varney. At the least they expected a rational and sympathetic response from school board members who were themselves parents. But all of these officials stonewalled her requests and trivialized the pain and humiliation Shelly suffered. As a result Ms. Gaspersohn became traumatized. But the trauma did not last. She became an activist while her daughter's case wended its way to final rejection by the North Carolina Supreme Court.

Identifying Abuse

The problem with identifying possible abuse is that the symptoms of maltreatment may be caused by stressors unrelated to school. One of the most telling symptoms is avoidance of school. Other changes in behavior may also occur.

The best insurance against undiscovered school abuse is to start talking about school when the child begins attending class or preschool. Many children perceive attempts by parents to discuss school as intrusive. They feel parents are checking up on them, particularly when discussions revolve around grades and discipline. Parents must establish early on that they are interested in all aspects of their children's school experiences.

It is especially important that children understand they will not receive double punishment for admitting misbehavior in school. A student who is punished first at school and then at home for the same offense may not tell parents what has happened in the future.

The major indicator of problems is an unexplained change in the child's behavior. The cases presented in this book point to scenarios that lead to abuse. A complete list of symptoms is presented in the latest version of our School Trauma Survey, which appears as appendix C. Parents can help analyze the possibility of abuse by filling out the checklist or having their child fill it out (it is at the fourth-grade reading level).

Cross-racial paddling often raises special hackles. A recent case in Florida involved a white principal who not only hit the black children harder than white children but called them such unpleasant names as "welfare brats." This so enraged the black community that the National Association for the Advancement of Colored People (NAACP) intervened. They were successful in having the principal transferred.

Proportionately, black children are subjected to corporal punishment many times oftener than white or Asian children in almost every school district in the nation, as documented by the Office of Civil Rights of the Department of Education. However, in the next case reported by Dr. Adah Maurer all of the stereotypes are inoperative, and it appears that socioeconomic factors were predominant.

St. Clair County, in the heart of rural Alabama and twenty miles from Birmingham, is only eight-percent black. But Elsie McGowan, the black teacher who paddled seven-year-old William "Red" Elmore, was voted most popular teacher for six of the eight years she taught business subjects at the local high school. Her three whacks with a paddle that was twenty-two inches long and five inches across left William with black and purple bruises.

As assistant principal at Moody Elementary, she had earned the respect of black and white parents. Her husband,

James McGowan, sat on the city council in Pell City and over-
saw the city's police force in addition to teaching at the county
vocational school. In contrast, the Elmores, a white family, are
dirt poor. They live outside town on a desolate road and are
considered country people. The *New York Times* reporter who
delved most deeply into the racial angle did not use the term
"poor white," but it is implicit in his story. Ms. Elmore made
the same point: "This is not a black versus white thing, but the
powerful versus the powerless."

The townspeople were divided but not along racial lines.
One white resident, Billie Todd, said, "This is the South, and a
lot of us have come a long way, but some have not. She wasn't
going to let a black woman paddle her little boy. The sentence
was justified." James Lawley, the principal, claimed "That same
day a white teacher paddled her [Ms. Elmore's] daughter in
another class, and she didn't do anything," a claim that Ms.
Elmore hotly denies.

No white-supremacy group has come to the Elmores' aid. Perhaps support for paddling supercedes racial bigotry in Alabama.

Family Stress

My colleagues and I have conducted extensive research into
studies of families whose children have been abused in school.
We have found that family stress is a common reaction and is
almost always present in cases of more severe school abuse. Typically when parents discover the symptoms and the causes of the
abuse, they seek redress from school authorities. In the majority
of cases that come to my attention, resistance, stonewalling, and
outright threats by school officials discourage parents from
going further. But some parents vow to carry the struggle up the
bureaucratic ladder and elsewhere.

When angry parents confront the school authorities, the bu-
reaucrats almost always support the action of the person who
administered the punishment. They may institute a mild penalty
such as a written reprimand, but in most cases the disciplinary
practices are considered appropriate. The school authorities
then begin to question the motives behind the parents' com-

plaints. The parents, especially the mothers, tend to become fearful, depressed, and anxious for their children. Unlike most precipitating events in adult traumatization, in these cases the child victims are forced to return to the environment in which the stressor occurred. Because of legal sanctions regarding school attendance and educational priorities, the parents are in a classical approach-avoidance dilemma. The result is frustration, anger, anxiety, and depression.

Because of the attitudes of the school authorities, complaining parents often fear their children will be harassed. Their fears are realistic, even when it is difficult to identify additional subtle stress placed on the children. Consider what happened to ten-year-old Jim Polk after his parents filed a suit against his school district for abusing his six-year-old sister.

> The Polk children attended school in the Midwest. In the early 1980s six-year-old Kim was grabbed by the neck and jerked roughly by her first-grade teacher. (This was not the first time the teacher had roughed up Kim.) Medical examination, including X-rays, revealed severe cervical strain and the possibility of ligament injury. Kim developed classical stress-related symptoms, including school avoidance, nervousness, fear of strangers, and withdrawn nonverbal reactions, and she lost weight. The Polks' attempts to obtain an apology from and change in the teacher's alleged abusive behavior were treated with contempt.
>
> Jim, also a student in Kim's school building, was an academically gifted child whose behavior in school had been exemplary. He was a hard worker, extremely conscientious, and in his seven years in school had never had a problem. After his parents filed suit against the school, Jim suddenly received a six-week detention assignment for a minor talking-out-of-turn incident. Next, the principal threatened Jim with punishment for running between school buildings.
>
> By this time, Jim's parents recognized the pattern of vindictiveness of school authorities they had feared. They complained to the principal and he backed off. Jim, however, was not immune from sarcastic statement by his teachers, typically snide remarks about fear of being sued if they were not nice to Jim.

Teachers as Caregivers or Betrayers

Teachers have tremendous power over the lives of children and the aspirations of their parents. This is especially true in the case of preschool and primary school children. Teachers are empowered as trusted caregivers by society. They are given the power of in loco parentis, the authority of parents. They thus have tremendous potential to do good—or bad—to children.

During normal developmental stages, children are dependent on their caregivers to fulfill appropriate needs. Trust is a crucial factor when caregivers physically or verbally assault children. A number of studies indicate a variety of later psychopathologies related to early abuse by caregivers. With the exception of the studies conducted at NCSCPAS, most of the research has been done in familial settings or with special institutional populations; however, the findings of these studies apply to school children.

Carmen, Reiker, and Mills (1984) found that almost half of 188 psychiatric inpatients in their study had histories of physical and/or sexual abuse and that 90 percent of these abused patients had been victimized by family members. They cited the profound betrayal of trust and an ongoing vulnerability among the critical factors in chronic abuse situations that may have led to the more severe psychological and behavioral symptoms shown in this population. They noted extreme difficulties with anger and aggression, self-image, and trust as typical of victims of more chronic abuse. They differentiated between men and women. Abused females typically directed their anger and aggression against themselves, whereas the males most often directed their aggression toward others. Of particular interest is the finding that adolescents who are abused even once display the same types of emotional and behavioral reactions as adolescents who have been chronically abused from childhood (Carmen, Reiker, and Mills 1984). This would lend weight to the import of the abusive parent–caregiver interaction itself rather than the development, severity, or regularity of the abuse. These findings apply to situations in extremely punitive schools or where teachers regularly target specific children for severe disciplinary measures or ridicule.

Some experts (Finkelhor and Browne 1985) propose a theory of "traumagenic" dynamics to explain the psychic damage caused in children who have been sexually abused by significant caregivers. As in the swatting of Shelly Gaspersohn, however, the actions of the teacher do not necessarily have to be sexual, since the violence is what results in severe symptoms. The betrayal, powerlessness, and stigmatization lead to feelings of low self-esteem. The betrayal may be a specific contributor to an intense need to regain trust and faith or an intense distrust, loss of faith, and aversion (numbing) to intimacy. Other reactions related to betrayal by caregivers are nightmares, phobias, hypervigilance, and somatic complaints that may extend into adulthood.

Witnessing

The effects of direct abuse seem clear. It is also possible the witnesses in close physical or psychological proximity may be just as vulnerable to the development of stress disorders. Frederick (1986) reports intense avoidance symptoms in children at a playground who witnessed their friends being shot by a sniper from a building across the street. Surprisingly, children who were not present at the time also developed avoidance behaviors and other symptoms as a result of the shooting.

A comparison of corporal punishment and psychological abuse with murder may seem farfetched. Nevertheless, the dynamics of the situation are similar in terms of witnessing or hearing. In many cases I have found that siblings develop negative attitudes toward teachers and schooling when they are close to a victim.

Relevant to reactions of siblings to the stress of the victim is a study (Jaffe et al. 1986) of the degree of adjustment of two groups of boys who were either direct or indirect victims of family violence. The boys, ages four to sixteen, were measured on social competence (activities, social participation, school performance) and behavioral problems (hyperactivity, aggression, withdrawal). The study found that the adjustment difficulties for children who were directly victimized and those who merely observed the victimization were comparable. Also, both groups evidenced poorer adjustment than boys who had never been abused.

There were, however, some differences between those directly abused and witnesses. The directly abused boys demonstrated significantly more externalized symptoms. They were disobedient at home and/or school, and they were described as lying and cheating, destroying things belonging to themselves or others, being cruel, associating with bad friends, and fighting. The children who witnessed the abuse tended to internalize symptoms. They were described as clinging to adults, complaining of loneliness, feeling unloved, unhappy, sad, or jealous, and worrying.

In addition to scientific evidence on the effects of witnessing traumatic events, anecdotal information can help to determine the extent of the problem. The boxes contain samples of letters received at NCSCPAS on the problem.

I read story in Parade Sunday Gazett Mail when teachers hit kids in school. I think this should not happen in our schools this law should be changed and also prayer back in school. I know children isn't that bad to be treated like that story and I have read in paper about the children in West Virginia. I was one of the children in third grade to see several children punish for know wrong. One day this teacher beat a boy all over the school house and blood was coming from his face. We lived across road from school house and all us children was crying and my mother hurd us all and she came in school and stop the teacher from beating this boy. I never liked school after that happened and I couldn't learn. I was afraid of teachers so I am eighty two years in October, but I remember this was always on my mind when I read this story. I just thought I must tell you about this. We mustn't let this happen. God bless you for taken part in this. Excus my writing.

I am writing you today out of a response from a recent article on the use of corporal punishment in *Children*, a magazine for parents. I am extremely concerned with the issue of corporal punishment in the schools as well as a form of parenting.

I have a very valid reason. Twenty-five years ago when I was in kindergarten, I was a very enthusiastic child. I had changed schools in mid-year and went to a larger school. I had a boy in the same class with me who was hyperactive. The teacher couldn't control him, so she sent for the principal. I was new and was wondering why the whole class got scared when she called for the principal—everyone got quiet. When the little boy that was acting up saw the principal coming in the classroom he hid under a table. The principal had a thick black belt in his hand! Both the teacher and principal physically dragged this little boy out by his legs! Then the principal proceeded to beat this little boy!

I had never been so scared in my life. I came from a family that didn't hit! This incident marked me for school the rest of my school years. I was afraid of school. I became too shy, afraid to talk to the teachers. Afraid to ask for help. Afraid to participate. I was out sick a lot from that day until the twelfth grade.

I never told my parents, and I'm thirty-one years old. I've been in therapy for battered women for two years. I've recovered, and now I have concerns for the future of my beautiful two-and-a-half year old son.

I would appreciate any information you have and any locations in New York that I could help out with public awareness, and also how to start a public awareness group in my town. Thank you [from] a concerned mother and citizen who wants to help prevent child abuse.

Striking Back

Parents frequently experience intense rage when they learn that their children have been the victims of corporal punishment in school. Some have physically attacked school authorities (Clarke,

Erdlen, and Hyman 1984; Clarke, Liberman-Lascoe, and Hyman 1982). One of them was Vicki Elmore, a soft-spoken mother from Leeds, Alabama. I had talked with her on the telephone after her son was paddled in school. When I met her on the Donahue show, it was hard to believe that she was a convicted criminal. Here is her story as pieced together by Adah Maurer in the winter 1987–1988 issue of *Last Resort*.

Vicki Elmore had been in the news since February 13, 1987, when she hit Elsie McGowan with a wooden board, causing a four-inch gash from the hairline to the eyebrow. She was arrested, tried, and convicted of first-degree assault. On November 23 she was sentenced to a six-month to five-year term in the women's prison. However, she finally served six months in the county jail.

With that much information, one could conclude that she was a villain and deserved to be punished. "You can't go around beating up people with paddles," said St. Clair County assistant district attorney Lamar Williamson. "There is a process to go through, and it must be followed," added St. Clair County superintendent of schools Charles Ray.

Vicki Elmore agrees wholeheartedly. That is exactly what she was trying to do: to go through channels to stop Elsie McGowan, the assistant principal of the Moody Elementary School, from beating up people with a paddle. It was only after she had tried everything—appealed to every bureaucracy—and had been shunted away from all of them that, as a last resort, she used the paddle on the paddler. She told Judge Hugh E. Holladay that she would not have struck Ms. McGowan if the officials to whom she had appealed had heeded her complaints that her child had been abused.

Her first effort was to write a courteous request to the school not to paddle her children. She asked administrators to call her if any of her children needed disciplining, and she would come at once.

Jo Elmore, age eleven, carried this note to Elsie McGowan. He told the jury that Ms. McGowan tore the note up and laughed. (She denies this. In any case, she ignored the request.)

One day William "Red" Elmore, age seven, "hollered" on the bus (no one yet has asked the background reason for that. Did another child poke him?), and the bus driver, Anita

Middlebrooks, took him to the office (dragged him there by the hair, according to Red) to be disciplined. Without the courtesy of a call to his mother, as requested, disciplinarian McGowan gave William three blows with a paddle twenty-two inches long and five inches across that left black and purple bruises from broken blood vessels under the skin of his gluteals. Tearfully he told his mother that evening that he had been hit so hard that he had landed on the floor, the breath knocked out of him.

Vicki Elmore went to school the next day to find out why her request that her children not be paddled had been ignored. She was brushed off. The law in Alabama does not require that parents be consulted before their children are hit nor does it specify how many blows may be given, how hard the hitting, or for what offenses. She asked to see the paddle used on her son. She took it as evidence, she said, and left the school with it.

Paddle in hand, Ms. Elmore took Red to see the family doctor, Laura Pound, who examined the boy, noting the bruises. (At the trial, Pound was permitted to testify as to the size of the hematomas but not as to whether the paddling constituted child abuse because the judge ruled that she was not a competent authority to judge abuse.)

Next, Mr. and Mrs. Elmore went with the paddle to the Moody Police Department. Sergeant Bobby Clements wrote up a complaint, took pictures of the child's bruises and referred the Elmores to the Department of Human Resources (DHR). The next morning they went to the Pell City DHR office, where social worker Melinda Morrow advised them that the case would be investigated and a report filed.

The Elmores next consulted with St. Clair County district attorney Van Davis about the options available to them. They did not ask for a warrant, nor did he suggest that this was possible. Said Davis, "I do not think the child abuse statutes fit the facts as you have related them." But he promised to call the county superintendent of schools and voice the Elmores' concern about the paddling.

During all of these visits, Ms. Elmore carried the wooden paddle wrapped in tape. She wanted to leave it with someone in authority as evidence of the weapon used on their son, but all declined to accept it. Frustrated but still not defeated, she took it home. There one of her children handed over a note from the school, warning that school officials would take action against her if the paddle was not returned. She would be arrested for theft of school property.

That threat was the last straw. Ms. Elmore took the letter to city hall and asked, "Where will they put me if I clobber someone?" Sergeant Clements, called to city hall to answer the question, told her to take it back, so back to school she went.

In the outer office, Ms. Elmore asked Elsie McGowan, "Do you want this paddle back?" She was upstaged with a command: "Come with me." When they reached the inner office, Ms. Elmore asked again, "Do you want this paddle back?" When the principal answered, "Yes, if you don't mind," Ms. Elmore brought the paddle down on Ms. McGowan's head. In the effort to retrieve the paddle, the principal slammed the angry parent against the wall, causing a gash in her head.

The national press presented the story as one of the dangers of unrestrained corporal punishment. Vicki Elmore was provoked to action by the fact that her child had been hit with a weapon for so mild an offense as a shout on the school bus and after she had specifically requested, in writing, that her children not be paddled.

At trial, the prosecution denied that corporal punishment was involved. John Dobson, assistant district attorney, said, "I cannot condemn a mother's concern over her child. But that is not what this case is about. This case is about a vicious assault. Are we going to have to come in here on a murder case because people are solving their problems with sticks?"

This episode illustrates two major issues: it is a good example of violence begetting violence, and it demonstrates that despite the cruelty and unfairness of the system in some areas, the legal establishment is arrayed against parents in cases such as this.

Schools Protect Their Own

School authorities are quick to sign complaints against outraged parents; they are less likely to file charges against their own staff. Even when outrageous abuses occur, school authorities find it easier to defend the teacher than to attempt lengthy bureaucratic procedures necessary to discipline the offender. An exacerbating factor, which works to the advantage of the schools, is the longevity and expense of most cases.

Parents are forced to move through various bureaucratic levels that seem designed to cool their ardor and discourage them. Without a lawyer, they are usually lost. In order to get a lawyer, they either have to be well off enough financially to pay a retainer or convincing enough for the lawyer to take the case on a contingency basis (in the latter, the lawyer agrees to take a percentage of any settlement). If the parents are poor enough, they may be able to convince legal services or some other poverty law group to take the case. But overworked poverty lawyers often consider school abuse cases to have low priority.

At each bureaucratic level and legal step, parents and children must relive the incident, telling the story over and over. If the abused child is back in school, not only faculty but other students may harass him or her. Harassment usually takes the form of ridicule because the victim "couldn't take" the punishment or anger because the victim's family is suing an educator whose get-tough approach is popular with some or most elements of the community. This is especially true if the abuser is a coach. Exhausted by the continual drain of emotional energy and often financial resources, many parents give up.

What If It's Your Child?

Credibility has become a major issue in child abuse cases. As a result of media publicity about how easily children are manipulated in their testimony, the credibility of children is in doubt in the eyes of many.

In my research I have found that children's symptoms are a good indicator of what has been done to them. It is especially important to be sensitive to any negative changes in behavior that may appear suddenly and then become increasingly negative. It is especially important to understand how parents, educators, and the community react to these symptoms or negative changes in behavior.

A good example of symptom development that was misread by at least seventeen families is illustrated in the case of Gauley

Bridge, West Virginia. (The following material is culled from my personal experience with the case, newspaper clippings, material gathered by the Appalachian Research and Defense Fund, and the attorney general's office of West Virginia.

In 1983, a teacher of first-grade children in a small West Virginia town decided that stern measures were needed to keep her pupils well behaved. Children alleged that if they did not remain in their seats some were tied to them; some of those who were not quiet had their mouths taped; and others were told that they must assume more responsibility for their bodily functions. These six- and seven-year-old children were allowed to go to the bathroom only during specified times. If they needed to go at other times, they were required to raise their hands; although they were allowed to go to the bathroom, they lost their play period, and their names were put on the board. The result was an abnormally large number of cases of enuresis and encopresis in the group. The children alleged that the teacher verbally denigrated children and warned them that if they told their parents of some of her practices and she found out, they would have to wear "tattletale" buttons.

These children began to develop somatic symptoms associated with going to school. The parents, not understanding what was happening, resorted to the usual practice of forcing their children to go to school and punishing them for not wanting to do their schoolwork. In the late spring, one of the children talked to her mother about having her mouth taped. The parent, incredulous, checked with some of the other parents, who questioned their children. Their questioning revealed a systematic series of punitive actions by the teacher.

During the following school year, according to some of her students, the teacher stopped taping and tying them, but she continued verbal assaults and threatened the new group of pupils. The Department of Human Services of West Virginia filed child abuse charges against the teacher, an unusual step because child abuse agencies do not generally become involved with school abuse. In addition, the Appalachian Research and Defense Fund joined the fray on behalf of the parents. The parents' litigation was initiated with great trepidation since the teacher's husband was a business associate of the county superintendent of schools and a member of a politically powerful family.

I conducted psychological evaluations of the seventeen children and their families who requested help, with the help of a team of psychologists and graduate students. These evaluations required a flexible approach due to temporal, financial, and logistical limitations. Diagnostic assessments were conducted by three senior psychologists and seven advanced students from a local school psychology program. Testing took place in a large, unused storefront over a weekend. The assessment procedure included examination of available school records, individual family histories, descriptions of the traumatic events by parents and children, and a structured interview based on questions derived from the diagnosis of posttraumatic stress disorder. Each parent was requested to fill out a behavior rating scale to indicate their child's functioning before and after first grade. Each child was administered a standard battery of tests.

As the assessments progressed, individual children were administered specialized tests to rule out certain problems that would have made the children even more vulnerable, such as previous emotional, educational, or learning problems.

Evaluation revealed twenty-one stress-related symptoms in the children who attended school during the two-year period: vomiting, nausea, headaches, stomachaches, nightmares, earaches, fear of the dark, thumb sucking, crying, enuresis, encopresis, hair pulling, insomnia, excessive dependency, difficulty concentrating, excessive shyness, depression, hyperalertness, fear of strangers, withdrawal, and avoidance of school. One child pulled out all of her eyelashes. The interviewers were not able to elicit sufficient information to determine whether any of the children experienced flashbacks.

The symptoms could be documented in only the seventeen children whose families sought help; the remainder chose not to participate in the litigation. Since it was anticipated that diagnostic information would need to be used to prove proximate cause in the courtroom, it was crucial to establish that the teacher's actions were in fact the cause of the children's symptoms.

An ideal solution to the problem of determining cause and effect would have been the collection of data from a control group of local first graders. This was impossible because of the lack of cooperation by school authorities, who were being sued, and the animosity or fear of reprisal on the part of other parents in the community. However, serendipity intervened. During the initial school year, while the parents were unaware of the events taking place in the classroom, the teacher was out of school for surgery for approximately three months. The parents reported that most of their children's symptoms had ceased during that period. Especially startling was the decrease in somatic problems and the refusal to go to school. When the teacher returned to the classroom, the children's symptoms returned.

To a great extent, this case hinged on retrospective information, based primarily on parent reports. That is, all of the information was collected after much of the abuse had occurred. Therefore, in order to determine if the teacher had caused the symptoms, we had to rely on past school records about the children and parents' descriptions. It might be argued that the respondents had an obvious axe to grind and might benefit financially by establishing that their children had been abused. However, political pressure, community resentment, and economic realities contradicted this. In fact, these parents were basically conservative, conforming members of the community. Some had children who were currently enrolled in this teacher's class and were extremely fearful of the consequences for their children. The clinical team felt strongly that the evidence was heavily weighted in favor of the diagnosis of posttraumatic stress disorder (PTSD) in approximately half the children and that the problem was directly caused by the teacher. This syndrome is discussed in the next chapter.

The lawsuit on behalf of the parents by the Appalachian Research and Defense Fund and the West Virginia Department of Human Services did not make it to trial. A local judge sent the case back to the school board, which heard the parents' complaints but refused to hold hearings on the expert testimony. They did agree, after much pressure, to hold closed hearings in which only their attorney and the plaintiffs' attorneys heard witnesses. The West Virginia Supreme Court issued an injunction against the teacher's presence in the classroom for a specific period of time, which expired without any action taken by the local court. The parents petitioned the West Virginia Supreme Court to force the case to trial. By this time, about two years after the initial events occurred, the case had generated a hot political struggle between the educational establishment and the child abuse authorities. There had been extensive media coverage and a real threat to the network that protects local oligarchies. The parents' request was rejected, ending their hopes to obtain justice for their children. The teacher received tenure and remained in the school.

Based on my testimony in a closed hearing and reference to the case on a PBS broadcast, the teacher sued me for $2 million. The case was thrown out by the judge, and the teacher appealed. After the second pleading by the teacher, her whole case was thrown out since she had no legitimate reason to sue me.

The West Virginia case involved combinations of verbal and physical assault. Despite the symptoms, the stressors were not as severe as in many other cases I have studied. The following case study is an example of a severe single paddling in which the loss of trust in the teacher was significant.

> In a southern state, Patty Carr, an exuberant, bright, and creative first-grade girl, whispered to another child in her class. The strict fundamentalist philosophy of the Christian school she attended required that the child be paddled. The child, who had rarely been spanked at home, had a choice of having the teacher or an administrator conduct the paddling. She chose the teacher, a person whom she loved, respected, and trusted. The paddling was administered by using several Ping-Pong paddles taped together. The beating caused muscle spasms and large bruises, which horrified her mother, who immediately took the child to their family physician. Following this, child abuse charges were filed. The child became withdrawn, fearful, and clinging, and she developed enuresis and sleep disturbances. She lost interest in learning and refused to go to school.
>
> Four years later, after extensive psychotherapy, most of Patty's symptoms had disappeared. The parents sought relief in the local county court. A jury trial, in which the judge refused to allow testimony by the state child abuse authorities, resulted in an acquittal for the teacher.

Children who are forced to return to the classroom may become angry, and they may retaliate. Others model the teacher's aggression; parents are puzzled and distressed when formerly good-natured children start picking on siblings and getting into fights at school.

4

The Aftermath:

Educator-Induced Posttraumatic Stress Disorder

W HEN I first saw Shelly Gaspersohn, two years after she had been severely swatted, she still could not talk about the incident without crying. Despite what the psychiatric expert for the defense said, despite what the jury decided, I knew she was continuing to suffer.

Shelly had not been to war, nor had she suffered the effects of a terrible natural disaster, such as an earthquake or a tornado. She had not been raped or witnessed a murder. Yet she had many of the symptoms of victims who have suffered through those types of traumas. I thought her problem was posttraumatic stress disorder (PTSD), but what I observed in her did not fully conform to the textbook definition.

Child victims of maltreatment such as physical and sexual abuse have received a great deal of attention, but the focus is generally on the physical acts and damage; the psychological results of these abuses have not been well studied. Not only was the research on childhood PTSD practically nonexistent; nothing I could find referred to educator-caused PTSD.

How Children React to Trauma

Most of the scanty evidence regarding PTSD in children is related to exceptional stressors that result in symptoms often similar to but not identical with those observed in adults. The distinctions between adult and childhood PTSD are especially crucial for use in expert testimony when establishing the exact cause of the problems.

I believe that one of the reasons Shelly lost her case was that her swatter was a teacher and coach who was holding up the long-revered standards of rural America; he was not a lurking stranger or sadistic child molester.

I am sure that many people in Harnett County thought that Shelly would have to learn to be tougher. A few swats on the behind could hardly be classified in the same league of stressors such as war, earthquakes, or child abuse. How could Shelly's suffering be compared to that of a Vietnam veteran? In fact, if it is assumed that the stressor in PTSD must be beyond the range of normal experience, this standard is not met in a school where paddlings are common and accepted.

I believe that children are more vulnerable to less extreme stressors than those that may cause PTSD in adults. Children and adults may be equally vulnerable to unpredictable disasters, but children may be more at risk in relation to stressors in society over which they have relatively little control. For instance, increasing poverty, especially in cities, has led to rising numbers of children with symptoms similar to those witnessed in PTSD (Stein 1986). Do the increasing numbers of these children exclude them from a PTSD diagnosis because the traumas that cause the symptoms do not fulfill the criterion of stressors outside the range of common human experience?

Disciplinary excesses of educators provide examples of a wide range of unusual and severe traumatic events over which children have little or no control. Yet many of these stressors such as corporal punishment and verbal abuse are generally not severe enough to cause PTSD. When they are severe, however, the diagnostic and legal results are troubling. The child's ability to deal with the trauma is greatly affected by the interaction and support available from his or her immediate caretakers.

If fear turns to anger, the child may retaliate against the teacher or the school. Others model the teacher's aggression and may turn their displaced anger against siblings with whom they formerly had few disputes, or they may start getting into fights at school.

It is clear that many students who initially feel protected and loved in school can be devastated by abuse by their teachers. The impact may be as certain as if their parents had maltreated them.

Parents, teachers, and other caregivers may have trouble understanding children's reactions and not be alert to recognizing stress symptoms. For instance, a group that studied children's and parents' reactions to the Three Mile Island nuclear accident (Handford et al. 1986) found that the parents of the children in the immediate area did not recognize the extent of the anxiety that the children experienced. A group of researchers who studied children who survived the horrors of the Pol Pot massacres in Cambodia (Sack et al. 1986) found that the children reported more distress with school grades, peers, and themselves than was observed by their caretakers. Another study focused on a group of school children who were kidnapped and buried alive in a trailer. They finally dug themselves out and were rescued. In follow-up studies of the effects of the trauma, the parents underestimated their children's reactions; many initially denied their children's need for professional help, despite the growing number of stress symptoms (Terr 1979). Professional evaluations demonstrated that the trauma had significantly affected the children's psychological adjustment.

These examples are beyond the range of normal experience and seem far removed from the kind of stresses that children might experience at the hands of even the nastiest educator. Yet the symptoms suffered in EIPTSD are not much different from those suffered by the children described. Nevertheless, the disciplinary excesses of educators are generally considered too common to cause PTSD.

PTSD in children should be considered within the context of age and a wide range of stressors. A review of current research shows that children of different ages react differently to stress.

Developmental Factors

EARLY CHILDHOOD

Children at the preschool and early primary school ages (up to about age nine) react differently to stress than do adults. For instance, bedwetting is a frequent reaction in five and six year olds who have been abused in schools.

After being traumatized, young children may become withdrawn, subdued, or even mute (Pynoos and Eth 1985, 1985b). They may not tell their parents of the abuse because of fear of retribution by the teacher. They may even fear that they will be punished by their parents for doing something wrong. They may become overly dependent, as well as clingy and whiny. They may suddenly act more immaturely. Sleep disorders—sleep talking, night terror, and sleepwalking—are a common reaction in this age group. Avoidant behaviors, new fears, and increased levels of anxiety are often observed.

In order not to think about the trauma, many young children deny to themselves that it really happened or is happening. They make it "go away." Yet they often reenact the event in their play. This is their way of mastering the trauma. School phobia is common.

Table 4–1 shows the symptoms of two groups of children suffering from school trauma: the West Virginia first graders who were tied to their seats, had their mouths taped, and were psychologically assaulted, and a group of eight and nine year olds from Colorado whose teacher scapegoated, humiliated, pinched, shoved, and punched them (Krugman and Krugman 1984). The investigators used a different set of descriptors from that used in the West Virginia case. For purposes of comparison, the data were collapsed and recategorized.

CHILDHOOD

My research defines childhood as the period from age nine to adolescence. Younger children seem to have the ability to make believe that traumas did not happen. As children become older, stressors begin to have greater impact on their thinking. Their schoolwork may be impaired by intrusive recollections, inhibition of spontaneous thought, and general depression.

Children who are entering the last stages of childhood may begin to become obsessed with revenge against the offending teacher. They may fixate on the details of the trauma to try to understand it or explain it away. Or they may become highly

Table 4-1
COLLAPSED SYMPTOM LIST OF TRAUMATIZED
ELEMENTARY SCHOOL CHILDREN IN WEST VIRGINIA AND
DENVER

Symptom	West Virginia First Graders (N = 17)		Denver Third and Fourth Graders (N = 17)	
	N	%	N	%
Reexperiencing trauma	0	—	NR	—
Personality change	9	53	13	76
Memory and concentration problems	5	29	NR	—
Psychic numbing	6	35	5	29
Avoidance reactions	12	71	15	88
Sleep disturbances	12	71	4	24
Somatic complaints	16	94	6	35
Habit disorders	2	12	NR	—

Notes: The number of symptoms and percentages do not equal 100 percent because some children in each sample reported multiple symptoms.

NR (no response) indicates that that type of symptom was not reported, although it might have existed.

anxious and live in constant fear as they anticipate further trauma. A variety of behavioral and personality changes may develop: poor peer relationships, tenseness, unprovoked aggressive outbursts, and distrust of adults. Particularly characteristic of this age group is a susceptibility to the development of somatic complaints, such as headaches and stomachaches, and elaborate and sophisticated reenactments of the trauma in play.

Lenore Terr (1983) studied the children in Chowchilla, California, who were kidnapped and buried in a trailer, and documented differences in PTSD between adults and children. Unlike adults, the children did not become fully or partly amnesiac, evidence psychic numbing, or exhibit unwanted flashbacks, but

they did exhibit relatively frequent declines in school performance, frequent posttraumatic reenactment play, a skewed sense
of time, and limited views of the future. Our clinical evaluations
of children with EIPTSD also indicate lack of flashbacks and
amnesia.

Calvin Frederick (1986) assessed children who were victims
of adult violence. In one case, a sniper in a house across from an
elementary school in Los Angeles pinned down a group of teachers and children. Children were killed and wounded during the
siege. Frederick studied children who were shot, who saw play-
mates shot, and who went to the school but did not actually witness the shooting. He found a series of symptoms similar to
those I have observed in EIPTSD, which included fear of school,
nightmares, and phobias.

ADOLESCENCE

The adolescent experience of PTSD is most similar to that of
adults. Anger against the aggressing teacher and the school may
play a major role. More-than-normal adolescent rebellion may
develop following a traumatic event.

Trauma may result in substance abuse, precocious sexual behavior, and school truancy. Substance abuse may be the teenager's way of dealing with depression resulting from traumatic
experience. Too old to engage in play acting, adolescents may
resort to self-destructive behavior as a defense against anxiety
and painful memories and as a reaction to their guilt.

A study of the emotional and behavioral reactions of seventy-
seven adolescents who were physically maltreated for an average
of five-and-one-half years, identified six patterns of adolescent
reaction: aggression, dependency, generalized anxiety, extreme
problems with normal issues of adolescent adjustment, emotional and thought disturbance, and helplessness and dependency reactions. The authors noted that 70 percent of the respondents had academic performance difficulties, 52 percent
had sleep disturbances, 31 percent admitted to substance abuse,
and 35 percent reported aggressive behaviors (Farber and
Joseph 1985).

Research on EIPTSD

Two series of studies conducted by NCSCPAS researchers sought to understand EIPTSD. The first examined the extent of physical and psychological abuse that teachers had experienced when they were students. That research found that between 40 percent and 60 percent of teachers from different samples had developed stress symptoms as a result of being abused by their teachers in elementary or high school. The study helps us to understand that many educators are modeling the abusive teaching techniques of their own teachers.

The second study surveyed students in a high school in suburban Philadelphia (Lambert et al. 1988). The school has students from predominantly middle-class with some lower-middle-class families.

We developed a questionnaire that asked students to check as many aspects of their worst school experience as they wished and to check the single worst thing an educator had ever done. Of the 372 teenagers in the sample, 60 percent replied. A summary of the results follows. (The questionnaire is reprinted as appendix C.)

Summary of Results

Ridicule. Thirty-four percent of the students reported that they were ridiculed by educators to such an extent that they developed some stress symptoms. The types of ridicule (1) "put you down for not doing well," (2) "made fun of you," and (3) "made you feel that you were not as good as everyone else."

Overly Punitive Sanctions. Twenty-one percent of the students said that their worst school experience resulted from overly punitive sanctions—those that they felt were grossly unfair and/or undeserved. They were: (1) "gave you detention for no reason," (2) "suspended you for no reason," (3) "expelled you from school for no reason," (4) "wouldn't let you go to the bathroom as punishment," (5) "threw things at you like a book, eraser, or something else," and (6) "lied about you so that you got in trouble."

Verbal Assaults. Twenty-one percent of the students said they were severely verbally assaulted. Offenses were (1) "yelled at you" and (2) "said they would do something bad to you (made a threat)."

Physical Assault. Thirteen percent said they were physically assaulted. The assaults included (1) "pinched or squeezed you so that it hurt," (2) "slapped or punched you," (3) "pushed you," (4) "grabbed you hard," (5) "shook you hard," (6) "pulled your ears or hair," and (7) "hit you with a ruler, paddle, or something else."

Isolation/Rejection. Eight percent said they were isolated or rejected. This included (1) "didn't let you be a part of special subjects or activities, such as music, sports, trips, or art," (2) "ignored you," (3) "would not pay attention to you," and (4) "made you stay alone, away from everybody."

Verbal Discrimination. Two percent said that educators (1) "called you names because of what you looked like" and/or (2) "put you down because of your religion or race (color)."

Peer Humiliation. Two percent were humiliated by peers with teacher assent. Teachers (1) "let other children tease you" and/or (2) "let other children hit, slap, or push you."

Corruption. Sexual comments or advances by educators caused stress symptoms for 2 percent of the students. This included (1) "made sexual comments that you did not like," (2) "touched you sexually but did not force you," (3) "touched you sexually and forced you to let it happen," and/or (4) "forced you to have sex."

TRAUMATIC STRESS SYMPTOMS

The major purpose of this study was to determine the extent of symptoms that children may develop as a result of their worst school experiences. Most of the students said they recovered from the experiences and were not seriously damaged. But the experiences reported in this and other studies have later effects on attitudes toward educators, schooling, and schools. (Perhaps with such large numbers remembering negative experiences, this might account for Americans' generally low regard for schools.)

We were interested in the frequency (how many times), duration (how long), and intensity (how much of a problem it caused) of traumatic stress symptoms. We found that almost 10 percent of the students experienced symptoms of such frequency, duration, and intensity that they suffered. My colleagues and I collapsed the responses into twelve categories, and students could indicate as many individual symptoms as they felt. (Because students could list symptoms in more than one category, the total percentages do not equal 100 percent.)

Problems in School. Sixty-nine percent of the students said they had school-related stress symptoms after they were maltreated at some level. The symptoms included hatred, worry, and crying about school grades and attendance. Students skipped school, cut classes, stopped doing homework, and got lower grades.

Aggressive Behavior. Sixty-four percent of the students developed aggressive responses. These included rapid loss of temper, loss of control, desire for revenge, and disrespect to teachers. Some students acted out their angry feelings by picking on others and fighting.

Avoidance Behaviors. Avoidance is one of the most common symptoms of PTSD. Fifty-eight percent of the students developed some type of avoidance responses such as staying away from their abusers and the place where they were humiliated. They also tried not to think about or talk about what happened.

Changes in Personality. One of the most dramatic events in PTSD is sudden or even gradual behavioral changes that do not seem to be related to any recent events known by the parents. Even in EIPTSD, when the parents know what happened, they find it hard to believe that one cruel experience in school could make such a difference. Fifty-five percent of the students said that they experienced changes in the way they felt or acted. These included feelings of depression, hopelessness, guilt, anxiety, self-deprecation, and loss of trust in adults.

Reexperiencing the Trauma. Our early studies showed that children do not reexperience the traumatic event as adults do. Adults, for example, often have vivid flashbacks. But by using statements about a variety of ways that children might reexperience the traumatic events in school, we found that 49 percent of the students said that they had some reexperiencing; pictures of the event popped into their minds, they had unwanted recollections of the event, and they talked obsessively about the event.

Fearful Reactions. Hyperalertness—a condition in which the person is always on the lookout for a similar bad experience—affected 27 percent of the students. Responses included fearful anticipation of further harm by the abuser, other adults, and even peers. Some reported becoming jumpy.

Somatic Complaints. Twenty percent of the students developed somatic complaints: headaches, stomachaches, tiredness, loss of appetite, body aches, nausea when thinking about school, enuresis, and daytime urinary accidents.

Withdrawal. Nineteen percent of the students began to withdraw, a common indicator of depression. They withdrew from friends, family, people who were present at the time of the trauma, and previously enjoyed activities. They spent more time alone and lost enthusiasm and motivation that they had previously.

Memory and Concentration Problems. Thirteen percent of the students reported memory and concentration problems as a result of worry over their treatment by educators. These problems were mostly focused on their ability to function in school or to do homework.

Dependency and Regression. Ten percent of the students said that at some time they had acted immaturely after the abuse. This regression takes many forms, such as a desire to be younger, a fear of going to bed, and clinging to parents.

Habit Disorders. Ten percent of the students suffered twitches, thumb sucking, nail biting, and stuttering.

Sleep Disturbances. Sleep disturbances occur in almost all cases of PTSD. While only 10 percent of the responding students reported them, they were among the students with the most severe symptoms. These included nightmares and/or trouble falling or staying asleep.

PTSD and Self-Esteem

Good self-esteem is probably the most important quality needed for mental health. People who do not feel good about themselves have trouble treating others well. In over thirty years as a professional, I have yet to meet a troubled child who has a positive self-image. Events that erode self-confidence and cause feelings of helplessness, anxiety, uncontrollable anger, guilt, and rejection are bound to result in problems. While there appears to be a correlation between lowered self-esteem and PTSD in children, the interaction and causality are not so clear. Does PTSD cause lowered self-esteem, or is latent low self-esteem one of the preconditions that make a child vulnerable to PTSD? Some studies shed light on this issue.

Childhood traumas may have specific long-lasting effects on self-esteem in relation to the developmental stage at which the stressors occur (Eth and Pynoos 1985a). A number of studies suggest that family violence and sexual abuse at an early age may lead to seriously lowered self-esteem of indeterminant length.

Hughes and Barad (1983) studied sixty-five children who were residents of a battered women's shelter to determine their degree of adjustment. Using self-report measures and checklists completed by mothers, staff, and teachers, they found a below-average self-concept score for the preschool group and more aggressive behavior in school-age sheltered boys than girls.

Another group (Oates, Forrest, and Peacock 1985) compared thirty-seven children between the ages of four and fourteen who had been admitted to a hospital with the diagnosis of child abuse with thirty-seven nonabused children. They were matched for age, sex, ethnicity, school, and socioeconomic status. Abused children saw themselves as having significantly fewer friends than comparison groups, showed less ambition with regard to future occupation, and had significantly lower self-concepts, as measured by the Piers-Harris Self-Concept Scale.

Poor self-esteem and feelings of hopelessness and helplessness are frequently associated with suicide in adolescents. One study (Deykin, Alpert, and McNamara 1985) demonstrated the association between exposure to child abuse and neglect with suicidal behaviors in adolescents. One hundred and fifty-nine adolescents who had made suicide attempts were matched for age and sex with others who were treated for medical conditions unrelated to suicide attempts. They found that prior contact with the state Department of Social Services, which handles child abuse and neglect cases, was three to six times more likely than for the comparison group. I have worked with at least three cases of school paddlings that resulted in overt suicide threats by the victimized children.

Where You Live Makes a Difference

If a child has a cold or a cut, it does not matter where he or she lives in order for a doctor to diagnose the problem. If a child has a learning disability, a good psychologist, no matter where he or she lives, will be able to determine what is wrong. But with EIPTSD, where one lives may determine how a child is diagnosed and treated. This is especially true in relation to physical abuse. Psychological maltreatment is so little studied that school and community attitudes and professional responses in different areas of the country are not fully understood.

In determining PTSD, a normative approach is used. That is, based on normal experiences, a person cannot have PTSD. The trauma must be beyond normal experience. That is why war, earthquakes, and witnessing or experiencing violence are considered to be associated with PTSD. A normative reference refers here to a statistical interpretation of how stressful a stressor should be.

The guidelines that psychologists and psychiatrists generally use to diagnose PTSD rely on a normative interpretation. Those guidelines say that for PTSD to be diagnosed, stressors must be beyond the range of normal human experience; that is, they must be statistically rare or highly unusual. Therefore, in order for a stressor to be associated with PTSD, it must be normally experienced by an extremely small percentage of the population.

The idiographic model, which I propose instead, suggests that a wide variety of individual factors must be considered in diagnosing PTSD in children. Individual coping styles, as they interact with developmental stages and environmental stressors, must be considered in order to understand the full extent of PTSD in children.

Common stressors, such as death and divorce, may have a wide range of effects on different children, for example. Similarly, common school disciplinary procedures affect different students differently. How children react may depend on such factors as the degree of general punitiveness of their teacher and the severity of the specific punishment that causes the most severe reactions. Other issues, such as students' previous experiences with the particular offending teacher and with other teachers, may be important.

Children from homes in which corporal punishment is rarely or never used may be particularly vulnerable to the effects of a beating by the teacher. On the other hand, children who are abused at home may find that the abuse at school overwhelms them. Or, the abuse in school may be minimal in comparison to what they experience at home.

In many cases, I have found that children's self-esteem and previous successes in school can make a big difference in how they recover. Children who have handicapping conditions and have been left back two or three times, in addition to being frequently punished, tend to suffer greatly. Factors such as these put the lie to the belief that you can use statistics on rates of punishment to tell how much emotional pain an individual child is allowed to feel before diagnosing PTSD.

In the South and Southwest and in rural areas and inner cities, too many students are exposed to overly severe punitiveness that can result in EIPTSD. When maltreatment is a routine disciplinary practice, it is accepted as normal. For instance, corporal punishment in schools is a revered aspect of southern culture (Clarke, Erdlen, and Hyman 1984). Should we accept battered buttocks in South Carolina but not in New Jersey?

Community sentiment and legal standards also affect teachers' attitudes and understandings of the limits of punishment. Where corporal punishment is illegal, teachers' attitudes change. Bogacki (1981) demonstrated that teachers in New Jersey were much less favorable to the use of corporal punishment than were those in Texas and Pennsylvania, where it is legally permissible.

Using EIPTSD in Court

When students are abused in school, parents may wish to sue if they do not receive appropriate apologies and restitution. Depending on where they live and how influential they are, they may have difficulty proving that the educators should not have done what they did or even that they did anything wrong.

In 1977, in the case of *Ingraham v. Wright*, the U.S. Supreme Court, in a five-to-four decision, denied school children constitutional protection from corporal punishment. Specifically, school children have no protection from cruel and unusual punishment and are not entitled to procedural due process. The Court, however, has allowed contradictory federal circuit court decisions regarding substantive due process to stand. In the Texas case of *Cunningham v. Beavers*, in 1988 the Court let stand a state law that allows corporal punishment up to the point "of deadly force," yet in refusing to rule on *Garcia v. Miera* (1987) in New Mexico, it allowed the paddled child to sue the school board for relief based on substantive due process guarantees of the Constitution. In both cases the children were represented by New Mexico attorney John Roessler, who believes in the possibility of a substantive due process remedy, which would require the Court to define the line separating corporal punishment from child abuse in a case in which an educator inflicted such heinous damage as to shock the public conscience. Given the makeup of the current Court, I think this is unlikely. Meanwhile, when parents of severely paddled children sue schools, educators invariably rely on *Ingraham* as their defense.

The state supreme courts are unlikely to offer relief. For example, in *Mathis v. Berrian County Schools* (1988), the Georgia Court of Appeals allowed that "it is to be anticipated that corporal punishment will produce pain and the potential for bruising" and therefore denied the parents and child the right to go to trial.

There has been increasing success in litigation by seeking redress under personal injury or tort law. By use of clinical case studies and large-scale research, staff at the NCSCPAS have validated the existence of long-term psychic injury as a result of overly severe corporal punishment. The cases may be won by establishing that the child has EIPTSD.

By shifting legal arguments in corporal punishment cases from the physical injuries to the long-lasting emotional harm, we have entered a realm of law with well-established guidelines that work in favor of injured school children, who are increasingly winning in litigation. This may help to change local and regional school policy through pressure from insurance companies that place themselves at risk by covering schools that allow corporal punishment.

Within the framework of torts law, courts and insurance companies are familiar with the concept of long-term psychological or psychic injury, which is frequently used in litigation involving workmen's compensation and disability. I have stopped trying to prove to courts that corporal punishment or psychological abuse should not be allowed. If state laws allow these types of maltreatment, the plaintiffs generally cannot win unless the abuse outrages the local populace. Therefore, I have reframed the problem within the context of torts law. That is, what lifelong damage does a particular abuse cause a child who is obviously suffering?

Handicapped children, especially those with learning disabilities and emotional problems, are particularly vulnerable to excessive corporal punishment. In recognition of this, there have been recent attempts to amend federal legislation for the education of handicapped children to forbid hitting them.

5

Long-Lasting Effects of Physical and Psychological Maltreatment in School

Research on Long-Lasting Effects

There are compelling clinical and legal reasons to determine the longevity of symptoms and underlying emotional trauma in children who have EIPTSD. Improved diagnostic and treatment strategies may be derived from this knowledge. In litigation, awarding of compensatory damages often determines whether resources will be available for treatment or, if treatment has been ongoing, whether the stress on the family is exacerbated by financial problems. Research efforts at the NCSCPAS indicate that an increase in punitive damages will convince educators to recognize the counterproductive nature of the kinds of disciplinary practices that lead to litigation.

The long-term emotional effects of physical and psychological abuse in the schools are reflected in the letters received at the NCSCPAS. Three (largely unedited) are printed here in the boxes. Such letters promoted a study of thirty-one families of school-abused children who were identified through press clippings, correspondence, and a search of court rulings (Clarke 1986). The cases were confined to Appalachia because of funding stipulations. From the families interviewed, Clarke obtained information on observable symptoms that occurred from six event. The median was two and a half years. In order of frequency, long-lasting symptoms reported by parents were avoidance of school and fear associated with educators (nine cases); loss of trust and fear of adults, especially educators (six); loss of interest in school (five); denial of or refusal to discuss the traumatic event (three); nightmares (two); and excessive crying (two). Three other symptoms were observed in at least one child: excessive need of praise, aggressive behavior, and fear of going to bed alone.

Dear Dr. Hyman:

Please keep up your good work in the area of corporal punishment. I was a victim in the second grade and know that it should be outlawed.

When I was eight years old another girl and I picked flowers from people's yards on the way home from school. When my mother found out she told me in a nice way that it wasn't the right thing to do and I vowed never to do it again.

Well, I had a surprise waiting for me the next day at school. Miss W. my teacher was friends with Beth's mother, she was the other flower picker. Beth's mother had spanked her for picking the flowers and Miss W. had decided that if Mary Beth got spanked, I deserved it too. So when I went to school, she took me in the coat closet and beat the hell out of me. She smacked me in the face more times than I care to remember. After the assault she made me stand in front of the class crying and tell the entire class who I had crush on. It was a horrible experience that I wouldn't wish on my worst enemy.

Afterward, I came home from school, in a terrible state, telling my mother that I never wanted to go back. My parents were blue-collar and taken advantage of when they tried to make some sense out of this madness. The principal told them that poor Miss W. was nervous and she might lose her job if they complained. He didn't really give a damn about me or my feelings. He just didn't want the school to look bad. I didn't even get an apology and was still stuck in her class. I

---

still remember how one time she gave everyone a treat and a card for a holiday except me.

The woman was not fit to teach, she was a couch case herself, I only hope she never got mad at any other student. I'll tell you, to my dying day I will never forget that day and its been almost twenty-five years.

It's funny, but later during my college days, I always went out of my way to avoid female teachers, especially single ones. I always hated school and closets. Please do your best to help naive students and parents to avoid similar experiences.

Lots of luck.

Dear Dr. Hyman:

As I was reading my newspaper today I was alarmed to see the picture of a young lady, Nicole Fathman, 16 years old of Marysville, Ohio, with the story of her abuse at school from a teacher hitting her. . . . Governor Richard Celeste himself signed, in Ohio, a new law giving local school boards the option to ban spanking. I am very happy that I live in one of these seven states that bans corporal punishment, and glad to hear . . . New York [is] to have corporal punishment banned this September, and Ohio last January 8, 1985.

I feel so fortunate, Dr. Hyman, to have this great opportunity to speak out on corporal punishment. I am 50 years old and never believed that I would hear the same things going on that happened when I was a young boy. I am just petrified. I went to a small one-room school house with 35 kindergarten to eighth-graders. My second teacher used a razor strap. We held out our hand until the tears run down our face. I had this strap used on me many times.

My third teacher [grade school to eighth grade]:

1. used a razor strap on our hands

2. Made us go out from of classroom and bend over with fingers on our toes of shoes for 2–3 hours
3. put us under her desk for a few hours
4. put us in coatroom for a few hours
5. kept us after school
6. hit the side of our heads with a large geography book

   . . . I walked three miles home in a Northeast snowstorm, my face got almost frozen. I got hit beside the head once with a large geography book at 13 years old . . . as I had to smile at a friend making funny faces to get me to laugh. I got stunned for a few seconds with that old geography book beside my head, I see a room fun of stars, I could feel my legs bucklin [sic], I thought I was going to hit the floor. My head did swell up some. I got my eyesight back to jump and threaten to do the same to her if she ever hit me again with that geography book.

   Awhile [sic] back my friend at school she said she cried and run out the door for [that] afternoon, crying because I got hit by the geography book. The next morning the teacher was waiting to slap her but she was too angry for the teacher to touch her and said she would leave again and tell her mother about me being hit. Never to touch Guy again, or she would look into it. Two years ago [the friend] asked if I remembered her leaving. I did . . . afterward someone told me Kataline run home crying her heart out. She would tell you the same thing today.

   The superintendent came twice a month, I was under the desk [and] his feet almost touched me, but I kept out of his way . . . I was rounded up far as possible under the teachers desk. My dad went to the teacher and said if she did any more to me he would contact the superintendent of schools.

   . . . I know of three or four more who will say I'm right. They got the works themselves from a cruel teacher. . . . I hope to see the day 41 more states will also ban corporal punishment. A child should never be hit by a teacher, or parents, they automatically become shy, scared, nervousness, mean, they need love, respect, honor, and not even shouted at for a small mistake, and will remember all their life . . . as I [and] my school mates remember to this day. As I and my school mates remember to this day that this abuse forced us to hate these two teachers.

Dear Dr. Hyman

I have just read your very interesting article in *Parade* Magazine, "Should School Children Be Hit?" (3/24/85).

I will attempt to relate to you my own personal case and you, the sociologist, can draw your own conclusions.

I am a man of forty years and attended school in North Carolina from 1950 through 1962 at which time I was graduated.

Until I reached the third grade I remember myself as relatively happy and fairly well adjusted. I had attended a Catholic kindergarten at age four and was allowed to enter the first grade at age five.

Although, no one to this day has ever been told, my first negative experiences in school began in this pre-school setting. My mother, a born-again fundamentalist, wanted me to go to kindergarten as a way of accelerating my interest in learning. The only pre-school at this time in our town was CATHOLIC, so that is where I was enrolled. As you may know, Catholic's are required to say a prayer to the Mary, the Mother of Jesus, several times each day. This consisted of facing a STATUE and repeating the lines of a "standard" prayer.

I remember well my Mother's instructions regarding this little ritual. "When the other little Catholic children are facing 'Mary' and praying to her each day, you should asked to be excused." Even though my parents explained this situation prior to my enrollment it didn't really set well with the Sisters. Anytime something went wrong I was blamed. Once a water glass from the teacher's desk was found to be cracked and even though I knew nothing about it, I was traumatized severely and paddled. I still have a vivid recall of this incident.

Upon entering the first grade in the public school system, all went rather well until Third Grade. My parents were going through a divorce and argued a lot. Loving them both, but especially my father, my little world went into a nosedive. Instead of have someone to help me get off to school each day, now with my father gone, I had to go it alone. On occasion I would be late to school (mother worked, leaving at 5:00 A.M. each day) and as a result I was humiliated and on a couple of occasions spanked with a ruler across the hands. Once I was spanked because a dog followed me to school right in front of the class. These things build resentment in children and to this day, I look back with genuine hatred towards that third grade teacher and the Principal who would be called into the room to administer the punishment. I recall much about these two individuals even beyond their actions towards me as a student. Things such as how they sounded when speaking, certain words they would use and even the pronouncement of their words. It seems that teachers of that day were filled with negative and sometimes abusive perspectives.

This stream of unpleasant day in, day out experiences has certain indirect negative spillovers. I was made aware by the fourth grade teacher, that the third grade teacher had given her a full rundown on my disruptive actions and my battle went on for another year. This fourth grade teacher took up where the previous one left off, even though I was never spanked again. Ridicule in the classroom in front of my peers during these two early years have had an effect on me as a person.

In addition, these attitudes are often passed from teacher to teacher. The child is in a completely defenseless position. The negatives that he encounters, real or not are perceived as valid, thus producing a child growing to adulthood with a somewhat distorted viewpoint.

> Today, I am somewhat of a loner, but I have been able to earn a good living since leaving the U.S. Army in 1967. However, I haven't forgotten and probably never will. "As the twig is bent . . ."

A review (Lamphear 1985) of seventeen studies of the psychosocial results of abuse identified fifteen that were good enough so that the results were considered valid. Compared to nonabused children, those who were physically abused had a greater frequency of problems. These included noncompliance, tantrums, and aggression toward peers and adults. They had poorer peer relationships and social skill deficits, were less socially involved, had less empathy, and performed poorly in school.

Another study (Chandler, Shermis, and Marsh 1985) focused on symptoms of stress in terms of children's coping strategies. Although this work does not deal directly with PTSD, it is of interest nevertheless. The researchers identified four types of maladaptive stress responses in children. The first is characterized by resignation, an acceptance of helplessness, and a tendency to relegate the course of events to adults who appear to be in control. The second group is characterized by impulsive acting-out behavior. These children may have little emotional control and may be quick to cry, lose their temper, or attack others. A third common maladaptive response style which we have observed in EIPTSD is characterized by an avoidant strategy. This can range from avoidance of school and previously enjoyed people to activities related to school. Emotional withdrawal and cognitive denial are other symptoms. The last style is characterized by the use of passive-aggressive behavior familiar to professionals who work with underachieving children.

Our investigations of EIPTSD led to the question of the longevity of symptoms that never received attention from parents or mental health professionals. One approach to this research problem is to develop a normative data base. We did this with the school trauma study of high school students. But we were also interested in the perceptions of adults, particularly teachers, of their worst school experiences. At NCSCPAS we are just beginning to study the effects of teachers' experiences of psychological maltreatment by their own teachers. Eventually we hope to determine if there is a relationship between the teachers' past experiences and the psychological atmosphere of their own classrooms.

A School Trauma Survey of Teachers and College Students

Wendy Zelikoff-Simkin worked with me in our first studies of teachers' experiences of being maltreated in school. Before turning to the results of our studies, let us examine some of the actual experiences related by the teachers and college students who responded to our survey. I have selected samples from the hundreds of cases we have studied. They are organized loosely by categories that have some overlap and are all written in the first person; I have reproduced them almost exactly as they were written by the respondents.

LONG-TERM EFFECTS OF ABUSE

The first group of anecdotes illustrates some of the experiences that reflect the long-term effects of abuse.

> My fifth-grade teacher was looking over school photos of all students in the class during milk break. When he came to mine, he held it up and exclaimed, "What a face!" Students were standing all around the teacher's desk. I was horribly embarrassed. I felt my face get hot. I still feel like crying when I think about it. I am now 36 years old. I know he didn't mean what I thought he meant, but that doesn't change how I feel. He was one of my favorite teachers. I have always seen myself as ugly since that time.

> I had been taking violin lessons for three years and had just (within months) transferred from the conservatory main campus to a new suburban campus. This caused a change in teachers. I had had a gentle older man and then got a younger

woman. She was very intent on perfection and complained about my lack of progress (I did not practice as much as I was supposed to). One afternoon, she became angry because I obviously had not practiced. She started hitting me on the hands and arms with her bow. I threw my bow down, started to cry and left, telling her I was calling my mother. My mother came. I was given a choice to go back or to quit music lessons. I quit. My violin was put away until my mother died.

In fifth grade I had difficulty with multiplication. Each day one teacher would orally quiz us on our facts. I was chosen to relay the multiplication tables for the number seven and had great difficulty with the exercise. The teacher stopped the class and drew everyone's attention to me. At this point he began to tell me how stupid I was and that I probably didn't study (although I did). I was so embarrassed I was in tears and had to leave the room. I never forgot it.

My third-grade teacher ridiculed me in front of my reading group while I was reading out loud. It was an advanced reading group but not difficult for me. I made the mistake of pronouncing bow (BO) as bough. She screamed at me and made fun of me for this mistake in front of my classmates. I was humiliated and felt her reaction was unjustified. Yet it was so devastating I became more self-conscious and afraid to speak up for fear of making more mistakes. My self-consciousness and low self-esteem has only now, at the age of 22, begun to heal (not that this was the only contributing factor to my low self-esteem).

I had a fourth-grade teacher who simply did not like me (personality conflict). During the whole school year she made my life very difficult. After I was grown my mother and I discussed it and she told me how upsetting that year was for her. Until that point in my life I believed I was at fault. Not until I was a grown woman did I resolve my feelings and realize through my mother that this teacher was at fault.

I recall spending several nights preparing and completing a composition. When I handed it in, the teacher grabbed it—

read it aloud and criticized everything about it. To this day I have had difficulty accepting positive recognition of my writing skills.

HUMILIATION

The following accounts illustrate how a variety of teacher behaviors can result in humiliation. In some cases the actions were overtly vicious; sadly, in other cases the teachers probably never knew the damage they caused.

> A teaching sister pulled up my dress and spanked me in front of the whole class in second grade for talking in church when I was in fact reciting prayers! She did not allow me to walk in a church procession and threatened to prevent me from making my first Communion.

> My teacher noticed that I was scratching my rear end and commented on it in class. I was utterly humiliated.

> In tenth grade a teacher identified me, in front of the whole class, as someone who never does well on history tests. She then stated that if I could pass the test, anyone could.

> I once had a sixth-grade teacher put a cut-out cardboard box on my head to project my voice because I was shy.

> In third grade, a teacher ridiculed [another] student who had an urinary infection for "going in his pants."

> In third grade I had trouble telling time. For many days, the entire class had to wait for me to say the correct time until we could go to lunch.

> I did not hear that boys were called at bathroom time in kindergarten, so I went into a stall and started to go to the bathroom. The teacher came in, saw me in with the boys and dragged me out with my panties at my ankles while she yelled and screamed about listening.

Name Calling

Name calling is a common form of maltreatment toward school children. Types of name calling range from the mundane to the inventive.

> In the sixth grade I was in a school play and put lipstick on. I tried to remove it, but some was left. The teacher yelled at me in front of the class to remove it because I looked like a "slut."

> In second grade I was told to go to the back of the room and stand there for talking. When I started to cry, I was yelled at and called a "baby" in front of my classmates.

> I wanted to play with the older girls who were jumping rope. They were in my brother's class. They wouldn't let me join, so I bit one of the girls. Their teacher then brought the whole class (including my brother) to look for the "Dog."

> Ms. ——— stood in her door as my first grade class passed her on the way to the auditorium. As I passed, she chided "cry baby, cry baby . . ." because I often cried.

> My high school gym teacher ridiculed me in front of the class for being clumsy.

> When I did not understand a lesson in eighth grade English, I asked the teacher to explain it again. She yelled at me, called me stupid, and sent me to the vice principal.

> In eleventh grade, my French teacher announced to class that I was failing second-year French and that I was so stupid she could not understand how I had been put in her class. She raved on for at least ten minutes and made me come in every morning and every day after school to work with her.

Abuse of Bright Students

Many of the abuses refer to students' lack of ability. But even bright students are vulnerable.

One of my teachers looked up IQ scores of students and referred to them in class, saying in front of everyone—you should be doing better—your I.Q. is such and such—you are an overachiever—your I.Q. is such and such.

In first grade, my teacher reprimanded me for reading through our primer, *Dick and Jane,* and advancing beyond the point where she was instructing the class.

PHYSICAL APPEARANCE

One of the cruelist of verbal assaults involves comments about a child's appearance.

In fifth grade a teacher called me fat and meant it in a bad way.

In the tenth grade, my history teacher (a nun) had had my sister (a bit of a troublemaker) in a previous year. This teacher humiliated me in front of the class at every possible opportunity. One example: I was wearing the older version of the school uniform . . . she made me stand up in front of the class, and laughed at me saying, "why do you have that uniform on? Are you too *fat* for the other one?" etc. Yes, I was!

My coach told me that I was a disgrace as a captain of the team because my hair was long and I had lost a game in overtime because the person I was guarding scored.

I was in seventh grade and was very tall for my age. I was extremely self-conscious and nervous about giving an oral talk for my English class. My heart pounded as I walked up to give my speech, and [I] nervously began. My teacher interrupted my speech and said, "God, you have big feet! What size shoe do you wear?"

A dental hygienist came to our class and asked me to rinse with a solution that shows where food is left on your teeth. The teacher took me in front of the class and showed the class what was "wrong" with my teeth, even though it was after lunch.

BIGOTRY IN THE CLASSROOM

Teachers may reflect their own bigotry by both conscious and unconscious remarks. Often, subtle forms of prejudiced behavior are recognized by children.

When I was in fourth grade, the teacher told us to draw a pilgrim and cut it out. I couldn't draw well but did the best I could. The teacher called me in front of the class and said, "What is this? That's not a pilgrim. It's awful." I felt terrible. She told me to take it and show it to two other teachers, to show them how awful it was. They didn't know why I was showing it to them and they said it was good. They were kind but I never forgot it. It was so humiliating. I am Jewish, and I am sure the teacher was anti-Semitic.

I was observing a class in which the teacher was teaching about Martin Luther King. The children knew he was black and was fighting for civil rights. When the children were confused about the difference between black and white, she asked me (I am black) to come up and pointed out all of the supposed physical differences between black and white people.

I was the only Jewish person in the whole school. The teachers all knew this because I took off for the holidays. One day our math class was being very bad. Mr. ——— stood on his chair and pointed his finger at us and said "you kids are worse than the Jews that put Jesus on the cross!"

My fifth-grade teacher made me stand in the corner because she said I was talking. There was someone in the room talking, but it wasn't me. I tried to tell her but she wouldn't listen to me. I always felt that she didn't listen because I was black and she was white.

Mrs. ———, my white third-grade teacher, told me that black children (I am black) "don't live like that" regarding my written composition on my summer vacation in Florida.

An English teacher—whose rule was "miss a test, take a "C"—even when tests were scheduled on the Jewish holidays, caused me to be excluded from twelfth-grade college English because of a "C." (I majored in journalism in college.)

BEHINDS ARE NOT THE ONLY TARGETS

The following excerpts reveal that some teachers prefer to slap faces and bang heads.

My teacher used to physically punish the boys by holding and slamming their heads against walls. He also seemed to like making the whole class exercise in the winter with no jackets for entire recess as punishment. . . . He was very sarcastic, always putting us down, yelling, demeaning.

I was waiting in line at the lavatory to go in a stall when two girls came out at the same time. I was second in line and went into the second stall. When I came out, the nun was waiting for me. Apparently, the girl behind me claimed I had cut in front of her. The nun proceeded to yell and to take my head and bang it into the tiled wall.

In second grade my teacher accused me of screaming out in the class. When I told her it wasn't me and the girl who had screamed admitted it was her, she still insisted that it was me and banged the side of my head into the chalkboard.

One day the teacher was checking homework. Each boy who didn't do his homework got a slap in the face. Each girl who didn't do her homework was told to turn it in the next day.

When I was in sixth grade, my teacher hit a fellow student with a paddle causing him to fall into the concrete block wall. . . . His skull [was] fractured.

If a student did not know an answer or rustled a paper at the wrong time, he would be set upon by the teacher. Ridicule and physical abuse were most often used by this teacher. Most distressing of all was when the teacher would rip a student out of his seat (for what appeared to be innocuous behavior) and smash his head against the blackboard. As a witness to this event, I would cover my eyes for fear of seeing blood and brains all over the blackboard.

I was slapped across the face by a nun for not folding a paper properly. Before this incident she would pull hair, pinch, etc. She did not single me out; very few students escaped her wrath.

In fourth grade I was supposed to cover all of my books for school and I was given specific directions on how to do it by my teacher. All were covered correctly except one because I didn't have sufficient materials—when she checked my books, she became very angry and slapped me across the face.

A POTPOURRI OF PUNITIVENESS

The following submissions represent the wide range of maltreatments reported by the respondents.

I was punished in Parochial School for not kneeling appropriately during a church service. I was told to kneel on a cement floor for a forty-five minute period while others in class were eating lunch.

In twelfth grade, I was three minutes late for a class due to circumstances beyond my control. My trigonometry teacher wouldn't allow me into class. After receiving a late slip from the office and my principal's intervention, I was allowed to enter class. To spite me, the teacher gave a quiz in my absence, which I wasn't allowed to make up. I volunteered to do an extra assignment to make up the quiz, but was denied.

I witnessed my brother being spanked with a ruler when I was in the first grade.

My second-grade teacher was very strict and, on occasion, abusive to the class. She put tape on the mouth for talking, spanked the students with a ruler, put them in the corner, removed them from the classroom, and made many threats. Though I was never physically harmed, I was terrified of her overall treatment of the class.

I hurt my wrist and could not participate in gym class for a few weeks. My gym teacher insisted I do push ups even though I was in pain.

I was instructed to hit another student in class because he did poorly in the weekly spelling tests.

The data about the nature and extent of abuse in schools experienced by teachers and a sample of college students reveal that psychological trauma is not uncommon. Remember that this sample is made up of people who were able to achieve enough in school to get accepted in college and earn their degrees. Because we have not yet studied a cross section of adults, we can only imagine the extent of negative experiences of students who *didn't* do well in school, including those who dropped out.

Some of the incidents reported seem horrendous; others seem trivial. The point is that these were the worst school experiences caused by an educator that these teachers remembered. The amount of stress caused by each incident cannot be gauged by someone else.

OTHER SAMPLES AND SURVEYS

Our first sample consisted of forty teachers from a wealthy, midwestern, suburban school district who were attending a workshop on psychological abuse. Almost all were experienced teachers and were highly educated. In terms of background, socioeconomic class, and affluence of the district in which they were employed, they represented an elite group. Therefore, it might be expected that the data presented represent an underestimation of the amount of abuse observed and experienced during the average teacher's youth.

All of the respondents indicated that they had witnessed abusive acts by teachers. Twenty-five (60 percent) reported a personal experience of denigration that they still remembered clearly. The following list places the abuses in order from most to least frequent: (1) sarcasm and ridicule, (2) criticism for poor performance, (3) abusive tone of voice, (4) withdrawal from non-academic activities such as recess and art, (5) name calling based on the student's physical characteristics, (6) unwarranted expulsion from class or detention, (7) allowing other children to harass or belittle the student, (8) painful pinching or squeezing, (9) throwing objects at the student, and (10) pulling student's ear or hair.

The second sample consisted of thirty-five undergraduate students at a large urban university on the East Coast. All were members of a sorority that volunteered to participate in the study. (The respondents were volunteers; we do not expect that what they report represents the general population.) Seventeen (48 percent) never witnessed abuse in their school days. Of the remaining eighteen, twelve (34 percent of the total sample) reported having been traumatized.

The third group consisted of forty-one special education teachers from suburban Philadelphia school districts who were attending a workshop on psychological abuse. Although six reported never having witnessed or experienced a traumatic school stressor, thirty-five (85 percent) reported some such instance.

The ranking of frequency of type of traumatic incidents for all three groups indicates verbal assaults were the most common. On the average, 65 percent of the respondents reported that their worst school experience had consisted of verbal assaults, including put-downs and ridicule. Thirty-two percent reported that social isolation was involved in their worst school experience, 18 percent reported the teacher encouraged humiliation by peers, 17 percent reported physical abuse, 17 percent reported being ignored, 12 percent reported overly severe punishment, and none reported being sexually harassed. The total percentages in this study did not equal 100 since respondents could report more than one abuse as part of their worst school experience. Also, some of the averages only include responses from the Pennsylvania study which included more types of abuse in the checklist than appeared in our earlier survey form.

The background information about the respondents suggests that they were from relatively privileged groups (they were college students or graduates). Despite this, a surprising number had witnessed or had been the object of some sort of abusive teacher behavior. It might be objected that many of the behaviors described could hardly rate as child abuse, either psychological or physical; nevertheless, the fact that they are so well remembered suggests the impact they made.

Of those who reported an incident and symptoms following it, the most frequently occurring symptom of the midwestern schoolteachers (80 percent) and the Pennsylvania special educators (89 percent) was a personality change. This included such reactions as "developed a lowered positive self-image and sense of competency," "became more nervous and anxious than before," and "became more sensitive to criticism," in order of frequency.

The East Coast undergraduates reported reexperiencing the trauma and memory and concentration problems as their most frequently occurring symptoms, with a full 60 percent of the sample experiencing these two types of reactions. Both of the other groups reported these as their next most frequently occurring type of symptom, with between 44 and 71 percent of the subjects reporting incidences of reexperiencing the trauma. Reexperiencing the trauma included "repeated flashbacks" and "recurrent nightmares related to school and the incident." Memory and concentration problems included "excessive worry about school performance" and "had a shorter attention span than before the incident."

Some form of psychic numbing was reported by 40 percent of the midwestern teachers, 47 percent of the undergraduates, and 31 percent of the special educators. Most frequently reported psychic numbing reactions included "a decline in school performance as noted by grades and/or incomplete homework assignments," "appeared unhappy or depressed after incident," and "became more withdrawn and spent more time alone."

Somatic complaints and physical reactions associated with autonomic arousal were reported by 34 percent of the Pennsylvanian special educators, 16 percent of the midwestern teachers, and 13 percent of the undergraduates. Stomachaches and headaches were most frequent of these. Sleep disturbances were the next most commonly experienced symptom, with 27 percent of the undergraduates, 14 percent of the special educators, and 12 percent of the teachers reporting this. Most commonly reported were "experienced greater fatigue" and "sleep disturbances." Least common were habit disorders, with between 8 and 13 percent of those reporting symptoms experiencing reactions such as nervous tics and nail biting.

We were interested in determining if there was a relationship between the age at which the trauma occurred and the length that the symptoms lasted. The samples were combined into those who were maltreated during primary school and were ages four to eight; a latency group of those maltreated when they were ages nine to twelve; and an adolescent group made up of those who were maltreated between ages thirteen and nineteen (table 5–1).

The most frequently occurring symptom, which was reported for those who were maltreated at all developmental levels, was a personality change. Between 74 percent (adolescent group) and 95 percent (primary group) reported some form of personality change. Due to the small sample size, it is not meaningful to discuss the differences in frequencies of the particular types of larger psychological changes, such as type of personality changes noted.

Those who reported that they were maltreated in the primary grades reexperienced the trauma incidents more than those who were maltreated at other ages. In fact, in a statistical analysis, there was a significant difference between developmental levels in the incidence of reexperiencing the trauma for a full year or more after the initial traumatic school stressor. The primary-aged group reported a greater frequency in the general presence of reexperiencing symptoms and in the continued presence for a year or more of this reaction. When all data from the studies are pooled, however, analysis did not yield a statistically significant difference among developmental levels for the reexperiencing of the trauma.

Clinical studies of traumatized children have generally not indicated the presence of flashbacks. It could be that the item used in our retrospective survey is not clear. The descriptor was "repeated flashbacks (i.e., undesired memories of the event)." Possibly children are unable to report flashbacks, clinicians do not ask the right questions, flashbacks occur in only a small per-

Table 5-1
FREQUENCIES OF SYMPTOMS LASTING LESS OR MORE
THAN A YEAR, BY AGE WHEN MALTREATMENT OCCURRED

		Primary (N = 21)		Latency (N = 16)		Adolescent (N = 19)	
				Longevity of Symptom			
Symptom		Less[a]	More[b]	Less	More	Less	More
Reexperiencing	N	14	8	6	1	8	2
the trauma	%	71	38	38	6	42	11
Personality	N	20	11	15	6	14	5
change	%	95	52	94	38	74	26
Memory and	N	9	6	5	2	5	2
concentration	%	43	29	31	13	26	11
problems							
Psychic	N	12	3	7	1	7	0
numbing	%	57	14	44	6	37	
Avoidance	N	16	5	11	2	11	5
reactions	%	76	24	69	13	58	26
Sleep	N	3	0	1	1	2	0
disturbances	%	14		6	6	11	
Somatic	N	5	1	3	1	3	1
complaints	%	24	5	19	6	16	5
Habit disorders	N	4	3	2	1	0	0
	%	19	14	13	6		

Notes: Percentages will not sum to 100 percent since subjects may have experienced multiple symptoms.

Percentages of total samples experiencing symptoms are not reported because individuals may have chosen not to respond to the survey when approached if they did not experience a traumatic school stressor.

[a]Symptoms experienced up to a year.

[b]Symptomatology experienced for a year or more.

centage of children, or adults' recollections are confounded. Our latest research is investigating this issue.

A group of thirty-one subjects reported a traumatic school incident occurring between the ages of 9 to 13. Of this latency-aged group, 48 percent (fifteen subjects) reported flashback symptoms for over a year or more, 13 percent for one month to a year, and 40 percent for more than a week but less than a month.

A limitation of these studies is that they do not tap the longevity of the symptoms, since the highest category was "one year or more" after the incident. Also, since the responses are retrospective, we must rely on long-term memory. These limitations are being addressed in current research. Nevertheless, the studies reported here reveal, in three disparate samples, a quite high rate of reported abuse. While the actual events reported were not as severe as the cases presented previously, it is clear that the development of baseline data will be of great help in establishing parameters for diagnosing EIPTSD.

6

What You Should Know about School Discipline

A sk most people to define discipline, and they will tell you that it is punishment. Yet discipline is not punishment, although punishment is a type of it. The term *discipline* comes from the Latin *disciplina,* which originally referred to learning and teaching. It is also associated with the concept of the disciple.

Several studies conducted at the NCSCPAS suggest that definitions of misbehavior in schools vary widely. Moreover, the perception of how "bad" a particular type of misbehavior is may be the result of a complex set of forces concerning the neighborhood where the school is located, community standards, the reputation of the child being disciplined, the background of the individual teacher, and recent events in the school.

No one approach to discipline has yet proved best (Hyman and Lally 1982). Some may work better in some situations than others. And teachers are not automatons into which you can plug any approach and expect it to work. But as this chapter demonstrates, there are more than enough alternatives to psychological and physical punitiveness. The approaches discussed here, if used correctly, will work most of the time to prevent the need for punishment. The emphasis should always be on prevention.

Withdrawal of privilege should be used to discipline students for unacceptable behavior. If procedures such as time-out, detention, and in-school suspension do not work, the problems are probably serious. That is the time to call in the school psychologist, not hit the student or psychologically demean him or her for the misbehavior.

Research conducted over ten years at the NCSCPAS and by others has repeatedly revealed that there is no consistent pattern of offenses that results in the use of corporal punishment. Our studies of psychological abuse further suggest that it is not the student offense that determines the punishment but a variety of other factors, ranging from the level of punitiveness in the school to whether the teacher got up on the wrong side of the bed.

Considering the importance of the issue of discipline, relatively little ongoing or intensive training about discipline occurs in the training of teachers. Parents may be familiar with their child's school, with the homework assignments, and the school rules, but they probably have little information about the teacher's or the principal's underlying philosophy of how children are best motivated to learn. In fact, school personnel probably do not fully understand it themselves.

In the fall of 1957, for my first teaching assignment, I entered a third-grade classroom of thiry-four unruly children in a small, rural New Jersey school. Between kindergarten and my appearance, my charges had had seven teachers. Unlike my unsuccessful predecessors, I had not been trained in education, but like them, I had received no formal courses in theory, research, and practice in school discipline. I had little more to go on than the practical examples of the teachers of my own childhood and the advice and examples offered by my colleagues. What to do with Bobby, who was constantly moving; with Jane, who still did not recognize preprimer words; and Susan, who wanted to read fifth-grade books and was bored with the class? What about Jimmy and Joe of the ready fists?

The conventional wisdom about discipline from fellow teachers could have been reduced to a few simple maxims: "Don't be too friendly; you're not here to win a popularity contest"; "Don't smile until Christmas"; and "If you have to get rough, don't leave any marks on the children." The last bit of advice was rather puzzling; I knew that corporal punishment had been illegal in New Jersey schools since before the turn of the century.

As I began to read about discipline, I ran into the age-old conflict between opposing views of the nature of children. Democracy suggests that concepts of childhood be based on the belief that each child is unique and deserving of the right to develop that uniqueness. Teaching methods and discipline should emphasize cooperation, methods of dissent, and respect for the rights of others. Schools should be exemplars of due process and reflect principles of participatory democracy.

Authoritarian societies emphasize unquestioning loyalty to leaders, reflexive obedience to authority, and the foolishness of dissent. Examples may be found in the educational approaches used in contemporary totalitarian or fascist societies. Even in modern democracies, the discipline in schools often reflects the traditional and/or religious beliefs of the society. It all boils down to whether one's views are more influenced by those who try to teach democracy as a process in education as opposed to those who think children are incapable of benefiting from that process.

When I attempted to discuss these issues with many experienced teachers in the 1950s, I was shocked by their lack of attempts to connect the concepts of democracy with approaches to school discipline. I was also told that all that "democracy stuff" comes from progressive education promoted by John Dewey and his followers, whom my colleagues accused of being a bunch of "pseudointellectuals" (I never heard my colleagues identify anyone who was a real intellectual), a popular term during the late 1950s and early 1960s. Many teachers claimed that the pseudointellectuals were trying to destroy traditional education. Many of my colleagues stated that research had nothing useful to say to educators and that the best single advice to new teachers was not to "let the kids get the upper hand on you."

Since I was fresh out of undergraduate school where I had majored in liberal arts, the massive anti-intellectualism of most of my fellow teachers was surprising. When faced with a problem such as discipline, they had no desire to think past the end of their yardsticks.

The anti-intellectualism that once pervaded education is no longer as apparent as it was in 1957. However, among teachers and administrators, there is still a significant and counterproductive undercurrent of suspicion and hostility toward intellectually oriented practitioners, such as psychologists, who attempt to use contemporary theory and research as a base for solving the problems of discipline.

Most of my fellow teachers were decent people who were very helpful in many ways. The principal was a gem who supported my innovative approaches, which included five reading groups instead of the usual one-to-three, writing plays with the class, and democratic methods of establishing rules. But in my first year as a teacher, I decided that my peers were as ignorant as I was about theory, research, and the literature on school discipline, and I decided to find out as much as I could.

The following three years I taught fifth and sixth grades in the same school and began to study part time in a school psychology program. I became especially interested in ways to integrate democratic principles into the process of education, especially discipline, and I began to experiment with democratic teaching methods. After sufficient study I realized that, in a democracy, children should behave because they want to, not because of fear of getting caught. Therefore, they would have to develop internal controls, as opposed to external controls. Intermediate-level children proved to be perfect candidates. My students and I mutually developed rules for the classroom and held regular class meetings to discuss and solve problems ranging over such issues as seating, free time, and projects. Most important, I focused on developing a climate of trust, friendship, and respect. The students knew I was the boss but that all suggestions received fair and just consideration.

In 1964, in research I conducted for my doctoral dissertation, I arranged for an experiment with a large number of fifth-grade classes. After measuring authoritarian and democratic climate through a student-administered scale (the Hyman A–D Scale), teachers were told by their administrators to leave their classrooms for forty-five minutes. The students from the authoritarian classes went crazy. They fought, yelled, and threw things at each other. Some tried to physically control others, and several students threatened to get the teacher. Their model for control was punishment by an external authority, the teacher. In the democratic classes, you would not have known the teacher was missing. These children had internalized the values of their classroom.

The Inconsistencies of Discipline

Although some teachers take pride in being tough, most would deny that they are authoritarians. But the discrepancies between what teachers often think they do and what they actually do are often startling. I once conducted a study of junior high school teachers to explore that issue. I wanted to determine if teachers used different control techniques with classes of bright children as compared to classes of average and low-ability students. Thirty teachers took part in the study, and each teacher taught classes in each of the three ability groups. The study used the Hyman A–D Scale.

The students filled out the Hyman A–D Scale, and average scores were obtained for each class. In addition, the teachers were asked to fill out one form for each class. However, they were asked to respond as if they were the typical student in each of the ability groups.

The findings were startling for many of the teachers. They tended to view themselves as much more democratic with their high-ability students than did the students. Although there were discrepancies in the middle-level groups between teacher and pupil perceptions, some very interesting findings emerged with the low-level students.

The students in the lowest tracks in secondary schools present difficult problems. They are hard to motivate, and many have long histories of misbehavior. They are not retarded, yet they are often several years behind academically (unless they are mainstreamed retarded children). Because they are not in special education, they are not legally entitled to extra services. They often come from homes where positive motivation toward school is lacking. Their parents may be hostile to teachers, and they may rely on punitive methods to make their children behave at home and in school. These children are most frequently from homes of the working poor, or their parents are on welfare.

This lowest group perceived their teachers as more authori-

tarian than did any other group. And there were major distinctions between male and female teachers. Most of the male teachers were able to guess how their classes would respond. The
female teachers underestimated how democratic their students
felt they were. The explanation? Female teachers tended to recognize the lack of nurturance and sense of academic failure of
these students and in response tended to focus on the emotional
needs of the youngsters. They recognized the hostility of the students for what it really was: the students' inadequate defenses
against teachers and other students who made them feel inferior
was to act indifferent to school.

The women teachers tried to motivate the students by finding or developing appropriate reading materials that would be
interesting and relevant, by understanding their pupils' backgrounds, by use of humor (not sarcasm) and patience in the face
of adversity, and by being fair and consistent in discipline.

The male teachers thought that the best way to handle the
students was to be "tough." One of the men summed up his feelings about his lowest group: "With those kids you have to let
them know who is boss. From the first day I keep my thumb on
them. They know they can't screw around with me. I won't take
any crap from any of them. Most of them are here only because
they are forced to go to school until they are sixteen. You think
their parents give a damn if they stay in school or not? If their
parents don't care, why should I?" With this attitude, it is little
wonder that these teachers received the most authoritarian
scores from the students. This study and others suggest that
what goes on in authoritarian classrooms with the lower ability
groups is a major reason for high dropout rates.

A Case of Overreaction

Why are children being psychologically and physically maltreated in the name of discipline? Overreaction to discipline
problems is all too common, as is illustrated in the following.

I was invited by a rural school district to do a workshop on
school discipline and violence. This was not an unusual request
except that I was somewhat surprised by the emphasis on deal-

ing with problems of violence. Initial conversations with the administrators who hired me suggested that they were having a real problem with school violence. When I arrived, I was told of an incident that had happened the previous year.

A 16 year old, usually considered an isolate by his peers, had stabbed another teenager with a pair of scissors. The episode caused great consternation in the school and the community. Committees were set up to develop better discipline codes, to bring in experts on self-defense (for teachers), and to develop better methods of discipline. But in fact, in spite of the flurry of activity, this incident was quite atypical of the school. My conversations with school staff indicated that despite policy decisions by people who should have been well informed, few knew the relevant factors in the background of the boy who committed the act, few knew the actual details of the event, and they all agreed that this was a highly unusual event for their school. Yet the reaction of the school and community was an almost total knee-jerk response of the need to get tough with unruly teenagers. Most of the disciplinary measures developed, such as suspension and detention, were punitive in nature. In other words, a single incident, despite past data concerning the generally good behavior of students in this school, had stirred up latent emotions to become more punitive with students, an atmosphere that inevitably leads to abuse.

This example illustrates a major problem: educators generally have an impoverished repertoire of responses to deal with misbehavior; they tend to rely on a few simple maxims. This is partly due to the lack of systematic training in their college and graduate school programs. Whenever I present speeches or workshops, I always ask for a show of hands by those who have had at least one college or graduate-level course devoted to discipline. Few, if any, hands are raised by teachers or administrators trained before the 1980s. Of more recent graduates, perhaps 5 percent raise their hands. Schools have tried to compensate by offering in-service training. Unfortunately, most of the training consists of half-day or one-day workshops on the latest pop discipline program. The workshops can hardly scratch the surface.

Discipline is a highly personal and emotionally charged issue. It cuts across all aspects of our lives, and new concepts need to be carefully considered, tried out, and then modified according to each teacher's feelings and the nature of the class and the students. The improvement of discipline is a task requiring the commitment of time and resources. The school needs to begin by identifying what behaviors are desirable and how those behaviors may be encouraged and rewarded. Many schools, however, begin by defining those behaviors that are forbidden.

In several research studies, my colleagues and I looked at the rules in schools around the country and found that educators' definitions of misbehavior and feelings about appropriate disciplinary responses vary greatly. The following is a list of misbehaviors gleaned from our studies: excessive talking in unauthorized areas, obscene language, insolence, stealing, drug-related activities, smoking, fighting, defacing school property, gambling, littering, loitering, dishonesty, petting, tardiness, rudeness, class cutting, gang-related activities, failure to complete homework, disobeying requests of school staff, inattention to classroom activities, making unauthorized eye contact, possession of weapons, wearing hair in unauthorized styles, breaking the dress code, cheating, having body odor, not doing as well on tests as required, bringing banned reading materials to school, printing unauthorized material in the school paper, breaking training rules in sports, masturbation, holding hands, kissing in public, and extortion.

Not only are there regional differences in the way schools define the seriousness of particular offenses and acceptable punishments for particular misbehaviors; there may be great differences among schools in a district. For instance, we conducted a study of offenses leading to suspensions in an inner-city school district. Certain schools had an inordinate number of suspensions related to the category of defiance; others in the same district suspended relatively few students, and those almost exclusively for violent behavior. Most interesting was the school with the highest rate of suspensions related to truancy. Clearly they also had a high dropout rate, yet few school officials questioned this obvious connection.

Effective Alternative Approaches
to Punitiveness

In 1977, the NCSCPAS received a grant from the National Institute of Education to examine the literature on the effectiveness of training programs designed to help teachers improve discipline. This study set the stage for an exhaustive review of all research available. It also provided data for additional research studies and the development of training.

In the studies we conducted, we classified the approaches to discipline in seven categories: behavioral, psychodynamic/interpersonal, classroom ecological, humanistic, sociological, and biophysical. The first three are discussed here. We call this the teacher variance approach; it is based on the belief that the best discipline occurs when a teacher's philosophical outlook is matched to an appropriate training program.

BEHAVIORAL APPROACHES

Reinforcement. Behavioral approaches are based on the assumption that all behavior, including misbehavior, is learned. The principles for learning behavior and misbehavior are based on reward and punishment. Extensive research shows that reward, usually referred to as reinforcement, is the most effective way to change behavior. Reinforcements vary according to each person's preference; what is appropriate for one child may not be appropriate for another. Basically the behavioral approach suggests catching children being good. That is, great emphasis is put on reinforcing children for their good behavior and ignoring the poor behavior so that it is not reinforced. Reinforcement in the classroom can be done by verbal praise, a pat on the back, or even free time for good behavior.

The chief problem with behavioral approaches is that some teachers may not believe that children should be reinforced for being good; they believe that children should be good anyway. They tend to look at reinforcement as bribery. (Once a teacher talks about bribery, I know the chances that he or she will use behavioral approaches are slim.)

One characteristic of a well-managed, behaviorally oriented classroom is that teachers frequently praise children for behaving appropriately. One useful technique is called modeling. If, for example, three children are sitting together and one is misbehaving, the teacher can merely say to the other two, "I appreciate how you are doing your work," without saying anything to the misbehaving child. The teacher thus provides a positive model of good behavior without calling attention to the bad behavior.

For children with extensive behavioral problems, school psychologists can help teachers set up specific behavioral modification programs. These approaches require the counting of the inappropriate behaviors, the determination of a reinforcer that will work to change this behavior, and the implementation of the reinforcement system with the child, along with a counting of the number of misbehaviors that still remain. If this approach is done appropriately, a written tally of misbehaviors should show a substantial decrease once reinforcement schedules are set up.

Parents can play a vital role by using similar behavioral programs at home, and they can frequently provide effective reinforcers for good school behavior. With some children, parental cooperation is crucial, and in all cases parents need to be informed and involved at some level.

Most inappropriate behaviors in the classroom can be easily managed with behavioral techniques. However, there are certain behaviors, such as fighting, loud disruptions of the class, and bizarre mannerisms, that cannot easily be ignored. In these cases, the teacher must ask a school psychologist for help in determining the meaning of these behaviors. In many instances where the child is not emotionally disturbed, simple punishment procedures have proved very effective. Time-out is one of these procedures.

Time-Out. Time-out is a widely used punishment in schools—and it has been greatly abused. It has increasingly entered the list of causes of EIPTSD in young children.

When twelve-year-old Jim and his mother moved to a predominantly rural school district in southern Illinois, she had hopes for a new beginning for her son. She informed Mr. Jones, the principal of her son's new school, that she had recently divorced her husband, Jim's stepfather. She and her children had left their former home primarily because he had abused them. Assuming that Mr. Jones would understand, she said, "I know Jim has emotional problems and will sometimes misbehave. He may get into fights. Please let me know immediately if he needs to be disciplined, and I will cooperate with you. The child abuse counselor said that severe punishment will only make matters worse. The school psychologist told me to give Jim lots of support, encouragement, and opportunities to talk about his feelings of anger. If punishment is necessary, I have learned to use withdrawal of privilege or time-out."

Mr. Jones, a tough guy from the "old school," was glad to learn that Jim's mother approved of time-out. Much to her dismay, he informed her of his "reasonable" use of paddling. He assured her that he believed in time-out and would be happy to use it if necessary. He had a special time-out/in-school suspension room that worked very well. Woe to any student in Mr. Jones's school who tried to get away with anything. A man from the "don't smile until Christmas" school and an ex-military man, he stated, "I know the importance of discipline and punishment"!

Sensing the potential for trouble, Mr. Jones laid in wait for Jim's first indiscretion. It wasn't long before Jim was subjected to the testing and teasing that bullies so often feel they must inflict on newcomers. Jim controlled himself as he had been taught in therapy and did not use his fists in response to the teasing, an accomplishment he was proud of. Unfortunately, he did refer to certain alleged unsavory traits of the bully and the bully's mother. These were reported to Mr. Jones, who was waiting for the chance to bring Jim to heel.

Aware that he should go easy on the paddling, he used it sparingly, giving Jim three licks. Then the boy was consigned to the time-out room, a windowless, poorly ventilated supply closet. He was sentenced to spend five full consecutive school days there, with nothing to do. Despite her request, Mr. Jones neglected to inform Jim's mother, nor did the hapless, resentful Jim, who became more and more angry at the principal.

In a predictably increasing spiral of misbehavior and punishment, Jim became a regular visitor to the time-out room. Conditions finally became unbearable for Jim when he was sentenced to spend two weeks in the room during a heat wave in June. He finally told his mother what had been going on.

I was asked to provide expert testimony in the ensuing litigation against the school. The school could find no credible experts who would testify that Mr. Jones's use of time-out had any professional or effective purpose in helping Jim improve his behavior. I found that it had caused severe problems. After expensive initial litigation, the school and the insurance company settled out of court. No one won since much of the settlement money went to provide psychotherapy for Jim and his angry, depressed, and distraught mother.

The story of Jim may seem bizarre to those who understand the use of time-out, but similar cases occur all too often. During the past few years, I have been increasingly asked to testify against educators who send children to extended periods of solitary confinement for offenses and under conditions never recommended by the psychologists who developed the procedure.

Children with learning disabilities and behavioral problems seem to be the most frequent victims of misuse of time-out in spite of the fact that most of the research on this method was conducted to help children with these problems. Time-out, however, was developed as part of a whole system; used alone, it may be useless or even harmful.

Time-out is a type of punishment based on behavioral research. The theory is that if a student is taken out of a pleasant or reinforcing situation, that in itself may be sufficient punishment to convince the child not to repeat the offense.

The use of time-out has grown out of an extensive body of experimental and classroom research and practice on effective classroom management. It is based on methods of contingency management, which itself is based on research demonstrating that children's behavior in the classroom can be shaped by the judicious use of rewards and punishments. Giving and removing rewards and punishments can increase or decrease behaviors.

Also, rewards and reinforcers are much more effective than punishments.

Anything given to increase a student's good behavior is considered a reinforcer. Both giving and removing rewards can change behavior. If what a teacher gives, does, or says does not increase the desired behavior, by definition it is not reinforcing. If what is done to stop misbehavior does not stop it, by definition it is not a punishment. Punishments can be both given and removed as a way of decreasing behavior. If a punishment does not work, there are several options. The most popular—and usually least effective—choice is to increase the amount of punishment. Instead, the teacher can try a different and, he or she hopes, more effective punishment, or the teacher could give up on punishment and try to focus on increasing the desired behaviors through rewards. A teacher who uses time-out repeatedly without eliminating poor behavior, as in the case of Mr. Jones, is not meting out a punishment. In fact, too often, it becomes a reinforcement by getting the student out of a classroom situation he or she dislikes. Therefore, if a teacher uses time-out repeatedly and the misbehavior does not cease, it is probably a reward.

Figure 6–1 summarizes the methods of using time-out within the framework of contingency management. Before a teacher turns to time-out, he or she should use this matrix by listing everything he or she can do in the upper left quadrant, which represents the most effective approach, followed by the lower left and then the lower right. The last resort should be positive punishment, and it should be carefully considered and then monitored.

Four Types of Time-Out. There are four types of time-out: isolation, seclusion, exclusion, and nonexclusion.

Isolation occurs when the student is temporarily removed from the classroom. The rule of thumb is that the removal time in minutes should not exceed the child's age; however, the research on effectiveness shows that the correct duration is best determined by what works. In school settings, short periods of time-out can be very effective when used in conjunction with positive reinforcement programs. Long periods of time-out

RESPONSE OUTCOME

	INCREASE GOOD BEHAVIORS BY USING	DECREASE BAD BEHAVIORS BY USING
G I V E	POSITIVE REINFORCEMENT such as praise, tokens, merit points	POSITIVE PUNISHMENT such as verbal reprimands, unpleasant consequences
R E M O V E	NEGATIVE REINFORCEMENT such as stopping or removing unpleasant consequences	NEGATIVE PUNISHMENT such as time out from a rewarding or pleasant class situation

Figure 6–1. Contingency Management of Behavior

(over thirty minutes) begin to pose ethical problems. It may lead to seclusion, a form of long-term solitary confinement in which students are locked up for long periods in uncomfortable, unsafe, and unsupervised areas. This is an open invitation for a lawsuit.

Some classes use a cardboard box or a special booth to isolate students from the rest of the class. The presence of these enclosures, however, all too often leads to their overuse. A tired and frustrated teacher may be tempted to remove children with behavioral problems. Out of sight and out of mind may make life easier for the teacher in the short run, but it is a formula for long-term problems.

If reasonable use of time-out does not decrease the unwanted behaviors after several sessions, it is likely that increasing the duration will not work. Perhaps it is time for the teacher to think about why removal from class is not a punishment.

Exclusion occurs when a student remains in the room but is asked to sit away from the rest of the class, perhaps behind a screen or in a corner. Nonexclusion is used to limit the extent of a student's involvement in ongoing activities. The student may be required to continue working while the others have free time.

When and How to Use Time-Out. Time-out should be reserved for extreme behaviors such as hitting, cursing, or lying. These are actions that are not only inappropriate but also unacceptable. Minor misbehaviors such as talking out of turn, pushing in line, and other daily irritants should not be punished with time-out. If time-out becomes routine, it probably will lose its effectiveness.

Time-out can be effective only if the student enjoys class. Also, the process of sending a student to time-out should not be reinforcing. For instance, if a student enjoys irritating the teacher and the teacher responds by yelling as the youngster goes off to time-out, the teacher has been defeated.

Below is a list of do's and don'ts for the effective use of time-out:

- Do establish clear procedures and time limits for going to and remaining in time-out. Post a description of the offenses deserving time-out in a prominent place.
- Do tell students what rules they have broken and calmly request that they go to time-out.
- Do prepare options for students who refuse time-out. Calmly repeat those options if a student refuses and give him or her time to consider what to do.
- Don't send an errant student to the friendly counselor for time-out where he or she will be counseled instead of punished.
- Don't send students to the principal where they may sit in the outer office to be entertained by the comings and goings of secretaries, other students, and school staff.
- Don't yell, scream, or threaten students when you send them to time-out.

Time-out, when used as part of a total system of contingency management, can be an effective method for reducing misbehavior. It should not be the equivalent of a sentence in the gulag or solitary confinement in a federal penitentiary. Nor should it be confused with in-school suspensions, detentions, or other exclusionary procedures, which are rarely used as part of a systematic approach to improving behavior.

Time-out is a technique based on the theory of negative punishment. It is a short-term removal of a child from a pleasant situation to an unpleasant one. It is most effective with young children.

A great deal of controversy has swirled around the concept of time-out as teachers have begun to misunderstand and exaggerate the techniques. For instance, a time-out room that is dark and secluded is completely inappropriate for young children. Some teachers have constructed time-out boxes; others have put children in vaults, closets, or darkened cellars. This is not time-out; this is cruel and unusual punishment. Time-out merely consists of placing the child behind a screen in a corner of the room or facing the wall for a few minutes. This must be done unemotionally; it must be an accepted practice in the classroom; and other children must learn not to pay attention to the secluded child. A number of research studies have shown that time-out can be effective when children are being reinforced for their inappropriate behavior by the attention they get from the teacher and other children.

Summary. A visit to a well-run classroom that uses behavioral principles will reveal the following:

1. Instruction will be geared so that each child receives some reinforcement for accomplishing tasks each day.
2. The teacher will constantly praise children in a genuine and warm (rather than gratuitous) manner. He or she will also pat children on the back, congratulate them, and may even have a system of stickers, tokens, or other types of rewards that can be added up to achieve a goal.
3. Often free time will be used as a motivator for children to finish their work efficiently and well.
4. Children will never receive negative, deprecating statements from the teacher.

5. If children are misbehaving, someone—the teacher, an aide, or another adult—will keep track of the misbehavior, or the children will make individual contracts with the teacher and keep track of their own behavior.

6. Time-out will be used as a last resort for children whose behavior cannot be tolerated in the classroom. It will be done in an unemotional way, and the children will understand that their misbehavior will result in placement in time-out as a consequence.

THE PSYCHODYNAMIC/INTERPERSONAL APPROACH

The psychodynamic/interpersonal approach is based on the assumption that children, in order to learn to behave appropriately, must go through various developmental stages. Adequate personalities are developed in conjunction with relationships to parents, other important adults, and siblings. Using this approach, we tend to view behavior in the school as a manifestation of problems in the home. If a child is misbehaving, it is incumbent on the teacher, social worker, or psychologist to discover what is going on in the home.

In the psychodynamic/interpersonal approach, misbehavior is always understood as a symptom of an underlying problem. Therefore, rather than treating the symptoms, a teacher who utilizes this approach tries to understand why the child is misbehaving. (I find this to be a tremendous problem when working in consultation with teachers, since they are more concerned with symptoms rather than the underlying causes for the behavior.) Once the reasons for the child's misbehavior are determined, a number of approaches should be used. The following is a checklist:

1. The teacher talks with the parents to try to discover if the behavior at home is similar to that displayed in school.

2. The teacher tries to analyze how the behavior in the home is related to behavior in school and what can be done to avoid it.

3. If the problem is severe, the teacher contacts the school psychologist to gather information and obtain recommendations.

4. Once the general nature of the problem is discovered, the teacher can spend some time talking with the child, getting to know the child better, and let the child understand that problems perceived at home are not necessarily perceived in school.

5. The student should be counseled by the school counselor, school psychologist, or social worker if the problem is severe.

6. Family counseling may be recommended.

7. Problems related to the home can be worked out through techniques such as bibliotherapy, art therapy, and various other approaches. In bibliotherapy, books with pertinent themes are selected. For example, if a child feels depressed and angry about his or her parents' divorce, books about children with similar problems can be used to show how the characters in the stories deal successfully with the issues. There are a wide range of topics written at various reading levels to help children with difficult life events.

8. A frequent and recurring problem is lack of communication in the home. Parents can be given materials on how to hold family meetings and how to strengthen family life.

9. The school can attempt to discover what the child is trying to accomplish by the misbehavior. Programs can be set up to help the child fulfill his or her needs in legitimate and appropriate ways.

10. Sometimes personality clashes between teachers and students cannot be resolved. In these cases, administrators should change children to other classes.

CLASSROOM ECOLOGY

The classroom ecology approach might best be compared to the traditional effective classroom. In this approach, the teacher is considered to be in charge of the situation and is nonpunitive but firm and fair. Children are motivated by appropriate curriculum, stimulating instruction, and a desire to meet the expectations of the teacher. Good classroom management is based on understanding a number of dimensions of classroom functioning. The following checklist can be used to determine whether ecological factors in a classroom need improvement:

1. Physical setting: Recent research has shown that a semicircular seating arrangement is best if discipline problems are to be decreased. Seating should be in such a manner that children who are constantly interacting inappropriately are separated. If they are seated together, they should be kept busy with projects.

2. Classroom temperature: If the temperature in the classroom varies significantly from the norm, behavioral problems can develop. This is especially true in the fall and spring, when classrooms can become hot because of the large windows. Studies have shown that children become restless and have difficulty concentrating when the temperature is extremely high. Fans and frequent drinks of water can alleviate this situation. And any sensible administrator will remove the children from the classroom when the temperature is so high that even the teachers are perspiring profusely.

3. Lighting: Inadequate lighting can contribute to misbehavior in classrooms. On the other hand, lighting should not be overstimulating.

4. Classroom decoration: Although there is no research to show the relationship between a well-maintained classroom and good discipline, common sense suggests that a motivated, interested teacher will update bulletin boards and keep the material on the walls current. Good use of the wall space and bulletin boards includes samples of students' work to increase their self-esteem and motivate them.

5. Teacher demeanor: Enthusiasm is an important factor in good classroom management. A dull, uninteresting teacher who overemphasizes the use of Dittoed materials and lectures in a monotonous, uninteresting manner is a definite signal for children not to be interested. Student-teacher interaction is important to good discipline. Good teachers frequently praise children

and do not demean them. Poor teachers are full of sarcasm, which generates resentment, anger, and lack of achievement.

6. Style of presentation: Lecturing is an art that most teachers need to develop. Every lecture should have a beginning, middle, and end. The beginning should never start until the teacher has the full attention of all the children, and it should review material presented in the previous lesson. The review should link to the body of the lecture, which should include student answers, questions, and participation. The end of the lecture should be tied to assignments and linked to work that will be covered the next day.

7. Curriculum: Curriculum is a major key to good discipline. Each child should be working at his or her level. One of the great problems in some rural and inner-city areas is that there is not enough diversity of curricular materials to individualize instruction. While many children can work at the same level, some will find the work too easy and some too difficult. A change in curriculum for these children often solves discipline problems. Teachers who are dependent on boring and repetitive busywork are bound to develop discipline problems. (A sign of this is stacks of duplicated worksheets in the room and the children spending most of their time with them.) Be careful not to confuse this with an individualized program in which the teacher prepares individualized materials for each child. These are usually self-correcting lessons that require minimal teacher help.

8. Management of errors: A number of management errors have been identified in the research (Kounin 1977).

> Disciplining the wrong child: Nothing can cause more resentment than punishing a child who was not misbehaving. Often teachers justify this by saying that the child in question had misbehaved at other times. This logic is lost on the child, who sees the teacher as being unfair.

> Group alerting: A good technique for keeping children on the ball is not to call on them in a set order but to call on them in a random manner.

> Transition periods: Many teachers have difficulty handling transitions between various activities or between classes. Some teachers take an inordinate period of time to change

activities. For example, if the class is preparing for play period, a poor manager will call on children one at a time. This usually requires that many children are sitting with hands folded, waiting to be called while others are standing in line with nothing to do but talk or shove. At the secondary school level, poor monitoring of halls between classes invites trouble.

Stopping bad behaviors: Teachers may use a variety of ineffective methods to stop misbehavior. The most glaring are nagging, screaming, use of sarcasm or ridicule, or frequently sending students to the principal. Ignoring more serious behaviors while disciplining trivial offenses is a mistake.

Engaged time: Well-managed classrooms are often business-like but supportive. Children spend a good deal of time on task. They may not always be working on academic activities, but they are engaged productively and cooperatively with the teacher, other students, or projects.

Smoothness: Teachers who have discipline problems frequently overreact. When I do workshops, I always ask the teachers to describe a series of procedures to stop two students sitting together from talking. I request that they go through a hierarchy from the least to the most disruptive procedure if they are giving a lecture and want to continue without losing the class's attention. Most teachers say that they start with verbal reprimands. But before doing that I advise them to look at the student, make direct eye contact, frown in disapproval (use the "laser glare"), move toward the students (proximity control), and finally gently touch the students. All of these can be done without interrupting the lecture.

THE PROCESS APPROACH

As part of our research on teacher variance, we looked at all of the programs we could identify and then identified what processes each program taught teachers to do and overlapped the various process.

Whenever possible, teachers should use information feedback. They should reflect, restate, and accept each student's feelings and ideas. They do not have to approve of everything a student does or says, but they can accept that the student's thoughts and feelings are genuine.

Teachers should praise and reinforce good behavior, although if they do this gratuitously or automatically, it will have no effect. A pat on the back is always a good idea. Teachers should try to ignore minor misbehavior. If they must punish students, they should use loss of privilege and try to do it in an unemotional manner.

If a child is being particularly difficult, the teacher should try to observe and record what the student does, and when he or she does it. Notes on behavior can be used to discern patterns and thus help to diagnose the student's problem.

The physical aspects of classroom ecology should facilitate good behavior. For instance, 90-degree temperatures on a hot Friday afternoon are bound to lead to problems if teachers try to push the students. Also, a well-organized classroom will set the climate for orderly behavior.

Educators can teach students problem-solving strategies to deal with aggression, name calling, and so forth. They can have class meetings to discuss movies, television programs, and newspaper accounts that inappropriately portray the use of aggression to solve problems. In this way students can generate age-appropriate nonaggressive solutions.

Teachers should appropriately express feelings. They too become tired, short-tempered, and angry. A teacher who has overslept and gotten caught in a traffic jam on the way to work or who does not feel well can share his or her feelings of frustration and anger. This will help students not to feel that they are somehow at fault for the teacher's changed mood. If both teachers and students recognize the teacher's mood, it may help the teacher to condemn a misbehaving student's behavior rather than condemning the child as a result of the teacher's own frustration.

OTHER APPROACHES

Alternative Schools. Every public school should have an alternative program for disaffected, alienated students. In the long run, alternative schools will aid society by dealing with children who normally would be dropouts. Alternative schools should operate with specific theoretical approaches. They should continuously monitor their successes and modify techniques as needed. For instance, an open, humanistic atmosphere may be effective with bright, mildly disturbed children who are bored with regular school and hostile to authority. For students with problems of self-control who tend toward delinquent behavior, a structured, behavioral approach might be recommended. Lack of both adequate planning and psychological consultation have resulted in many fiascos that have given alternative schools a bad name.

In-School Suspensions and Detentions. One of the great absurdities in education has been the practice of suspension as a punishment for truant or tardy students. Most educators agree but keep right on doing it. If punishment is needed, it should be on school grounds. Some students break rules so that they can be suspended. This may keep them in situations that sustain their problem behavior. When punishment must be used, it cannot work if it is what the transgressor wants. Therefore, all schools should have the physical facilities and personnel to conduct in-school punishments that work. If the punishment is effective, it will work after a few trials. Some students are constantly sent to in-school suspension, proving it was an ineffective punishment. Repeat offenders often need to be evaluated by the school psychologist to determine the causes of the misbehavior.

Discipline Codes. During the last decade there has been great interest in the use of discipline codes. This interest has arisen from a type of law-and-order approach that emphasizes the identification of specific misbehaviors and specific punishments associated with them. Most states have either mandated or suggested models for the development of discipline codes by local districts, yet there is almost no empirical research to link the use of discipline codes with improved school behavior.

Both parents and students should know the rules and punishments. Each school should have a designated list of misbehaviors with appropriate guidelines for discipline.

Consistency in discipline is not always the best indicator of effective management, however. Some administrators hide behind a discipline code in order not to use their own judgment about the appropriateness of their discipline procedures. In a large city high school, I was visiting with the chief disciplinarian and an assistant principal. The case in point was one brought to the attention of the disciplinarian.

A high school girl who had no previous discipline problems was suspended. She had gone into the girl's bathroom and seen her name written on the wall with a felt-tip marker. It was an unflattering statement: "Jane ————— is a whore." The girl got out her own marker and started to cover up the graffiti. She was subsequently caught and suspended for three days, the penalty indicated in the school's discipline guidelines. The assistant principal, however, did not recognize the difference between the unknown person who originally wrote on the wall and the young girl who was trying to defend her reputation. When questioned, he pointed to the exact punishment for defacing school property. The disciplinarian pointed out (too late for Jane) that the administrator's discretion should be used in cases with extenuating circumstances in determining the punishment. Clearly discipline codes can set up rules but do not provide for justice, which can come only from well-intentioned, thoughtful administrators.

Teacher Consultation. Often discipline problems in the classroom can be related to inadequacies on the part of teachers. For instance, in dealing with particular problems, teachers might have a lack of knowledge about the appropriate thing to do, a lack of skills to carry out the appropriate procedures, a lack of objectivity in dealing with the problem, or a lack of self-confidence that interferes with acting effectively. These basic precepts, described by Gerald Caplan (1970), a well-known psychiatrist at Harvard University, were utilized initially to develop a whole field of teacher consultation that is a focus of the training of modern school psychologists.

Often discipline problems are related to teacher inadequacies, which can be relatively easily corrected if teachers are willing to work with consultants. One of the advantages of consultation is that a teacher works with an experienced school psychologist. The school psychologist may never see the child in question directly but will help the teacher to deal with the problem at hand. In this way the teacher not only resolves the problem of this particular child but acquires new skills and understandings in order to deal with other similar situations, as illustrated in the following example.

Mrs. Jones was an experienced fifth-grade teacher in an inner-city school. She was well respected by staff and parents and generally considered a good disciplinarian. She had requested that I conduct a psychological evaluation of Sammy, a student she felt was emotionally disturbed.

When I observed Sammy in class, he did appear quite active. He spoke out of turn, left his seat without permission, and was sullen when corrected. What Mrs. Jones had not told me was how she handled these problems. Whenever Sammy did something wrong, she called him names such as "baby," "class clown," "brat," and "Mr. Sour Puss." She constantly rejected his efforts for help and never called on him when he raised his hand. Her interactions with him were negative, critical, and sarcastic. She never praised him but rather focused on reminding him of his past indiscretions and expected future misbehavior.

After about three consultation sessions with Mrs. Jones, it was apparent that she intensely disliked Sammy and she wanted him removed from her room. In previous years she had been able to deal with children like Sammy, but now she seemed helpless, angry, and overwhelmed.

After six consultation sessions, I told Mrs. Jones that she spent the first three consultation sessions complaining about how bad Sammy was. We had spent three meetings discussing, collaboratively, how to manage Sammy. I patiently waited for her to see how her abusive behavior toward Sammy was making things worse. Finally I pointed out that although she had the skills to manage Sammy, she always had excuses for not following through on approaches we had planned together. I also pointed out her successes in previous years with difficult children like Sammy. I suggested that maybe something else was wrong.

I told her that she seemed stressed, tense, and sometimes depressed. She immediately broke into tears. It was then that I discovered that her marriage was breaking up and that her

own son, about Sammy's age, had become a behavioral problem in home and school. It did not take much for her to realize
that her abuse of Sammy was a result of other frustrations in
life. Because her husband had left her, she had to deal with her
son by herself. She had to deal with him, but felt she did not
deserve to be stuck with Sammy also. I was able to convince
Mrs. Jones to obtain help and support in her personal life, and
after further consultation she was then able to stop abusing
Sammy and to begin to help him.

School Climate: The Good News and the Bad News

During the 1980s, the public and educators were subjected to
numerous reports on how to improve education. The first volley
against teachers occurred when they were told the nation was at
risk. Since then, sages from universities, business, government,
and even foreign countries have addressed this issue.

The solutions to better education include teaching educators
so-called effective teaching skills, raising teachers' salaries, using
statewide basic skills tests to evaluate and improve teacher performance, eliminating undergraduate teacher education, stress-
ing basic skills, providing automatic retentions for failing students, returning to "good old-fashioned" discipline, teaching
specific values, teaching only "great" books, and standardized
curricula. As with all other reform movements in education, it is
sometimes difficult to separate political rhetoric and posturing
from facts.

Throughout the hundreds of pages of reports by various
commissions, there has been surprisingly little emphasis on the
importance of teachers' individuality and creativity. Many of the
experts assume that there is a "right" way to teach, that there is
a universally "correct" curriculum, or that effective schools operate in specific ways. But based on my twenty-seven years of
experience and research, I have come to the conclusion that
there are many right ways to teach, that there are many different
successful curricula, and that good schools may be organized in
a variety of ways that match the needs of students, faculty, and
the community. Matching these elements for the best fit occurs

by establishing the right climate in which to nurture both teachers and students.

DEFINING SCHOOL CLIMATE

School climate encompasses all of the aspects of the environment of a school that may affect learning. Communities, parents, students, teachers, and even the school building contribute to the climate, but the most important factor in each school building is the principal. The principal sets the tone of the building.

Ask any psychologist, counselor, or special teacher who works in more than one school building about the differences among the schools. Sitting in the teachers' room, watching the students at lunch, observing the secretaries, watching students and teachers in the halls, and attending staff meetings offer valuable clues about the climate of a school. But the best method is to develop a questionnaire that is answered anonymously by students, staff, administrators, and even parents.

Let us take a few examples of how administrators determine different climates. At one extreme on a possible climate continuum is the type of school in which Mr. Macho, the ex-coach and heir to Hitler and Genghis Khan, rules supreme. Everything is orderly, the teachers are cowed, and the children's worst nightmare is being sent to the principal's office. Paperwork is always completed on time, staff meetings are always orderly, and the building is always clean. "You will obey" is the major communication from the principal to everybody in the school.

At the other extreme is the building led by Mr. or Ms. Wimp. The Wimps hide in their offices and do not want to hear about problems. They will promise you anything to get you off their backs but never come through. Deadlines always become crises, and teachers alternate between feelings of anger and despair. While most communication in Mr. Macho's school comes from him, in Mr. or Ms. Wimp's school, the communication generally flows from staff to the principal.

In both extremes people are unhappy, truancy and teacher absences are high, and achievement is low. Most school buildings have climates somewhere between the extremes, but each school building has its own particular climate, which in turn determines morale and learning.

Climate can be measured, described, and modified, but most administrators seem to be afraid of the process. The process takes time, energy, and commitment, and effective change usually requires three to four years of effort. Below is a brief outline of the steps I have used with schools over the last fifteen years. In every case, when the administrators were committed, the results were highly positive. When the administrators waffled, the projects died.

CHANGING THE CLIMATE

Problem Identification. The first step is to set up a steering committee representative of teachers, administrators, students, and parents, depending upon the extensiveness of the project. A school psychologist, university professor, or other outside consultant can help with the technical aspects of the committee.

The steering committee initially must identify possible problem areas, perhaps over several sessions. Members can meet with their constituents to confirm that all possible problem areas have been identified.

Items are then developed to measure the extent of problems. The goal is to develop a questionnaire that can be easily administered, scored, and interpreted. (I have always used answer sheets that can be scored by computer.) The questionnaire usually consists of statements to which the respondents can indicate their level of agreement. They are given a range of choices from "strongly agree" to "strongly disagree." Or they may be asked how important something is by indicating a range from "not very important" to "very important."

The steering committee generally should consider the following areas important to measure in order to determine school climate.

Physical Plant. At the most basic level, teachers need a safe, clean building that facilitates teaching. For instance, I have worked with teachers of very disturbed children in buildings where the intercom system was either nonexistent or did not work most of the time. They had to leave the class or send another pupil to get help from another teacher or adult when one of their students became highly aggressive. A sample item would be, "The hallways are kept clean." If 90 percent of the teachers strongly disagreed with this item, there is obviously a problem.

Physical Resources. Teachers know that there are limits on materials, but they are concerned about the adequacy of libraries and the availability of basic items like texts, pencils, chalk, and paper. A sample item might be, "There are adequate supplies of paper at the end of the year."

Personnel Resources. Teachers are concerned about the availability of nonteaching personnel to help in monitoring halls, playgrounds, lunchrooms, and security. A sample item is, "We need more lunchroom aides."

Financial Resources. Among important issues is the problem of teachers' salaries and distribution of monies. A sample item is, "Teacher compensation for coaching is adequate."

Communication. A major issue in all of the schools I have helped is communication—communication with and between administrators and between teachers and with parents. A major issue has frequently been that communication is almost always downward; that is, the administrators make all important decisions and communicate them down. A sample item is, "The principal implements suggestions made by teachers."

Discipline. Teachers always include discipline issues in the climate measures I have helped develop. Concerns usually focus on consistency of enforcement, administrative support, and adequate punishments other than suspension. Teachers in schools for children with emotional or learning problems are usually less concerned with punishment and more concerned with trying to provide for more adequate incentives or rewards to motivate the students to behave better. A sample item is, "Discipline is administered consistently by the principal."

Professional Support Services. Professional support services include psychologists, counselors, nurses, speech therapists, art teachers, and music teachers. Their availability and the nature of their service delivery is very important to teachers. A sample item is, "The school psychologist should spend more time directly helping teachers rather than just testing the children."

Morale. When teachers construct climate scales, they are always interested in measuring the morale of their peers. In inner-city schools, burnout is a big issue. This is most frequently related to feelings of helplessness and anger at administrators. In low socioeconomic status areas, the teachers often construct scales to give to parents to try to determine why the parents are not more involved in their children's schoolwork. Under the general category of morale, climate measures usually attempt to measure the type and extent of stress that typical teachers experience. A sample item might be, "I feel that I get no support from the school administration."

Using the Results. It usually takes about a year to introduce staff to the idea of climate assessment, to set up a steering committee, to develop the questionnaire, to administer it, and to get the results. Where I have consulted, we have always developed a brief written summary of the results, which is attached to the actual questionnaire. On the questionnaire, we give the percentage of responses to each item. This is presented to the staff, and a meeting is held to discuss the results.

Following the discussion of the results, the second year begins with the establishment of committees to begin problem solving on the major issues identified by the questionnaire. Once problems are identified, cooperative efforts by staff, students, administrators, and parents are needed to solve problems. I have found that any administrator who has been committed to the process of assessment and problem identification is motivated to follow through.

The NEA 1972 Task Force

In addition to the approaches I have discussed, in 1972 the National Education Association voted to take a stand against corporal punishment and offered a list of alternatives. Staff at the NCSCPAS have added to the list, which appears in appendix D.

7

Taking a Stand:

What to Do If Your Child Is Maltreated in School

So far this book has been about the nature and extent of abuses in the schools. Now we look at what to do about it. Before reading this chapter, however, ask your child (or someone else) if he or she was ever physically or psychologically abused in school. The School Trauma Survey can serve as a guide to the kinds of things you mean by abuse. You might not even want to use the word *abuse*; rather you could ask about the student's worst school experience or, better, ask the student to fill out the survey. Pay close attention to the nature and extent of symptoms. If the student you ask has not been personally victimized, ask if he or she has observed other students receiving abuse.

In general, there is a better than 50 percent chance that you will uncover some type of unnecessary maltreatment of students in your school. But discovering it is a lot different from doing something about it. The nature and extent of the maltreatment, who it happened to, whether it is continuing with your child or others, and your clout in the community will all determine what you will be able to accomplish if you want to stop the abuse of school children in your school. A mother in Georgia, whose twelve-year-old son was severely paddled, summed it up: "We always paid our taxes, respected authority, went to church, and thought the people in power would protect us. It just ain't so. When you are a little person, they try to tell you you ain't got no rights. But I'm not giving in, no matter what they do." She hired a lawyer from many miles away.

Psychological Maltreatment

Dealing with psychological abuse is more difficult than struggling against some of the worst cases of physical abuse because of the low level of public consciousness about it. Moreover, psychological maltreatment is more difficult to define than its physical counterpart. For instance, experts consider any type of name calling derogatory and therefore abusive, but children may react differently to the same denigrating terms. Since some students "go along" with this type of abuse, a teacher may rationalize that it is all right.

A good example of the problem occurred while I was presenting a workshop on psychological abuse to special education teachers. One teacher was offended when the other participants in listing abusive statements often made by teachers included nicknames suggesting obesity. The teacher argued with the other 150 participants in defense of her calling one of her students "chubs." She insisted that the particular obese, teenaged retarded student knew that the nickname was an expression of love. Finally, one of the other teachers told the group about her experience as an obese teenager. Her teachers had called her names, and in response she had joked back. But she said, "I was laughing outwardly, but I felt humiliated and shamed by those teachers. I will never forget what they did to me." We can never judge how each child accepts denigration and humiliation, especially in school where the teacher is the boss. Rather than trying to guess how a child can handle name calling, a teacher should never do it.

Gathering the proof of the cause and effects of psychological abuse may be more difficult than documenting physical maltreatment, but there are some interesting contrasts to note in preparing to confront abuse. Corporal punishment is based on tradition and is publicly defended by educators. Most educators who view pictures of the physical effects of severely paddled children are outraged and offended when it is suggested that this is an inevitable result of the practice. But with the exception of some few who think that fear of ridicule and actual verbal abuse are motivating, few educators will openly defend psychological assault of students. Most school board policy manuals and teacher guides stress the importance of building self-esteem and promoting the dignity of each child. Yet research suggests that practices such as name calling, put-downs, and scapegoating are much more pervasive than corporal punishment, and they do not appear to be confined to specific regions of the country.

Discovering the Abuse

The first indication that a child has been bruised, battered, denigrated, humiliated, or in any other way traumatized may not come from direct evidence. Rather, parents may sense that something is wrong because the child's behavior has changed. In one case a first grader with a generally cheerful disposition began to cry easily and complain about going to school, and she seemed depressed. The parents assumed she was avoiding the more difficult schoolwork and tended to ignore her. It was not until several months later that the parents discovered that the child was terrified of an unusually stern, punitive, and demanding teacher. The child had been severely scolded several times for mild misbehaviors such as whispering to a classmate. On one occasion she had not heard or understood the teacher's instructions for an assignment and was afraid to ask the teacher, and she had heard other children being paddled. This child was usually well behaved and compliant and was either ashamed or afraid to tell her parents that she felt terrified of her teacher, whom her parents had praised. Children's fear of reporting maltreatment by teachers is quite common, especially if parents threaten their children that they will be punished at home if they misbehave in school.

Young children who have been maltreated in school usually withdraw and cry frequently. Older children are more likely to react with anger and plan escape or revenge. In many cases of severe corporal punishment, the parents did not know anything happened until they bathed the child or saw the bruises when the child was changing clothes. A major noticeable symptom is that the children are visibly pained by sitting, and they may directly complain to the parents. Besides bruises, paddling can cause secondary damage. A child in Texas suffered a strangulated hernia and one in Michigan suffered partial deafness as a result of abusive paddlings by educators.

Overly severe discipline may not consist of just paddlings. Excessive physical drills, punches, kicks, shoves, slaps, and forced ingestion of noxious substances can all be abusive, though bruises may not occur. Specific types of abuse are associated with certain types of injuries. Excessive drills have resulted in deaths, ropes have caused rope burns, excessive time-outs in closed spaces have triggered phobias and seizures, and grabbing children by the hair has resulted in hair loss.

Taking Action

A parent who believes her or his child has been maltreated (or has witnessed another child being maltreated) needs to act quickly, rationally, and with clear goals. Six steps constitute the first action:

1. Identify the injury or maltreatment.
2. Document the injury or maltreatment.
3. Document the events surrounding the injury or maltreatment.
4. Determine culpability.
5. Decide on goals—for example, to obtain an apology from the offender and ensure that the abuse will not reoccur, file an assault complaint with the police and/or obtain a warrant for the teacher's arrest, file child abuse charges, or obtain an attorney and litigate.
6. Plan the strategy and take action.

IDENTIFY THE INJURY

It is difficult to generalize accurately about how to identify injuries. Younger children, for example, might not complain. They may still hold the teacher in awe. They tend to view misbehavior and punishment in concrete terms—as either black or white. They do not yet fully comprehend the limits of the teacher or principal's power to punish. They are easily intimidated. They believe that if they are bad, they deserve to be punished by the teacher. And they do not yet understand concepts such as due process, mitigating circumstances, and justice as opposed to legality.

In numerous cases of severely paddled primary school children, parents told me that they discovered the abuse when the children were bathing or changing clothes. In some cases, the children had gone several days without complaining.

Teachers with a reputation for being tough disciplinarians may use excessive amounts of verbal abuse. The best way to judge is whether students feel the teacher is fair. Good disciplinarians may be strict but do not enforce rules with sarcasm, ridicule, bias, and favoritism. Good discipline is not the same as punitiveness.

If a child's teacher seems overly punitive, the parent should keep track of what goes on in the classroom. The child may be more likely to tell what the teacher does to classmates than to himself or herself. This will provide a good barometer if the child's behavior starts to change.

Teachers who are inconsistent and appear unpredictable to a child may be going through emotional stress related to their personal lives. They may be kind and generous one day and sarcastic and demeaning the next day. The cause can range from financial to marital difficulties. Teachers with these problems need compassion and help, but their problems should not be allowed to serve as an excuse for abusing students, which is too often the case.

Frequently administrators and fellow teachers know about their colleagues' stress. This was the case with Mrs. Jones who was described in the previous chapter, but no one had connected her personal problems with her growing classroom difficulties since she had always been a good teacher. Even without consultation from the school psychologist, teachers who are abusive to students as a result of life stresses or personal problems can be helped. These include transferring difficult children from their classes, offering aides and additional classroom help, encouraging them to obtain psychotherapy, and helping them to find other outside resources. Unfortunately, the system often takes no action and lets the abuse continue.

velop an ongoing dialogue with your child about the daily events in the classroom. A parent who can establish a relationship in which his or her child feels free to talk about school will easily identify abusing teachers and traumatic events.

DOCUMENT THE INJURY

Just because *you* see teacher-inflicted bruises does not mean that anyone else will believe you. Just because your child develops stress symptoms from being publicly ridiculed and humiliated by his or her teacher does not mean that anyone else will take it seriously. Parents must obtain an official record of the abuse from people with recognized status and stature in the community.

In the case of physical abuse, you must immediately obtain clear color pictures of the injury the day it occurs. If you have a camera, take the pictures with a witness present. If you are not an experienced photographer, seek help from a friend. It is extremely important that these first pictures be clear since they may be used in court.

Besides using a regular camera, take some instant photographs as backup. If you depend on the instant pictures make sure to use high-quality film because poor film may not clearly show the redness of the bruises. If they do not clearly show the bruises, throw them away because they could be used against you in court. In the case of Jeremy Ward in Oklahoma, the parents relied on instant pictures that did not accurately depict the bruises left by a leather paddle shaped like the sole of a large cowboy boot. As a result, the physician's written description did not match what was portrayed in the pictures, which washed out the reds.

Once the bruises start to heal, it will be too late to document the original damage, although the blacks, blues, and browns of the healing areas should be documented during the two to three weeks they are present.

The next step is to go to an official to document the bruises— either a trusted family physician or a hospital. Because you may be filing child abuse charges, ask for a physician with experience in identifying child abuse. (Pediatricians are almost always trained to recognize abuse. Moreover, their professional association, the American Academy of Pediatrics, was one of the early national organizations to pass a resolution against corporal punishment in the schools.)

If the doctor takes instant pictures, ask for several copies immediately for your own records. If the bruises are not clearly shown, destroy the pictures or obtain a written statement from the physician about the disparity. If you have not already taken your own pictures, take them at the hospital or call a friend to meet you there to take the pictures. One of the most dramatic pictures I have seen was used in a case in Wyoming.

> A twelve year old in Wyoming did not do well in a math test. His teacher had told the class that if they all did well, he would give them some free time. In order to earn the free time, his teacher agreed that he and two other students who did not do well would be paddled by the whole class. The bruises were horrible. His parents were so furious that they hired a professional photographer. The eight-by-eleven-inch prints of the boy's multiply bruised buttocks provided such clear documentation that they helped immeasurably in litigation against the school. I determined that he had developed EIPTSD. After the deposition by the lawyer representing the school's insurance company, his family was offered a financial settlement by the school's insurance company in order to end the litigation.

Try to obtain a copy of the physician's diagnosis as soon as possible. This is usually what medical people call the parent's chart. You may have trouble getting this official chart, but you can ask the examining physician to write the diagnosis for you. Be persistent about obtaining a written record before leaving the office. I have become cautious about records because in a few cases pictures disappeared and physicians denied that they had told the parents that child abuse had occurred. If you litigate, the absence of this type of evidence can be devastating to your case.

You may want to take your child to your own physician. Make sure this is a person you know and trust. In many cases, local physicians have professional and personal ties to the schools and are reluctant to engage in anything as political as testifying as an expert witness against the community school board. Be sure that the physician knows that you may litigate the case. If he or she is not clear about helping you or expresses doubts about testifying, go to someone else immediately. Do not be timid in exploring with the physician his or her willingness to help you.

Most states protect educators from child abuse charges resulting from their attempts to discipline children. This protection occurs because the mandatory reporting laws and the processes for investigation do not encompass public schools. Parents can charge educators with assault and battery, but they may have difficulty obtaining cooperation from prosecutors. Prosecutors are guided by a generally conservative judicial tradition that suggests that the courts should avoid becoming embroiled in school disciplinary problems. This is not always the case; individual prosecutors have been outraged by abuses and have charged teachers with assault and battery. In most cases, however, parents have had to obtain legal help in order to make civil charges against the abuser. (This does not include the states where corporal punishment in schools is illegal.)

It is usually easy to document cases of psychological maltreatment. Unlike paddling, which usually occurs behind closed doors, teacher's sarcasm, ridicule, and name calling most often happen in front of the class. But although this type of maltreatment occurs far more often than physical abuse, it is less likely to be taken seriously by prosecutors. This is true even though psychological abuse and neglect are included in most state child abuse statutes and are becoming more recognized by professionals.

In the case of psychological traumatization by the teacher, the onset of symptoms is usually not as dramatic as in the case of physical abuse. Also, the symptoms may develop after a series of events rather than from a single episode. Your best initial step is to fill out the School Trauma Survey in appendix C. With this information available, you can help your child psychologist or psychiatrist to make the diagnosis. If possible, find one with experience with schools but with no political or financial connections to your school.

A local child psychologist, psychiatrist, or school psychologist who receives referrals from the local school district might be deterred from adequately helping you and your child for fear of losing referrals. Establish if there are any such connections.

DOCUMENT THE EVENT

It is extremely important to obtain facts about the incident. In many cases educators will deny that the events took place as described by the child. Once they hear the child's version, they may try to obtain support from other educators or students that the victim's story was false.

I have seen cases in which administrators have intimidated teachers, students, and other school employees into changing their stories. Once the school's economic and political juggernaught begins to roll, you will definitely recognize the intimidation attempts.

When you discover the abuse, immediately record your child's account of the event. Obtain the following information and try to make the account as detailed as possible: (1) date of the event, (2) time, (3) physical setting, (4) what the teacher and class were doing before the abuse, (5) what your child did or said that resulted in the abusive response, (6) whether classmates or other witnesses did anything, (7) what your child felt when the event happened, (8) what your child did while it was happening, (9) exactly what the abuser did, (10) what the abuser did afterward, (11) how your child felt afterward, and (12) what your child did afterward.

If your child has been abused publicly, find out which other children witnessed the event or heard the sounds from another room. Seeking help from your child's classmates may place you in a precarious position because you and other parents may be afraid that if you do anything to upset the teacher, the teacher will take it out on your child or the children of the other parents. Although parents have been able to gain the support of parents of other children who witnessed the event, getting other parents to cooperate is not always easy.

Ideally you should meet with these parents and their children and get written statements of what happened. These statements should be notarized if possible. I have found that in several cases, the children who witnessed the incident later changed their stories because of covert threats by the school. It is much more difficult to get witnesses to change stories after they have provided notarized accounts of the events.

Be sure you have a clear account of what happened before you take your child to the doctor. Younger children may be scared and confused, especially if they are taken to a hospital emergency room. When questioning your child, do not ask leading questions such as, "That teacher really hurt you, didn't she?" Instead ask, "How did it feel after the teacher hit you?" "What exactly did the teacher say that made you feel so bad?" Obtain a clear understanding of what happened, how the child felt, and who else saw it happen.

DETERMINE CULPABILITY

When severe punitiveness occurs, you need to be familiar with the disciplinary procedures of the school. Most schools have written guidelines for the administration of discipline, and they may state that corporal punishment is a last resort. Therefore, it is important to understand whether the teacher, in paddling your child or verbally assaulting him or her, followed the guidelines required by the school district. In almost every case in which I have been involved, the teachers did not follow the prescribed guidelines. Even when the guidelines have not listed specific hierarchies of steps to be taken before corporal punishment is used, it is often clear that teachers tried little else before paddling.

Although verbal maltreatment is relatively common, I have seen few guidelines spelling out what teachers should not do in this area. Some guidelines indicate that teachers should show respect for children if they want respect in return. I know of none that allows or even encourages teachers to call children names. Further, few educators will publicly admit to or encourage verbal abuse of school children; rather they generally agree that it is wrong to put children down.

In cases where teachers have done something that clearly and grossly violates the school's norms for discipline, you may be able to get support from other families and school authorities. In Florida, one of the most punitive states in the country, a teacher chained several students to his motorcycle and dragged them across a playground. He was suspended and eventually fired.

Here is what an eleven-year-old Ohio student told me about his experience in a fourth-grade art class: "We had to do a project with rope. The project was to make a bag out of a pants leg and use the rope for a drawstring. My teacher started to tease me and put the white clothesline I had around my neck. I felt silly and everyone was laughing. . . . It started to hurt as he tightened it. . . . It was burning and I was trying to take it off. . . . I wanted to cry but I didn't. Then during lunch I wanted to see the principal but the lunchroom teacher wouldn't let me go. . . . When I went to class my teacher kidded me about the red thing around my neck. . . . He let me go to the nurse and she put some cream on my neck." The teacher claimed he was only kidding around, and at the suggestion of the principal he apologized. The school superintendent stonewalled when the parents complained and invited them to sue if they wanted to. He said they lacked enough evidence of harm. Several board of education members agreed with the parents that the teacher used poor judgment. Since the teacher was not tenured, they did not renew his contract the following year.

If the method of discipline is other than paddling, punching, or shoving and borders on the bizarre, there is a reasonable chance that the school authorities will support your case. You at least have a much better chance of receiving action than if the abuse occurred as a result of "normal" paddling, slapping, or punching.

WHAT IS YOUR GOAL?

Your Child's Mental Health. Anyone who has been traumatized knows that the greatest fear is vulnerability to repeated traumatization. The event and the physical responses of fear, humiliation, and/or anger are paired. In any stress disorder, the person develops uncontrolled physiological reactions to the situation that produced the fear. The more traumatic the event was, the stronger is the physiological and psychological reaction to being placed in the situation again.

In school abuse cases, depending on the severity of symptoms and the teacher's or administrator's refusal to apologize, it may be necessary to remove the child from the class or school. An apology can go a long way in reestablishing trust just as a refusal can cause EIPTSD.

I have conducted psychotherapy with many adults who were psychologically, physically, and/or sexually abused by caregivers as children. In many cases the abuser was a parent, relative, or trusted family friend. Invariably the victims said that much of their pain would have been relieved if the abuser had recognized what he or she had done and apologized. When victims come for help, they still harbor the hope that the caregiver will eventually admit the mistake. Rarely does this happen. Therefore the goal of therapy is to help the victim adjust to reality.

I believe that the first goal should be to obtain an apology and assurances that the abuse will not reoccur. This means contacting the teacher directly and immediately setting up an appointment for the next day. Avoid appointments that start right before school unless the teacher assures you that he or she can provide class coverage. Otherwise you will get into the issue and the teacher will have to leave for class, feeling that you had your opportunity to present your case.

If the teacher feels defensive or threatened, he or she may ask the principal or even a union representative to be present. You are better off avoiding this at the first stage by not attacking the teacher on the telephone before the meeting. You might state that you want to clarify what happened between the teacher and your child. That alone may make the teacher defensive. Let the school be the first to become belligerent. Do not provide the ammunition to portray you as an angry, unreasonable parent who is out to get the teacher or the school.

Although it is obvious that you will be outraged that your child has been treated unfairly by an educator, before you go to school, consider carefully what you must do. In several cases, parents have confronted the abusing teacher or their principal physically. Some of these parents have been prosecuted for assault by the school and the case against the school was lost at the beginning.

If your goal is to relieve your child's symptoms, approach the school on that basis. You want cooperation. You want the perpetrator to apologize, and you want the child to be assured by the school authorities that it will not happen again. This is an ideal first step and an important goal to achieve. Unfortunately, it may not happen.

There are no data to determine how many cases of abuse are resolved in the first stages by apologies and assurances. In most of the cases we have studied, that did not happen. Therefore, we generally know about a case only when parents take it past the teacher and principal and it has usually received some media attention. By this time, the victimizers have developed their defenses.

Part of being a victimizer is developing rationalizations for one's acts. Child sexual abusers often claim that they loved the victim or that the sexual act did no harm to the child. Physical abuse is often justified by the claim that the child needed the discipline, the battered wife pushed the husband too far, or the victim deserved to get raped because she dressed provocatively. These irrational arguments are cover-ups for people with a proclivity toward violence. Collectively these arguments are based on blaming the victim, a subject of much study by social psychologists.

Unfortunately, too many people selectively accept the rationalizations for specific acts of violence against particular victim groups. They fail to realize that violence in a democratic milieu (unless in self-defense) should never be an acceptable solution to any problem.

Educators are not immune from blaming victims as a defense of abuse of children. But an even more common defense I have observed is to trivialize the incident or the effects of the abuse. When this happens, it is difficult to provide your child with immediate relief from stress. But you must try if your child's mental health is a major goal.

Even if the school authorities sympathize with your child, they may feel that admission of abuse will make them liable in litigation. Therefore, they are likely to stonewall until they obtain a clear understanding of the legal implications of admission of guilt. If this happens, you must decide whether you are committed to carrying forward or if you are willing to agree not to litigate in return for an apology. Make sure that any promises the school makes are in writing. In any case, do not let them delay your own plans if they are not willing to remediate the problem immediately.

Time and money are usually on the side of the school. They often wear parents down with bureaucratic procedures and delays. They know that the more they delay and communicate with your attorney (if you get one), the more it costs you. They also know that if you have taken your child out of school, you do not want to interrupt his or her education too long. If they wish to make things really difficult, they may try to force your child back to school through truancy laws. You may counter by placing your child in a private school, applying to pay tuition in a neighboring public school, or setting up home schooling. (In the last situation, check with your state department of education for guidelines.)

Filing Assault Charges. Anyone can file assault charges against anyone else. Whether the police or prosecutors will do anything about it is another story. Obviously this is not an option if your child has been psychologically abused; however, if the child has been physically abused, you do have the option of going to the police station and filing charges.

In many cases in rural areas and small towns, parents have reported that the police have discouraged them or refused to allow them to file charges. It is important to show them the evidence of the bruises. In the case of *Garcia v. Miera* in New Mexico, the investigating officer was so outraged when he observed the bruises on Teresa Garcia's legs and buttocks that he took the paddle away from the offending educator.

In Talladega, Alabama, law enforcement officers not only accepted charges but the district attorney vowed to prosecute a teacher for brutally paddling seven-year-old Jason Morris. The case was quickly brought to trial, and Judge John Coleman found the teacher guilty of third-degree assault and fined her $250 and court costs.

Filing Child Abuse Charges. Every state has a child abuse agency. It is usually in a department with a title such as Human Services, Youth and Family Services, or Child Welfare. Most states have child abuse hot lines that are listed in the telephone directory or may be reached easily through information. Despite the limitations of child-abuse statutes concerning schools, you should insist that the doctor who sees your child or the psychologist who examines him or her file abuse charges with the appropriate state authorities. This may help your case if you go to trial.

If you call to report abuse, you will be assigned a case worker who will investigate. Workers will respond most rapidly if they believe a child is in imminent, life-threatening peril. Most school abuse cases do not fit that profile and will probably receive low priority.

Typically child abuse caseworkers are usually overworked and not often well trained, and they have a high burnout rate. Further, since few states will investigate cases in schools or the workers may be unclear about what to do, they will probably seek help from a supervisor. The agency may be operated at the local or county rather than state level. If this is the case, the political implications of one agency (child abuse) investigating another agency (the school board) may deter the more timid or politically minded agency supervisors or directors. This is especially true in less populated areas where all the governmental agency personnel know each other.

If the agency is organized at the state level, political implications may still operate. But whichever agency you deal with, if the state laws protect teachers, you probably will not get too much help. However, I think it is important that all school abuse cases be reported by physicians and parents. Physicians have specific guidelines for diagnosing and reporting. Parents in most states can call child abuse hot lines to set the wheels in motion. Eventually the record of these cases will make an impact on lawmakers if parents and physicians keep reporting and following up to determine what happened.

Child abuse authorities have difficulty in dealing with school abuse in regard to reporting procedures. In every state it is mandatory that suspected child abuse be reported. That is, if you suspect child abuse and do not report it, you are liable for prosecution. In order to encourage reporting, there are strict rules protecting the confidentiality of the person reporting the suspected abuse.

Mandatory reporting laws were developed to deal primarily with abuse in the home. Neighbors, friends, and relatives would be reluctant to report suspected abuse if they feared retribution. Yet in the case of school abuse, the parents or physician are almost always the persons reporting. This is soon known to the alleged abuser and to the school community. Therefore, the potential investigation of the case presents additional problems of confidentiality for the workers and the reporters.

All states have elaborate laws to protect teachers from arbitrary suspension or firing. These are related to the tenure process and require that any punitive action against a teacher follow a series of due process procedures. While these personnel procedures are usually carried out behind closed doors, teachers are allowed rights such as being faced by their accusers, presentation of written charges, the right to counsel, and so forth. In any significant action against a teacher, the media eventually become involved as teachers, teachers' unions, administrators, school board members, parents, and sometimes students get drawn into the fray of charges and countercharges. This is not an arena familiar to most child abuse workers and certainly one that taxes their ability to function within their own guidelines of confidentiality.

INSTITUTING LITIGATION

There are three major issues important in determining who represents you and how successful your litigation may be: money, politics, and publicity.

Money. You may be morally outraged at the injustice and inequity in power between you and the school when you receive short shrift from the school authorities after your child has been abused. Although some lawyers may feel the same and be willing to offer immediate help, most will first weigh the probable cost against the possibility of successful litigation. There are two ways in which they can consider their fees. If the lawyer takes the case strictly on a fee per hour basis, he or she will make money whether or not you win the case. A lot of hours can be generated in dealing with the school board and their attorneys, who are usually on retainer. For the school, the initial financial drain from your case is negligible. The school will be much more concerned with the bad publicity than the initial costs of the case and will therefore attempt to keep the early maneuvering between lawyers out of the public spotlight. Meanwhile, the meter in your lawyer's office keeps ticking away.

If you do hire an attorney on an hourly basis, it is crucial that you make sure that he or she has no social, political, or religious ties to the educational establishment. (I know that lawyers are ethically bound not to take cases if they have a conflict of interest or dual relationships. Unfortunately, I know of too many abuse cases where attorneys were not straightforward with the distressed parents about past and present relationships with school authorities. The parents eventually either gave up, thinking they had gotten good legal advice, or ended up poorer but wiser after firing the attorney.) Additionally, try to find one with some experience in dealing with schools and with a record in disability (tort) litigation. Perhaps even more important is a background in advocacy law. Attorneys who have worked as public defenders, in poverty law centers, and in consumer rights movements are knowledgeable about fighting for the rights of individuals against government agencies or corporations.

But unless you have a strong case, a lawyer whom you know and trust, and/or adequate financial resources, I suggest trying to avoid hiring an attorney on a per hour basis. You may be better off finding a lawyer with experience in malpractice, liability, and/or workman's compensation who will take the case on a contingency basis. This means that the lawyer will defer payment for time with the anticipation of winning the case and receiving a percentage of the award or settlement as the fee. Depending on your financial status and the attorney's confidence in winning the case, you can negotiate how much of the secondary expenses you will pay up front. These include fixed costs such as secretarial services, and postage.

There is a major advantage and disadvantage in this type of relationship. In order to accept the case on a contingency basis, the attorney needs to be convinced that there is a good chance of either settling out of court (usually preferable) or winning. Therefore, if an experienced lawyer accepts your case on a contingency basis, you have a good chance of some settlement. You can be sure that the lawyer, who has invested his or her own time and money, will work hard on your behalf. The problem with the contingency approach is that the financial settlements in school abuse cases tend not to be very high compared to other types of awards in damage cases. Cases I am familiar with have ranged from settlements of a low of $13,000 in the rural South to a high of $80,000 in the Southwest.

Because of state laws and professional ethics, attorneys' fees usually top out between 30 percent and 40 percent of the settlement. This usually occurs after fixed expenses such as typing, travel, and fees for expert testimony are deducted. Because of the limited fees, very successful and experienced lawyers may not wish to take the case. Most of the lawyers with whom I have worked have tended to be young or at the mid-career level. Most have done excellent jobs. Another alternative is to obtain help through the American Civil Liberties Union, a poverty law center, or other advocacy group with legal resources to help children.

Politics. Regional differences and local politics have a profound effect on shaping the initial stages of a school abuse case.

I want to again warn of the dangers of attorneys who have any social, political, or even religious affiliation with the school. Once I was involved in a case in Florida where the initial attorney spent over a year making no progress in a case against a school. It turned out that he was a deacon in the church that sponsored the school. Most of his efforts seemed to have been aimed at keeping the case from the media and discouraging the parents from going to court.

Your potential attorney may have political aspirations in the community or county. If you are in a rural and/or conservative area, your attorney's political aspirations will not be helped by appearing to be so liberal as to defy traditional beliefs about discipline. Yet by taking the case and getting you to be "reasonable" with the school authorities, he can be viewed as an ally of the local political establishment and still collect his fee from you. Be very careful of that pattern, especially if the attorney keeps you out of the process so that you do not know what is happening.

Of course, politics could work to your advantage if the potential attorney feels that his or her career or political future will be helped by winning against a school board. The attorney may be very interested in child abuse and want to be identified as a politician who visibly works to correct abuse of children.

Whether politics refers to your attorney's desires to make good connections and further his or her career or actually maneuver in the real world of politics, try to determine what will help you most. This is perhaps a cynical view of the workings of our legal system, but it is a view tempered by reality.

Publicity. Schools are essentially political entities that above all else fear bad public relations. Most administrators struggle to maintain the status quo and avoid the media, except as a source of information to the public for announcing school functions. But even bad publicity in the long run does little harm to tenured educators. Superintendents and school board members are more vulnerable, however.

The media love nothing more than the classic American struggle between the little guy and city hall. Add a touch of child abuse and you have the ingredients that increase newspaper circulation and television viewing time. This is the worst nightmare of educators. This fear of confrontation, litigation, and public ridicule can be one of your best allies in moving a case toward settlement.

Some lawyers thrive on the publicity because it provides free advertising. In at least three cases, parents who had contacted me from various parts of the country had lawyers who were very tentative about taking the cases. I spoke with the three lawyers about media coverage and my opportunities to present their cases at the national level. I assured them of helping to get positive local and regional coverage. Immediately afterward they agreed to take the cases and intelligently used the media.

A negative factor in responding to the media is that the experience can be very painful for your child and family. Your child may be asked repeatedly to recount the traumatic events. Friends or sympathizers of the offending teacher or school may react to you in a hostile way. When popular coaches are the abusers, complaining parents may even receive threatening telephone calls.

It is clear that the media can be valuable in forcing the schools to settle cases quickly. But even if the school officials desire to settle, their hands may be tied by their own internal political pressures and the procedures required to take action against abusing teachers.

Understanding Educators' Rights and Due Process

In order to deal with the school, it is important to understand the thinking of the teachers, administrators, and school boards. They are confronted by a parent who is very upset, and they know that a lawsuit may be imminent. The first thing to understand is that in most states, a teacher cannot be summarily dismissed, suspended, or penalized without proper procedures being followed. Therefore, if you go into the school demanding that the teacher be immediately punished, you are seeking an impossible solution.

The most immediate action an administrator can take, even if he or she believes that the teacher has abused your child and wants to take strong action, is to suspend the teacher, usually with pay. This means that a substitute teacher will have to be hired and that the school board attorney will have to begin dealing with both the teacher's attorney and often the attorney from the teachers' union.

In general, all local teachers' unions, administrators, and teachers will deny that abuse is even a possibility in their schools. They will reassure you that if abuse were occurring, they would take immediate action. However, the truth is that it is very difficult to discipline a teacher who has maltreated a child. Further, in a number of cases I have dealt with, the coach, who is often quite popular in rural communities, is the abuser. He is nearly immune to criticism for anything but losing games.

The reality is that it is administratively easier to support an abusing teacher than it is to fire one. Therefore, rather than be defensive, the school authorities typically go on the offensive. If you sue, expect any of several reactions.

INTIMIDATION

Parents know that teachers have tremendous power to "get back" at children. When I was an idealistic, beginning teacher in a small rural school, I was shocked that one teacher scapegoated every child from a family he disliked. He even instigated his students to abuse one of the children of this family who was not in his class. Several of his students were ridiculing the child in the lunchroom when three of my students told them to stop. Name calling and threats emerged from both sides. The abusive teacher sent my students to the principal. When I found out what had happened, I was furious but relatively powerless to stop the abuse, despite my complaints to the principal. That teacher carried on a vendetta against the children of that family for years.

You must recognize a teacher's potential for getting back at your child or a sibling. A common technique is for educators to make snide remarks to the victim or siblings, alluding to the parents' willingness to sue about anything. Unfair disciplinary procedures may be used. Other students may be encouraged to scapegoat, ridicule, or isolate the victim.

Your best defense is to document everything that happens and let the educators know that you are keeping records. It is a good idea to demand that your child be immediately removed from the offending teacher's class. Schedule meetings with your lawyer and the offending educators. An especially effective countermaneuver is to become an expert on school policy and discipline rules. When they are not being followed, document the breach, and send copies to the offending educators. If you fight back vigorously, you can usually completely stop, or significantly reduce, scapegoating of your family.

BLAMING THE VICTIM

Invariably defendant school boards try to show that the victim deserved the punishment. They may explain the symptoms as resulting from abuse at home. They will try to find anything in the family that shows that the parents caused the child's emotional problems. They will dredge up divorce, parental squabbles, and previous spankings by the parents.

THE CHILD ALREADY HAD THE PROBLEMS

It is true that in some cases the victim already had problems. Many of the children I have evaluated had histories of learning disabilities or emotional difficulties previous to the school abuse. Some had been physically or sexually abused. But there is no one pattern of problems of victims except that the abuse precipitated PTSD. Other children had no previous problems.

The analogy lawyers often use is based on the eggshell theory. If a driver hits a person who receives serious long-term head injuries because his or her skull was abnormally thin (like an eggshell), the driver is not free from liability because of the abnormally thin skull of the victim. If a schoolchild already has emotional problems from abuse at home, that is all the more reason not to abuse him or her in school.

WEARING YOU DOWN

Predictably the school tries to wear you down. It has the time and resources to keep going longer than you do. School officials know that parents fear for their child and that they will become impatient with due process procedures and multiple levels of administrative meetings.

A lawyer working on a contingency basis can counterattack by calling for many depositions of school personnel. He or she can tie up busy administrators with paperwork and can bring in expert witnesses, which will cost money for the board to depose.

Time can also help you to publicize the case and to build up a coalition of allies: the media, experts, and professional groups.

OTHER ACCUSATIONS

Since schools are so much a part of the political fabric of communities, it is likely that a defendant school will attempt to generate sympathy for itself. One way is to point out that you are in essence suing the community; therefore it is citizens' tax money that is paying for the defense. The school may allege that you are suing just for the money and really do not care that continuing the case is causing pain to the child and costing the community.

Although most school boards have attorneys on retainer, the time they spend on abuse cases is not free. Often the teachers' union will also retain a lawyer to defend the abuser. In addition, the abuser, staff witnesses, student witnesses, and others are deposed by the school board attorney. Expert witnesses charge for their time preparing for the testifying in depositions. The expenses can mount up rapidly. When teaching staff are required to be present during legal proceedings, substitute teachers must be paid to cover their classes. Most of this eventually comes out of the taxpayers' pockets, if only in higher fees for school liability insurance.

Defendant schools frequently allege that the victim's parents have a grudge against the teacher or that they are out to "get" the school for some perceived past injustice. They will think of some way to show that the parents' primary motive is revenge.

In the case of a twelve-year-old boy in Wyoming, the elders of the Mormon church implied that the parents should drop the suit because all parties were Mormons and it would be an embarrassment to the church, according to his mother. In reply, the parents dropped out of the church and eventually won a settlement that enabled them to move out of the area. This case was handled by an excellent attorney in Jackson, Wyoming, David Claus, who has gone on to help other school abuse victims in Wyoming and Montana.

8

How to Debate the Issues

I N the summer of 1988 I met with Shelly Gaspersohn's mother, Marlene, at the Second Conference of the National Coalition to Abolish Corporal Punishment in the Schools. It was a long time since our first contact in 1983 when it seemed as if victims of school abuse were abused further by the schools, the courts, and their communities when they sought justice. When we went to court in Harnett County, North Carolina, it appeared to us that we were lonely figures, fighting an almost useless battle, but we realized that the battle had to be fought. Losing the battle in the courts regenerated the Gaspersohns' desire to fight in every arena possible.

After the trial, Shelly wanted to get on with her life; like many other victims, she wanted to forget about the events but couldn't, and probably never will. She gave up all interest in becoming a music teacher and switched to electronic engineering. She felt betrayed by the system of justice, which allowed her abuser to continue abusing other students. She made a few television appearances but devoted her energy to obtaining an education. Her parents carried on the battle. They and others are helping Americans to understand why physical and psychological abuse can no longer be tolerated in schools.

My high school geometry teacher frequently responded to students who confused the appearance of shapes with the mathematical realities that described them by saying, "Things aren't what they seem to be; they are what they are." This phrase often comes to my mind as I deal with apathy and/or approval of teacher use of sarcasm, ridicule, verbal assault, or corporal punishment.

Many fine educators remain open to parents' suggestions and concerns about the children with whom they are entrusted. They are open to change and invite constructive criticism from parents and other professionals. They want the appearance and reality of their schools to be consonant. Other educators base their functioning on political concerns. For them, appearances count most. They do not want parents meddling in their domain. These are the ones we must understand and defeat if appeal to reason, logic, and research evidence comes to naught. They can be defeated by strategies that include the examination of facts in a public forum, but when facts compete with personal beliefs, facts alone cannot bring about change. The different outlooks of school psychologists and educators illustrate some of the problems.

Psychologists and Educators: Different Outlooks

Psychology as a science and school psychologists as advocates for change in the schools have had an uneasy existence in the house of education. School psychologists have the potential obligation to bring to bear the knowledge and techniques of social science to the problems of contemporary schooling. This is especially true in regard to discipline problems since psychologists are trained to diagnose the causes of and remediation of children's misbehavior. Yet although the number of school psychologists has increased dramatically in the last two decades, their potential contributions to education have been largely untapped. I believe that this has led to a perceptible decline in the quality of people who apply to school psychology training programs, thus exacerbating the problem. Less qualified applicants drift toward the marginal training programs that produce psychological technicians rather than high-level problem solvers. The result is the proliferation of school psychologists' functioning as technicians. They put Band-Aids on the problems of discipline. Their roles and consequent frustrations often result in limited longevity of many of the best and brightest conceptualizers who wish to solve underlying problems rather than focus on short-term solutions such as corporal punishment.

There are a number of possible underlying root causes for the failure of education to utilize social science knowledge and the skills of school psychologists fully. We will look at some of them.

ANTI-INTELLECTUALISM

One of the abiding discrepancies between educators and psychologists is that intellectualism is emphasized and encouraged more in the selection, training, and ongoing careers of psychologists.

In 1957, with no background in education, I became an elementary school teacher. There I was told that "pseudointellectuals" were trying to destroy traditional education, that research had nothing useful to say to educators, and that the best advice to new teachers was "don't smile until Christmas." Since I was fresh out of undergraduate school where I had majored in liberal arts, the massive anti-intellectualism among my colleagues was surprising.

As an undergraduate student, my highest aspiration had been to be considered an intellectual—one who used scientific and/or rational systems of logic to solve problems. Intellectuals favored reason over emotion and experience to make sense of the world. Their sustenance was the written word, and their modus operandi was discourse, debate, and the search for ever more satisfactory solutions to problems. Why did this not apply to the process of education and the politics of schooling?

The anti-intellectualism that once pervaded education is no longer as apparent as it was in 1957. Nevertheless, there is still a significant and counterproductive undercurrent of suspicion and hostility toward intellectually oriented practitioners, such as psychologists, who attempt to use contemporary theory and research as a base for solving the problems of schooling.

CONCEPTUAL DIFFERENCES BETWEEN PSYCHOLOGISTS AND ADMINISTRATORS

Much of what school psychologists do is determined by their relationships with school administrators, especially building principals. Yet too many administrators do not understand the training and potential of school psychologists as behavioral and social scientists. They rarely rely on psychologists' problem-solving skills; rather, they view psychologists as personnel whose role ends after individual children are diagnosed and classified.

Too often administrators and psychologists become defensive and hostile when psychologists want to use social science research as a basis for solving problems. The views of these two groups seem to emerge from completely different frames of reference, a subject I have studied.

I began my research by examining the criteria for admitting each group into university training programs (Hyman 1988c). The scores of a pool of applicants at both the certification and doctoral level on combined Graduate Record Examination, a test widely used as a criterion for admission to graduate schools, evidence a wide discrepancy. Since 1975–1976 there has been a consistent difference of around 100 points between applicants to psychology programs and those to educational administration programs, with psychology applicants' mean scores being significantly higher than administrators'. Further, among all college of education applicants, educational administration, guidance, and physical education applicants have the lowest scores.

I was unable to obtain scores of actual enrollees of educational administration programs (for a variety of reasons too lengthy to discuss here). Mean scores for school psychology program enrollees are available, however, and reflect higher means than indicated in the applicant pool. Assuming that both groups accept students above the fiftieth percentile of applicants, the discrepancy still holds. The implication is that school psychologists as a group tend to be brighter than those who determine how their services will be used.

One consequence of the disparity between many administrators and psychologists in intellectual rigor and conceptual orientation to problem solving is covert resentment on both sides, especially in how to handle highly emotionally charged issues such as school discipline. In the worst cases of conflict—often on how to classify, place, or treat a child—administrators become defensive and psychologists become arrogant. As a result, available remedies based on social science evidence are never used because of mutual resentment, conflict, and ensuing power struggles. This is a major reason that many psychologists leave the schools and many administrators are hostile to psychologists.

Lack of Effective Communication between the Professions

Historically most educators have failed to tap the science of psychology effectively to improve education.

Almost all undergraduate and graduate training in education requires some coursework that demonstrates the relevance of psychology to teaching, learning, and schooling, yet most educators, once in the field, tend to view themselves as artisans who blend their own early experiences with trial-and-error approaches to develop strategies for use in the classroom or the administration of schools. They tend to reject theory and look for quick fixes to solve problems. Psychologists are taught that human behavior is complex, and there are few quick fixes for the problems they face. A good example of this discrepancy in outlook is provided by studies of approaches to discipline.

In previous chapters, I have discussed studies conducted at the NCSCPAS that demonstrate that teachers' own childhood experiences of being disciplined are the major predictors of how they will discipline their pupils. Number of courses taken, at least up to the master's level, seems to have little impact on actual practice. Psychological research with a direct bearing on most aspects of the educational enterprise remains remote and esoteric to the majority of classroom teachers (Dempster 1988).

Professional Orientation

In general, administrators and teachers are group oriented. Teachers are responsible for classes, group instruction, and group discipline. Administrators must attend to groups of students, teachers, parents, and others. Both must advocate for the maintenance of the group, sometimes at the expense of the individual.

Much of the training of school psychologists, in contrast, focuses on the diagnosis, remediation, and treatment of individuals. There is a strong focus on child advocacy and usually a course in ethical issues and responsibility to clients. Unlike educators, psychologists are liable for malpractice.

The psychologist's professional responsibility to advocate for individuals versus the school's concern for maintaining the group is a source of conflict that too frequently becomes personal and sometimes so acrimonious that the child gets hurt.

IDEOLOGICAL ORIENTATION

A high percentage of referrals to psychologists are discipline problems. Orientation toward discipline is a major determinant in diagnosis and remediation. Too often there is a serious discrepancy between educators and psychologists in conceptualizing the causes and remediation of misbehavior.

Workshops I have conducted all over the country include the use of a scale to measure punitiveness of participants. Invariably special educators, psychologists, and other personnel workers are least punitive; administrators, high school teachers, and coaches are significantly more punitive. These ideological differences in punitiveness are a common cause of serious disagreement about how to deal with behavioral problems of students.

It is possible that most educators and most schools are incapable of change and ongoing self-renewal based on the use of social science research. An alternate theory is that school psychologists are not adequately selected and/or trained to communicate social science information to fit into the school or to do more than educational diagnosis. Changes may be needed in both areas.

Meanwhile, we need to address those already in the field. I have worked with many outstanding administrators and teachers with highly successful results. It is clear that part of the solution to the successful utilization of psychology in the schools will begin when both sides accept the underlying causes of the problem and begin effective communication. I believe that parents, educators, and social scientists working together can make American schools nurturing and psychologically safe places where effective learning can take place.

Answering the Most Common
Defenses for Corporal Punishment

If you are interested in eliminating corporal punishment, become informed. If you have read this book up to this point, you are informed. It is a good idea to begin to gather local and state data so that you can document all of your statements. Practice debating, defending both sides of the issue. Fairly soon you will find that the other side uses a few meager arguments, which can be easily overcome if you answer in an authoritative, rational, and repetitive manner. Therefore, after you have gathered the information, you should be able to practice with some personal confrontations with advocates of corporal punishment. Let's review some of the arguments most often used by the pro–corporal punishment contingency.

Argument 1: "But we need the use of corporal punishment to maintain order in the school" or "We don't use corporal punishment very often, but we need to have the threat of it available to keep children from misbehaving." Several studies conducted at the NCSCPAS show that the elimination of corporal punishment does not do anything negative to the discipline atmosphere in the classroom or the school. The facts speak for themselves. New Jersey since 1867, Massachusetts since the 1950s, and many of the great cities and suburban school districts in affluent areas in other states have been able to survive without the use of corporal punishment. Japan, often touted as the example par excellence of academic achievement, does not use corporal punishment. All of the schools of continental Europe and communist and socialist countries function without the use of corporal punishment. There is no evidence that its use makes a bit of difference in terms of the behavior of children. Furthermore, why must educators base their discipline on fear? There is plenty of research evidence that the best way to get children to perform is by using positive reinforcement, not fear. There is no evidence that the fear of corporal punishment does anything to improve school discipline. As just one example, the Supreme Court in West Virginia in 1982 forbid teachers to use any instrument to hit children. Reduced to the use of their hand, most teachers stopped using corporal punishment altogether. Over the next year, the teachers' and the administrators' unions began to lobby for new legislation permitting corporal punishment, which was enacted. But there is no documented evidence that the schools of West Virginia suffered as a result of a complete lack of corporal punishment in the schools for a year until the legislation was passed.

Not only is there no evidence to indicate that eliminating corporal punishment will have any dramatic effect on the misbehavior of children; there is good evidence that a number of positive training programs for teachers result in the reduction in misbehavior. The elimination of corporal punishment and the implementation of appropriate training programs in discipline for teachers is a positive way to improve classroom discipline.

Argument 2: "Corporal punishment is used only as a last resort." There is a large amount of evidence that corporal punishment is not used as a last resort. In fact, the files at the NCSCPAS contain many examples of the fact that severe corporal punishment was used as a first resort. Research by Jacob Kounin and others showed that teachers make frequent management errors in handling school children. Teachers who are punitive tend to move toward punitiveness quickly and do not use a variety of alternative methods.

Argument 3: "You folks talk as though we're abusing children in the schools. We are only talking about reasonable paddlings." It is true that much of the paddling that occurs is not abusive if the term is defined as the extreme infliction of short-term or long-term damage. However, the infliction of pain at any time can be traumatic. Remember that the basic purpose of corporal punishment is to inflict pain. The teacher who is using a wooden paddle or other weapon is attempting to hurt the child.

Let us assume that most corporal punishment causes only a slight reddening of the skin. Without going into the argument about how red or sore the skin must be before child abuse occurs, it is easier to attack this argument on larger ground. It is not that so many of the cases of corporal punishment are abusive; it is that the ones that are abusive usually result in tremendous trauma for the children, the parents, and the community. Moreover, there is little question that the concept of hitting as an appropriate way to change children's behavior adds to the unacceptable level of violence in society. Although much of the paddling does not result in severe child abuse, it still gives children a clear message that violence is the way to solve problems.

Argument 4: "We only use corporal punishment to get the child's attention." This is one of the weakest arguments—that you have to beat a child to get his or her attention. What about talking to them? sitting down quietly with them? calling them aside? isolating them until they calm down? providing interesting curriculum or lessons so the child does pay attention? checking to be sure the child is able to do the work or if the work is too boring for the child because he or she is too advanced? All of these arguments are a sure counter to this argument.

Argument 5: "But the Bible says, 'spare the rod . . .'" If people literally interpret the Bible, it is probably hopeless to try to change their minds. Literalists as a group are more punitive than the masses. The only response to this argument is the suggestion to try alternatives before turning to corporal punishment. Moreover, the public schools have a secular approach to education. Therefore, biblical beliefs should not be supported in the public schools. A religious foundation for a pedagogical procedure is unacceptable.

Argument 6: "I got hit when I was a kid, and it didn't do me any harm" or *"I got hit when I was a kid, and look where I am now."* Undoubtedly the majority of contemporary Americans were spanked by their parents at some time in their lives, and an unknown but large number were either paddled or witnessed paddling in the school. In the past wife beating was tolerated; fighting was a generally acceptable method to teach children to resolve their problems; and sexual abuse and date rapes were kept in the closet. We know now that incest was practiced to a greater extent than we wanted to believe or we can still comprehend. We now know that the family is the most violent place in society. We as a nation have come to understand that there has been too much violence in the lives of children. These sobering facts have moved us to pass laws to protect children from violence in all settings—except the schools.

Allowing teachers to hit students adds to the high levels of violence to which children are exposed in society. This includes violence in homes, on the streets, and in the media. Although an adult's previous experience with paddling may seem inconsequential to him or her, acceptance of this practice adds to the general level of acceptance of violence as a way of solving problems.

Argument 7: "If you haven't been a teacher, you don't know what you are talking about." My favorite anecdote about this argument occurred on a hot October afternoon in a classroom packed with hostile inner-city teachers who wanted to go home. The principal had been requested by his boss to improve school discipline with the help of a project I directed. His main approach to misbehavior was suspension. If one suspension did not help, then surely repeated suspensions of recalcitrant students would convince them to change. The staff were experts at provoking students they disliked immediately after their return from suspension. It did not take much to provoke a snide comment or an angry response from alienated students who believed that they were not wanted in school. Most of them hated school and were happier at home or on the streets. These students were on permanent holiday because they were repeatedly suspended for short periods that did not require due process hearings.

As I began my presentation, one particularly hostile teacher stood up and interrupted me by challenging my competence:

> TEACHER: Dr. Hyman, did you ever teach?
> ME: Yes
> TEACHER: Dr. Hyman, where did you teach?
> ME: In Millstone Township.
> TEACHER: What did you teach?
> ME: Elementary school for four years.
> TEACHER: Did you ever teach in high school?
> ME: Yes. I have been a substitute teacher in high school.
> TEACHER: But you never really taught for a long time in a school like ours.

ME: No, but I have worked in schools for over twenty-five years and have worked with all of the schools in this community for over ten years.

TEACHER: If you are not in the classroom, you don't know what's going on.

At the time I began answering the challenger's questions, I naively thought that a few straightforward responses would suffice. But as we went on, it was obvious that I was a symbol of all that the teachers hated about the administration, the school board, and outside experts, especially university professors. I later found out that the morale and general climate of the school was so poor that no positive change was likely until the administration changed. It was obvious that my challenger was going to try to discredit me based on his premise that direct and ongoing experience as a teacher is the only qualification that is acceptable to establish expertise.

After a few more minutes of questioning, I extended my inquisitor's argument by saying, "Are you telling me that the only way that anyone can help anyone else is by having had the exact experience of the helpee? Are you saying that I would have to have cancer to help someone with cancer? That I couldn't coach baseball if I haven't played all positions or in fact that I couldn't coach any sport that I haven't played? Are you saying that I have to be emotionally disturbed to help someone who is emotionally disturbed?" At that point it was obvious that I knew the teachers were not open to change and they knew I was not going to be bullied. The bell signaling the end of the working day rang, and while I was in the middle of a sentence, the teachers (because of union rules) got up and left.

That was one of the most hostile group of teachers with whom I have ever worked. They had reason to be hostile because of a variety of factors, including the principal's lack of leadership, the deplorable condition of the school, and the politics of the school board. In such extreme situations, a change in climate must precede the use of logic to solve problems. But in most situations in which I have worked, there have always been some educators who will respond positively to logic. They will accept the premise that one may learn from reading history, research, and observations of others.

Argument 8: "I don't believe in all that research. I know from my own experiences what works." This is another version of the anti-intellectualism of argument #7. It is anti-intellectual because it is based on the belief that no one can learn by reading what others have to tell. If that were true, the scientific method would have nothing to offer. I heard this argument when I started teaching. It was not true then, and it is not true now.

I often ask proponents of this view if they believe in learning and if they believe one can learn from books. If they say yes to both, I ask them what research they have read on school discipline and with what programs they are familiar. This technique of exposing ignorance generally works when I do workshops with educators. A few always will point out the fallaciousness of their peers' rejection of knowledge that can be gained from the research of others. I sometimes suggest that if they do not believe in research, the next time they go to their doctor, they should tell him or her to ignore the research on a particular medication and give it to them because they heard from someone that it was effective.

Argument 9: "Teachers need the right to use corporal punishment to protect themselves." Most corporal punishment is done to small children, not older students who would hit back. Additionally, all states forbidding corporal punishment allow the use of force for self-protection. School employees have the right to use force to protect themselves or other people from bodily harm, to gain control of a dangerous weapon, or to protect property from damage.

Argument 10: "Most students who get paddled deserve it. They are usually the worst kids in class." This is relative since there is no universal standard for "worst." One of my former students (Minor and Hyman 1988), demonstrated that teachers with different personality types are upset by different types of behavior. Research by Junious Williams showed that black and white students are punished differently for the same misbehaviors. Data at the NCSCPAS show that a great deal of paddling of young children occurs as the result of minor offenses such as whispering in class or not completing assignments. This gives the lie to the contention that it is a last resort.

It may be that some frequent recipients of paddling are the "worst" kids. Invariably these are the children who are hostile, aggressive, and often bullies. Invariably they got that way from frequent physical and psychological maltreatment in the home and/or school. More of the same is far from being the cure.

Argument 11: "A little swat on the behind is good for some kids." There is no evidence that the infliction of pain has ever been good for anyone. One never knows if a "little swat" will have a horrendous effect on a particular child. The research shows that even wit nessing it can have lifelong negative consequences.

Argument 12: "Corporal punishment is the only thing some kids understand. Even their parents tell us to hit them." This statement is often made about children who are frequently hit at home. The parents who tell strangers to inflict pain on their own children often lack the education and ability to nurture and appropriately set limits for their children. In my experience these are often aggressive parents of aggressive children. Their children are often the most helpless and the ones with the lowest self-esteem.

Argument 13: "Don't tell me corporal punishment doesn't work. When I swat a kid for something, he doesn't do it again for awhile. The direct path to his brain is through his behind." It is true that pain temporarily suppresses behavior. It also causes anger, humiliation, and a desire to get revenge. It does not teach a new behavior; it does teach that violence is a way to solve problems. If one swat does work, it was not necessary, since the research shows that rational persuasion or some other punishment would have worked. Research also shows that young children who are hit frequently are less likely to behave than those whose parents set limits by positive methods that focus on reward and building positive self-esteem.

Answering the
Most Common Defenses for
Psychological Maltreatment

There is vigorous support for the use of physical punishment of school children, yet few educators will openly support the kind of verbal abuse that is clearly linked to stress symptoms in students. Based on our research, thousands of students each day are subjected to verbal assaults. The painful consequences of verbal assaults are unknown by most of the perpetrators. They do not even recognize what they are doing. When it is pointed out, here are their defenses.

Argument 1: "I was only kidding." This is the favorite defense of the name caller. This educator loves to give students nicknames such as "motor-mouth," "nerd," or "dirtball." Other names are more subtle but just as damaging. Once a teacher gives a student a label, even if it happens only once, the rest of the students may pick it up, and the child is labeled for a long time.

Argument 2: "That kid needed to be put in his place." This is a favorite defense of put-downs, the most numerous type of verbal assaults on children. It is also used to defend sarcasm. In most cases the teacher feels that the child deserved what was done because the child's behavior was considered inappropriate or offensive. Unfortunately, in many cases the student's offense is to think differently from the teacher or to demonstrate the teacher's inadequacy in some academic area.

Argument 3: "You should have heard what that kid said to me." I believe that two wrongs do not make a right. While it is true that students can be unruly and insulting, it does not follow that the educator should respond by demeaning the student. Often students who are disrespectful in school have been taught to respond in that way, because of a variety of reasons. Denigration and humiliation are counterproductive methods of helping chronically misbehaving students who generally already feel bad about themselves.

Argument 4: "He is a big boy and can handle it. Everybody has to deal with some verbal abuse in their lives." This is a common defense for treating children with the same level of verbal abuse that some adults are subjected to in the workplace. Coaches and vocational education teachers particularly too often think that they have to toughen kids for the realities of life. It may be true that adults can learn to handle verbal abuse, but few are happy with it. Children and adolescents, however, have not yet developed their sense of self. They still need to test themselves against the demands of the adult world. This must be done in a way that supports rather than breaks down their developing self-esteem.

Becoming Informed

In order to eliminate corporal punishment and psychological maltreatment, one must become informed and be aware of the arguments of the other side. When I attempt a rational academic discourse with strongly punitive people, I rarely make much progress. Direct and continuous challenges for them to support their beliefs with data is the best approach. I have not even found it beneath my dignity to attack the motives of those who support the use of overly severe punishments, including corporal punishment. Also, it is interesting that a study done of administrators in West Virginia showed a direct correlation between their lack of knowledge about research on corporal punishment and their support of it. That is, the less they read, the less they knew; the poorer they did on a test about this type of discipline, the more they supported it (Dennison 1984). This study confirms the findings of other studies in which the relationship between socioeconomic and educational background and incidence of abuse is defined.

A recent study by Risinger (1989) determined that the permissiveness of Texas law toward corporal punishment was a predictor of how favorable principals in that state were to the practice. Principals who condoned corporal punishment were quite familiar with how to use the law and its limitations to justify its practice (the law holds that a child can be punished up to the point of deadly force). As a group, the high school principals who viewed the practice favorably tended to work in poorer districts in which forty to sixty percent of the children were eligible for free lunch. These principals also tended to be former high school teachers or school counselors, were usually mainline Protestants, and usually came from blue-collar families. The group least favorable toward corporal punishment tended to be elementary school principals in suburban or urban districts. They were former elementary or middle school teachers, were usually Roman Catholic, and were aged fifty to sixty-five years. Members of this group tended to come from white-collar families.

FACTS ABOUT CORPORAL PUNISHMENT

Arguments against corporal punishment should be backed by facts and logical conclusions:

- Corporal punishment occurs more frequently at the primary and intermediate levels (Hyman and Wise 1979).
- Boys are hit much more frequently than girls (Glackman et al. 1978).
- Minority and poor white children receive lickings four to five times more frequently than middle- and upper-class white children (Farley 1983).
- Most of the corporal punishment in America occurs in the South and Southwest: Florida, Texas, Arkansas, and Alabama have consistently been among the leaders in the frequency of hitting school children (Farley 1983; Russell 1988).
- The least use of corporal punishment occurs in schools in the Northeast (Farley 1983; Russell 1988).
- Contrary to popular belief, corporal punishment is not used as a last resort. Studies suggest that corporal punishment is often the first punishment for nonviolent and minor misbehaviors (Hyman, Clarke, and Erdlen 1987).
- There is evidence that corporal punishment is one of the causes of school vandalism (Hyman and Wise 1979).
- In descending order of support for corporal punishment are school boards, school administrators, teachers, parents, and students (Hyman and Wise 1979).

- Very violent children are almost always frequent recipients of severe corporal punishment at home. Since hitting at home does not help them, it is just as useless and counterproductive in school. The old saw that violence breeds violence is supported by this finding (Hyman and Wise 1979).

- Corporal punishment is forbidden in the schools of continental Europe, Japan, Israel, the communist nations, Ireland, and other non–English speaking countries, Puerto Rico, nineteen states, many suburban upper-middle-class schools, and most of the largest cities of America (Hyman and Wise 1979).

- Teachers who frequently paddle tend to be authoritarian, dogmatic, relatively inexperienced, impulsive, and neurotic as compared to their peers (Hyman 1987).

- Teachers who do not paddle are most often those who were rarely, if ever, spanked or paddled as children. This modeling effect has been repeatedly demonstrated. The more teachers were hit as children, the more they tend to hit their students (Lennox 1982).

- People who indicate that they are fundamentalists, evangelicals, and/or Baptists tend to respond more punitively to disciplinary situations than those who identify themselves with other major religions and orientations. Demographic studies of corporal punishment in schools support these findings (Pokalo 1986).

- Schools with high rates of corporal punishment also have high rates of suspensions and are generally more punitive in all discipline responses than schools with low rates of corporal punishment (Farley 1983).

Proponents of corporal punishment may point out that it works because it immediately stops undesired behavior. They also argue that they behaved when they were young because they knew what would happen if they did not. They may swear that their swats did them a lot of good or that spankings and paddlings kept them from turning bad. Most of what they say is nonsense. It is the past turned rosy by the passage of time.

But some of what they say is true. It is true that corporal punishment temporarily suppresses undesired behaviors; however, that is only the beginning of the story. While common sense suggests that a good swat will stop the misbehavior of children, research demonstrates that corporal punishment is ineffective and counterproductive in the long run.

Following is a brief summary of reasons why corporal punishment is not a good idea (Hyman and Wise 1979; NCSCPAS 1988):

- Corporal punishment temporarily suppresses behavior, but it does not teach new behavior.
- Punishment generally is not effective in promoting new learning. The overwhelming evidence suggests that reward, praise, and interactions with children that promote the development of a positive self-concept are the most powerful motivators for learning.
- Excessive use of corporal punishment in the classroom decreases learning.
- Corporal punishment arouses aggression in pupils' aggression against the teacher, peers, or property (Bongiovanni 1979).
- The use of corporal punishment teaches children that violence is the way to solve problems. Research shows that this message is taught to those who inflict the pain, to those who receive it, and to those who witness it. It does not help children develop the internal controls that are necessary in a democracy.
- Eliminating corporal punishment does not increase misbehavior (Farley 1983).
- Even some psychologists, who should know better, distort research on punishment to recommend corporal punishment. This is a function of their own acceptance of this form of discipline when they were children (Sofer 1983).

The most devastating argument against the use of corporal punishment is its connection with child abuse. The acceptance of hitting as a way to change children's behavior serves only to sanction an already overwhelming amount of violence to which children are exposed.

FACTS ABOUT
PSYCHOLOGICAL MALTREATMENT

The data base on psychological maltreatment in schools is just beginning to emerge. But we do know how psychological maltreatment affects the development of personality:

- One in ten citizens at some time has a significant emotional problem. Many of them will be vulnerable because of low self-esteem and feelings of worthlessness planted in their psyches when they were young.
- Psychological maltreatment is as devastating as physical maltreatment in terms of severity and longevity of symptoms.
- Between 40 and 60 percent of teachers remember a traumatizing experience they suffered as students. An unknown number of them will unconsciously model some of the abusive behavior they received.
- In one study, 50 percent of high school students developed some stress symptoms as a result of psychological maltreatment by educators. About 2.5 percent developed symptoms of such duration, intensity, and frequency that they had some level of PTSD.
- Most psychological abuse in schools is in the form of put-downs by teachers.
- Research on the self-fulfilling prophecy demonstrates that subtle forms of psychological maltreatment occur when teachers unconsciously or consciously act on biases based on such factors as racial, ethnic, religious, or family stereotypes. This includes ignoring by not calling on children, lowering expectations and thereby using lower-level language with certain children, and comparing children unfavorably to their siblings.

- Almost all aggressive, impulse-ridden children live in homes where physical and psychological assaults are common.
- Psychologically demeaning and punitive teachers reduce learning rather than increase it by using these techniques.
- There is a common, unfounded belief among coaches that denigration, name calling, and verbal threats are good motivators for athletic performance. Although these practices may serve short-term goals of arousing aggression, they cause self-denigration in many high school athletes.

There is enough evidence to argue against psychological maltreatment. The problem is that most educators who do it are often unaware that they are causing emotional damage. Unlike corporal punishment and with the exception of coaching practices, most educators will not publicly defend the practices included under the rubric of psychological maltreatment. We need to sensitize them to the problem and help them to understand the value of "catching kids being good."

9

Eliminating Maltreatment in the Schools

THE vast majority of teachers enter education believing that they can help children and youth, but few are trained adequately to handle misbehavior in a positive and effective manner. Many would like to do a better job, but they are constrained by their own experiences as students, their own parents' disciplinary techniques, local tradition, and peer pressure to stick together when one of their ranks is accused of abuse. They generally know who the bad apples are, but few among them are willing to squeal on their colleagues.

Change at the Local Level

Abusive teachers, and often coaches, may remain unscathed for years because their behavior is ignored or covertly (sometimes overtly) supported by the administration and the local community. There may be many parents whose children were abused. They feel frustrated because they are unable to protect their children. When aroused, they may spew forth resentment, which falls on deaf ears. They are people who can be energized to fight against abuse in the schools.

It is rare that one family can bring about change. Personal litigation is often difficult, lengthy, and expensive. A better way is to obtain community support against the use of corporal punishment. One of the best methods is to focus on one teacher who has a reputation for maltreatment in the classroom. Surely there are other parents who are indignant, angry, and frustrated that their children have been psychologically abused or paddled without their consent.

In some communities, parents have not communicated with each other because they are not aware that their own children have been physically or psychologically assaulted. Very young children who are paddled are often threatened by their teachers and told not to tell their parents; some are afraid that they will be punished at home for misbehaving in school. But charges of abuse in the schools might receive media coverage and result in communication between parents of children previously abused by the offending educator. These and other interested parents frequently coalesce into a pressure group.

Gail Ernst of Allentown, Pennsylvania, provides a good example of an angry parent who convinced a resistant school board to change its policy. This case was well publicized in the local press. Ms. Ernst's son, Steven, and some of his classmates alleged that their teacher had paddled the entire class, except for one child who refused to be hit.

> At the beginning of a seventh-grade math class, one of the students reported that a book had been stolen. After a search through the room, the teacher informed the class that he was going to leave for a drink of water. When he returned, he said he expected the book to appear or he would paddle the whole class.
>
> While the teacher was gone, the entire class tried to figure out where the book was, but no one knew. When the teacher returned, he lined up the class of boys and girls and struck each of them with a wooden paddle. It later turned out that the book had been misplaced, not stolen.
>
> As allowed by state law, Ms. Ernst had previously placed a letter on file forbidding anyone in the school to hit her son. She complained about her son's treatment and was angered by the inadequate response she received. She began litigation against the school because her son, a child with a learning disability, was extremely upset by the paddling. My evaluation indicated EIPTSD.
>
> Ms. Ernst began a campaign to abolish corporal punishment in her school district. (The year before, I had debated the

former superintendent of the Allentown schools on Pennsylvania public television. He strongly defended the practice.) I called the new superintendent at the request of Ms. Ernst and other anti–corporal punishment members of the community and volunteered to testify before the school board at an upcoming meeting where the issue would be discussed. The school board declined, angering the parents even more.

Members of the parents' committee became familiar with the issues. They read materials from the NCSCPAS and knew how to respond to the defenses for corporal punishment. Some became experts on the local school discipline policy.

In order to effect change through the newspapers and media, Ms. Ernst organized parents and citizens, and they attended board meetings regularly. Their ranks grew as other parents of abused children became informed of their activities.

During these activities, the offending teacher struck again, this time at a parent. It was alleged that the teacher had grabbed a boy by both arms and slammed him against a locker. When the mother came to complain, he allegedly claimed that children lie and then proceeded to demonstrate to her what he had done. His actions were apparently enough to convince the school board to suspend and later fire him. He appealed and as of this writing is still not teaching in Allentown. This may have been the final factor in convincing school board members that out-of-control teachers must go. They gave in and abolished corporal punishment. It is clear that the pressure from parents and publicity forced a reluctant and conservative school board to change its policy.

Once a group is formed, its members will need a great deal of tenacity, persistence, and patience in order to change the thinking in the school and the community. It would be helpful if the parents could get a teacher or educator on the committee who is willing to help. (However, my experience is that this rarely happens because of peer pressure within the teachers' unions, especially in the South and Southwest, where the local values support the teachers.)

One strategy is to convince the school board to appoint a community committee to investigate school discipline policy and procedures. Although the board may try to load it with people sympathetic to its cause, the parents' committee can pressure for its own people, and the board generally will compromise so as not to look biased. Only a few people are needed to expose the committee and the public to all of the information available in this book and from other sources, including experts from nearby colleges, pediatricians, psychologists, and other professionals not allied to the school.

An important first step is to establish the rules and regulations the local school board has promulgated in terms of corporal punishment, to spotlight these rules, point out deficiencies, and examine the adequacy and number of alternatives. The committee must determine how often school psychologists, social workers, and trained counselors are consulted on discipline problems. They must find out if handicapped children are paddled, despite school psychologists' recommendations not to inflict pain on emotionally disturbed children. Perhaps the school psychologist can be persuaded to place anti–corporal punishment statements in the Individualized Education Plan of each child classified under public law 95-142. (Information about how this law works is available from school, county, or state special education officials.)

Once the committee obtains from the local school board the code of discipline or conduct, which usually spells out the behaviors that are not allowed and the penalties, it must determine any deficiencies that exist within the code. Most state departments of education have some guidelines on local discipline codes and will supply them on request.

The state regulations regarding corporal punishment need to be examined. Although some states are permissive, others suggest guidelines about who can administer it and how it should be administered. (See appendix E.)

It may be difficult to abolish corporal punishment in very conservative areas. In that case, a first step is to make using it more difficult for educators, perhaps by pressuring the school to develop specific guidelines for the protection of children:

1. Corporal punishment should not be administered immediately following a child's misbehavior since anger on the teacher's part might be involved.

2. It should not be administered in anger.

3. It should never be administered in front of anyone else except one or two neutral witnesses.

4. Parents should always be called before corporal punishment is administered, and they should be allowed to witness it.

5. Corporal punishment should always be administered with reasonable force. It should not leave bruises.

6. If possible, teachers should not be allowed to administer corporal punishment. It should be done by a principal or assistant principal, with witnesses present.

None of these guidelines is palatable to those who are completely against corporal punishment. In fact, some may object that they tacitly admit that corporal punishment is acceptable. Nevertheless, in communities devoted to the administration of pain, guidelines are a first step in ensuring children's rights. A school board can be sued more easily if it is discovered that it has not followed its own rules in the administration of corporal punishment. Moreover, trying to establish some criteria for reasonableness of force in the use of corporal punishment is especially important. This in some sense is a futile effort since those who favor corporal punishment may not be able to define or understand what is reasonable. Change can take place, though.

Changing Attitudes: An Experiment in the Deep South

An incident in the poor, rural community of Walterboro, South Carolina, which has one of the top swatting schools in the state and perhaps the country, galvanized action by a group of local citizens (Kija, Oropallo, and Hyman 1988). Carol Oropallo, a parent who grew up in New Jersey and spent ten years in France, was shocked to discover that her own children might be victims of a practice that seemed archaic. Her concerns focused on material published by the NCSCPAS and Adah Maurer's EVANG. With help from these groups and the National Coalition to Abolish Corporal Punishment in Schools, she organized the South Carolina Coalition for More Effective School Discipline.

As part of Ms. Oropallo's efforts, she and her husband, a lawyer, came to the aid of a middle school child in Walterboro who alleged that his principal had assaulted him. The parents went to the police after futile attempts to obtain help from the state child abuse authorities and officials of the board of education.

Attorneys for the boy and the school board negotiated an agreement whereby criminal charges would be dropped. In return, the school board agreed to a closed hearing for the boy and his family and a public school forum on the issue of corporal punishment. The forum was encouraged by Ms. Oropallo's group, which also did a great deal of work in organizing and publicizing the event.

The coalition had evidence that there was a serious countywide problem with the use of corporal punishment. The evidence was that Colletion County School District (the school authority that included Walterboro) had the highest rate of corporal punishment in South Carolina and ranked third highest among 82,999 schools nationwide, according to data gathered by the Office of Civil Rights.

As part of the public forum, the coalition arranged for me to make a presentation. While driving from the airport to Walterboro, Ms. Oropallo and I decided to conduct a survey. Since the purpose of the forum was to inform the public about the problem and to attempt to change community attitudes, we thought that a short pretest and posttest questionnaire of attitudes would be useful to determine the impact of the forum. (Of course, this is not the best way to plan research, but one must improvise when opportunities arise.)

Because of the nature of this field-based experiment, the exact number who attended the forum was not determined; however, estimates by the principal of the high school where the forum was held and others are that approximately 400 people attended. Some 198 participants returned one or both survey forms. Only 111 pairs of pretest-posttest cases were usable. This formed the sample size for the study.

The forum was attended by the school board members, school administrators, teachers, parents, and students. In addition, a small number were social workers and early elementary education students from a local extension program of the University of South Carolina. Although demographic information was not available at the time, it is estimated that the socioeconomic status of the audience ranged from lower to middle class.

We did not know why about half of those attending did not return completed forms, although several explanations are plausible. Ms. Oropallo indicated that one is the illiteracy rate. Approximately one in four adults in the Walterboro area is illiterate. Many people, upon entering the gymnasium where the forum was presented, refused to accept the forms when they were requested to fill them out. Probably many of these people were unable to read. Second, some of the participants stated that they had not changed their minds after the presentation and therefore did not return the posttest survey. Some returned neither. Finally, some participants might have felt that completing the surveys was not relevant to their reasons for attending the meeting.

The two survey forms were identical. Each included three categories of respondents (educator, parent, or student), indicated where to check for before and after the forum, and asked for comments. The four items are shown on the tables 9–1 through 9–3. Each participant received two forms with identical code numbers and the space checked for the form they were requested to fill out after they were seated. At the conclusion of the forum and using the second copy of the questionnaire, each participant was asked to respond again to the same survey.

The forum was extensively publicized through reminders in local and state newspapers, on local radio programs, flyers, and notices to all community agencies concerned with the issue. Every possible method of publicizing the meeting was utilized.

The forum began at 8:00 P.M., following a closed school board hearing. Participants were seated on the bleachers of a large gymnasium. On the floor was a long table at which the school board members were seated. In the center was a podium with a loudspeaker, and to the right were the lawyer for the child and three speakers.

Ms. Oropallo gave a twenty-minute talk explaining the problem in the community. A speaker from the University of South Carolina, Mary Willis, talked about local successful programs of

Table 9–1
PRE- AND POST-MEAN RESPONSE OF EDUCATORS
(N = 43)

	Pretest (%)		Posttest		
	Mean	*SD*	*Mean*	*SD*	*Change*
Corporal punishment should be allowed to discipline students in all high schools	4.60	1.45	4.47	1.61	− .14
Corporal punishment should be used to discipline students in elementary and middle schools	4.63	1.48	4.51	1.59	− .11
Okay to corporally punish children in front of their classmates	2.91	1.66	2.93	1.79	.02
If allowed, only principals and their assistants should administer corporal punishment	4.23	1.78	4.33	1.85	.09

Likert scale: 1 = strongly disagree, 2 = disagree, 3 = disagree somewhat, 4 = agree somewhat, 5 = agree, and 6 = strongly agree
*Significant at the 0.05 level

school discipline that did not depend on corporal punishment. I presented material for approximately an hour in which I showed slides of battered buttocks resulting from legal corporal punishment and discussed emotional issues and research findings. Then the audience responded; about ten of those attending made brief presentations, most of them against corporal punishment.

The preforum survey showed that as a group, parents, students, and educators "somewhat" agreed that corporal punishment should be allowed in public schools. About 25 percent "strongly" agreed that corporal punishment should be allowed. Although there was a significantly more negative attitude toward corporal punishment at the end of the forum, the proportion of participants who were strongly committed to allowing corporal punishment in public schools remained unchanged. Most people

Table 9–2
PRE- AND POST-MEAN RESPONSE OF STUDENTS
(N = 19)

	Pretest (%)		Posttest		
	Mean	SD	Mean	SD	Change
Corporal punishment should be allowed to discipline students in all high schools	3.21	1.96	3.05	2.07	−.18
Corporal punishment should be used to discipline students in elementary and middle schools	3.05	1.90	3.00	2.08	−.05
Okay to corporally punish children in front of their classmates	1.74	1.19	1.32	0.58	−.42
If allowed, only principals and their assistants should administer corporal punishment	4.94	1.08	4.47	1.68	−.47

Likert scale: 1 = strongly disagree, 2 = disagree, 3 = disagree somewhat, 4 = agree somewhat, 5 = agree, and 6 = strongly agree

agreed that when corporal punishment is allowed, it should not be done in the view of other students. Students were significantly less in favor of being punished in view of their classmates than were parents and educators. Furthermore, most agreed that the aunishment should be done only by the principals or their assistants.

Preforum attitudes toward corporal punishment among the three groups revealed that educators tended to be significantly more in favor of corporal punishment at all grade levels than did students and parents. After the forum, most of the educators present remained unmoved by the data, research, and case examples. They still held strong beliefs that corporal punishment should be allowed in public schools.

Table 9–3
PRE- AND POST-MEAN RESPONSE OF PARENTS
(N = 49)

	Pretest (%)		Posttest		
	Mean	SD	Mean	SD	Change
Corporal punishment should be allowed to discipline students in all high schools	3.41	1.88	3.06	1.96	− .37*
Corporal punishment should be used to discipline students in elementary and middle schools	3.33	1.91	2.92	2.06	− .41*
Okay to corporally punish children in front of their classmates	2.42	1.66	2.28	1.77	− .14
If allowed, only principals and their assistants should administer corporal punishment	3.98	1.96	4.26	1.89	.29

Likert scale: 1 = strongly disagree, 2 = disagree, 3 = disagree somewhat, 4 = agree somewhat, 5 = agree, and 6 = strongly agree
*Significant at the 0.05 level

Students in the audience were initially "somewhat against" corporal punishment before the forum; their attitudes after the forum did not change considerably. Unlike their peers in a study done in Pennsylvania (Hyman and Wise 1979), the students in Walterboro were against being hit but not very strongly against it after the forum.

The parents were significantly affected by the presentation. I think that the slides and my detailing of case histories had a real impact. I pointed out that in all the cases I presented, the parents had been thwarted by the schools. At the conclusion of the meeting, the parents shifted significantly to the belief that corporal punishment should not be allowed in the public schools.

In a postforum private conversation, one of the school administrators told me that he did not believe in research and statistics. His faith in the paddle was supported by his statement that "statistics can tell you anything you want." It appeared futile to try to explain the meaning of controlled research or to expect him to read about alternatives. He and other administrators seemed unfamiliar with the literature on discipline in their professional journals. The points he made reflected the feelings of many other responding educators. They were closed to research findings in their own field. Educators in this sample were much more in favor of corporal punishment than students or parents and are probably unlikely to change their attitudes without massive in-service training in positive methods of discipline.

Despite the policy of the National Education Association and almost all professional groups that deal with children, local and state teachers' associations have resisted abolishing corporal punishment. If the teachers in this study are representative of their state, they will probably continue to lobby against change.

This experience suggests that efforts to educate citizens to lobby against corporal punishment in the schools should focus on parents. They seem most likely to benefit from factual information. Grass-roots parent groups offer a strong base to influence legislators, who will continue to be pressured by teachers not to change laws allowing corporal punishment.

Abolishing Maltreatment through State Laws

When I began to conduct research on corporal punishment in the schools, it was illegal in only three states. As I finish this book in the fall of 1989, nineteen states have abolished it, and there are strong lobbying efforts against it in many others.

In 1984, the staff at the NCSCPAS began to investigate the extent of psychological maltreatment in the schools. At that time, the topic was on practically no one's agenda. In 1989, there has been a major conference on it, and the National Committee for the Prevention of Child Abuse has made psychological maltreatment in the home an issue. The government has begun to fund research on psychological maltreatment, and James Garbarino and colleagues have published a landmark book, *The Psychologi-*

cally Battered Child (1986). The state of California has recognized the importance of promoting self-esteem in schools and Stuart Hart has established the National Center for the Study of Children's Rights at the University of Indiana–Indianapolis.

Each state has abolished corporal punishment in a different way with pressure from different coalitions. There is no one way to do it. What seems universal is that the two groups that resist change are entrenched and defensive educators and the traditional conservative and religious right constituencies that support them.

There is a peculiar paradox in conservative philosophy in states such as North Carolina. There the Gaspersohns struggled in the courts, in their community, and at the state level to abolish corporal punishment. So far they and other child advocates have lost. Yet many citizens of North Carolina would probably protest strongly if anyone suggested that they lived in a state that supported child abuse. Also, much of the populace in this generally conservative state would probably agree that the government cannot tell parents how to raise their children. Feeling on this issue has been so strong among right-wing groups that they have opposed much of the child abuse legislation on the grounds that government has no right to interfere in the disciplining of children. Logically it would follow that those same citizens should resent the schools' attempt to subject children to discipline procedures considered unacceptable by parental or individual dictates. In other words, those who view less government as the best government do an about-face on the issue of the right of government officials (teachers) to paddle children against the parents' will.

North Carolina is the last state in the country that specifically empowers teachers to paddle children. School boards, administrators, judges, or local politicians cannot stop this treatment. The Gaspersohn case demonstrates the extent of support for paddlings that can be so severe as to be considered child abuse by physicians. This peculiar and frightening paradox suggests that concerns about child abuse stops at the schoolhouse door. Yet many times I have engaged parents, teachers, and administrators in North Carolina in discussion of this issue. Many accept that paddlings will bruise children and even cause bleeding. Legally, as long as the injury is not permanent and crippling, the abuse is considered all right.

There is little question that the best way to eliminate corporal punishment in American schools is with a state-by-state assault. When the NCSCPAS first organized, there was relatively little activity at the state legislative level in terms of attempts to eliminate corporal punishment in the schools. Since then the momentum has increased. Almost every major professional organization dealing with children has passed resolutions against corporal punishment. The active involvement of child abuse groups has added weight to the pressure against the pro–corporal punishment forces. Finally, great movement has occurred because of angry parents who have organized citizen's groups that have lobbied legislatures to work on the corporal punishment issue.

Organizing a State Lobbying Group

There is no substitute for political action in order to change policy in the United States. It is helpful for local groups to organize through a network. A number of state professional organizations, backed by national policy, are against the use of corporal punishment in the schools. These organizations include the American Psychological Association, the National Association of School Psychologists, and the American Academy of Pediatrics. The state chapters of the National Committee for the Prevention of Child Abuse (NCPCA) have been extremely active. In states such as Washington, Maryland, and Indiana, they have led the battles. Their efforts have been supplemented by a national coalition of organizations devoted to abolishing corporal punishment. The NCSCPAS has the information needed.

When state professional organizations hold yearly conventions, these meetings typically have themes. Corporal punishment and psychological maltreatment in schools is one that is of interest to all groups that are concerned with children. These conventions can be used to reach the public. Often the organizations have public relations committees or professionals in their state offices who can help to interest the media in the issue.

Theoretically, an important ally should be state education associations; however, although the National Education Association has a policy against corporal punishment, the state affiliates, especially in the South and Southwest, may strongly favor its use. My experience has been that the professional staff personnel are usually much more informed about issues such as school discipline and are likely to be against all forms of maltreatment. Usually the elected officers are also likely to be against overly severe disciplinary practices. However, the rank and file, through their delegate assemblies, control policy. The teachers in conservative areas keep the state education programs from agreeing with their national organization's policy.

It is helpful to contact the local chapters to identify individuals who might be favorable toward eliminating corporal punishment. Dedicated professionals can persuade their colleagues to change policy, as was done in Virginia.

Madeline Wade, president of the Virginia Education Association (VEA), led the battle to eliminate corporal punishment in 1989 in the first southern state to abolish it. When I met Ms. Wade in the summer of 1988, I predicted that she could not change policy in a southern state through the teachers' organization. But through quiet, persistent, and sophisticated behind-the-scenes lobbying, the VEA was responsible for changing the law in Virginia.

Although the national policy of the American Federation of Teachers is that teachers should have the right to use corporal punishment, some of the local associations, especially in urban and suburban areas, may be against that policy. The national organization, however, can be a powerful force against change. For example, half of the school children in Pennsylvania attend schools where the federation represents teachers. The state association president, Albert Fondy, supports corporal punishment. As late as the summer of 1989, the state legislators defeated a bill to support abolishment.

In Maryland, the state affiliate of the NCPCA had led a seesaw struggle against an almost evenly divided state legislature. The initial momentum came from Rosie Lamela, a single-minded, dedicated parent whose son was allegedly abused in his local school. The Maryland group was aided by Bill Bevan, former school administrator and state legislator. Each year, when they think a bill is going to pass, legislators meet behind closed doors at the eleventh hour and agree to exempt certain counties that desperately cling to tradition.

Parents who fight to abolish corporal punishment can expect a great deal of resistance from the school board. Every state has an association of school boards, and they generally have a lot of political power with state legislatures. The state school board associations generally have a predictable negative reaction to anything that would impose state control at the local level. Also, studies have shown that among educational groups, those most favorable to the use of corporal punishment have been school board members. Parents also can expect little help from state school administrators' associations, generally very conservative groups that favor local control. Therefore, the issue of eliminating corporal punishment is disguised as a struggle between local and state control. The real issue is whether children should be hit.

The national Parent-Teacher Association (PTA) is in the forefront of the battle. A major issue that might be used to galvanize PTA parents is the connection between child abuse and corporal punishment and how laws protect educators in most states. Because of the extent of psychological maltreatment, PTA members will be interested in this issue since their own children may be vulnerable.

In some states the local affiliate of the American Civil Liberties Union (ACLU) has been active in the battle. The ACLU leader in Georgia has helped organize state conferences and provided financial aid in litigation against school boards. In Pennsylvania, Susan Fritche of the ACLU helped legislator Michael Veon to draft a bill that was introduced in the 1989 fall session. Alan Reitman, the retired associate director of the national ACLU, has worked to convince state chapters of the importance of the issue.

Most university professors of psychology, education, and related fields will be helpful in the fight because almost all of the literature is against the use of corporal punishment as a disciplinary method. However, some may be involved with local school districts and therefore might not be a good resource.

It is important to identify sympathetic legislators who are willing to carry a bill forward. In Nebraska, state senator Ernie

Chambers worked behind the scenes successfully to change the law. He suggested to the state education association that if they worked against a bill abolishing corporal punishment, he might not be so vigorous in supporting a bill that was important to them. But in some other states, I have found that legislators who normally support education measures also feel that without support from the state education association, they cannot support abolishing corporal punishment. In some states, the state school boards have taken the matter into their own hands. Before abolishment in New York State, there was an on-again, off-again ruling about corporal punishment. The legislature could not pass a bill. The State Board of Regents passed a ruling to abolish but then reversed when one of their key members was absent—only to reverse again. The board was challenged, and the state attorney general ruled that the board had the authority to ban corporal punishment.

In 1989 the Alaska school authorities also took matters in their own hands as a result of the failure of the state legislature. Many native Americans there were particularly upset about the paddlings since hitting children is not part of their cultural heritage.

There are many routes to abolishment of abuse in schools. Interested citizens should try to obtain help from a professional lobbyist who works for a state organization, ranging from the ACLU to the state PTA. I have worked with lobbyists from state child advocacy federations or coalitions, state church councils, state psychological associations, and state legislators themselves.

In addition to lobbying by citizen advocacy groups and professional organizations, help may come from the state bureaucracy. In general, state child abuse authorities, much more than state education department officials, are likely to openly oppose corporal punishment in the schools. In some cases, as in West Virginia, the two departments debated whether child abuse authorities had jurisdiction to investigate abuse in the schools. In Illinois, the child abuse lobby was able to push legislation so that they could investigate alleged abuse in schools.

A unique approach was used in Florida. There the state Department of Health and Rehabilitative Services maintains a list of perpetrators on the State Child Abuse Registry. It uses this confidential list to screen applicants for work in child care facilities, with the disabled, and jobs that deal with adoption. It does not apply to schools, however.

The attorney for the Florida Teaching Profession–National Education Association complained that the health department is trying to stop corporal punishment in the schools with the threat of putting paddlers on the registry. His group endorses corporal punishment, which state laws authorize. The child abuse authorities claim that abuse is abuse. They apply a medical standard that if a bruise from a paddling lasts more than twenty-four hours, unreasonable force has been used and therefore abuse has occurred.

Between July 1, 1988 and June 30, 1989, the Department of Health and Rehabilitative Services investigated 820 educators and, as a result of the inquiries, 76 educators were put on the registry. Some are suing to be taken off. It is remarkable that educators go so far to prove that they should be allowed to abuse children. But they must be on the run. In 1989 the Florida legislature allowed local school boards to decide if they wanted to allow corporal punishment.

In some cases, unsuccessful litigation may mobilize support from many state organizations for an appeal, as it has in Oklahoma. In a case against the Muldrow Public Schools in eastern Oklahoma, Judge A.J. Henshaw clearly should have disqualified himself. He is the son of the retired superintendent of the school and a graduate of it. Although the judge failed to disqualify himself, against any precedent I am familiar with, he disqualified my psychological report of the victim. He also narrowed my testimony so it was hard to describe to the jury the effects of repeated beatings on the survivor, Jeremy Ward, with a leather paddle, thereby emasculating my testimony and credibility as an expert witness.

While Judge Henshaw limited my testimony about the case, he allowed the lawyer for the school board to harass me about my consulting work for the ACLU, which had no bearing on the case but was a clear signal to the Bible-belt conservative jury that I represented the "enemy."

Needless to say, Jeremy lost the case, although it is on appeal as this book is being written. Both the Gaspersohn and Ward cases reflect the problem of regional differences in law and definitions of reasonable punishment as they apply to the problem of child abuse in the schools. This topic was discussed at length in chapter 4.

Child abuse authorities can be invaluable in the attack on proponents of swatting in the schools. In some cases, a direct assault is required; in others, it is best to work behind the scenes.

Change at the National Level

There is probably little chance of any national legislation or Supreme Court decision that will help to abolish corporal punishment in the schools. The federal bureaucracy and the courts, especially in the matter of discipline, generally are loathe to interfere locally. Further, the Supreme Court has ruled out several of the most cogent constitutional arguments against the use of corporal punishment. The only argument left is one of substantive due process, and based on a number of state and circuit court rulings, there is not a great deal of hope in that area.

Recently the U.S. Supreme Court let two opposite decisions stand at the circuit court level. In the Tenth Circuit Court for the District of New Mexico, the Court said a child who was severely bruised had the right under constitutional law to sue the school district (*Miera v. Garcia*, 1987). Yet in Texas, the Fifth Circuit and the Supreme Court let stand a Texas law that school children may be corporally punished up to the point of "deadly force" (*Cunningham v. Jacksonville Independent School District*, 1988). Because of the Supreme Court's conflicting messages and because of its generally conservative approach to children's rights, it is unlikely that it will be the source of national abolition.

The National Association of School Psychologists, the NCSCPAS, and a coalition of other organizations have worked on an anti–corporal punishment amendment to the Education for the Handicapped Act (EHA) (public law 94-142) that would prevent infliction of pain on handicapped children. However, important potential backers in the House and Senate are reluctant to push too hard because they consider this change less important than others.

Meanwhile, attorney John Roessler of New Mexico advises litigants to avoid local and state courts and sue schools in federal courts, which he believes offer the best hope by claiming constitutional protection under substantive due process protections.

Despite decisions to the contrary, he still feels that in some cases procedural due process claims should be filed. Most important, federal laws allow both punitive and compensatory damages, whereas most state courts allow only compensatory damages under tort law.

Public Awareness of Alternatives

One way to attract attention to the corporal punishment issue is to talk about alternatives. Studies of teachers and my personal experience indicate a surprisingly small repertoire of methods of dealing with unruly and misbehaving children. Community groups, PTAs, and others can begin to focus on how to deal with children's misbehavior and, more important, how to prevent it. A community action group could focus on the kinds of training teachers are receiving to prevent discipline problems. An anti–corporal punishment group could start from the premise that discipline could be improved through better teacher training and a better climate. This is very intrusive to school officials, but more and more they are becoming aware that the public is taking a greater interest in what they do. Increasing pressure from home and from school advocates, increasing pressure on improving teacher efficacy, and recent demands for teachers to take competency tests are making administrators aware that they must be able to defend their methods and their knowledge base. A whole set of opportunities exists to begin to remind the educational establishment about its lack of knowledge or its lack of implementation of good classroom management and improved school climate.

Pushing for improvement in school discipline through prevention of misbehavior can be done in a nonconfrontational way by beginning to study teachers' knowledge of various methods to improve discipline and by providing consultation on discipline. Chapter 6 offered information on approaches to improving discipline. Armed with this knowledge, parents' groups can offer to cosponsor in-service training for school staff or to become involved in in-service training in discipline.

Often school psychologists, counselors, and social workers have training in positive approaches to discipline, but they are rarely utilized for this knowledge. Also, there are many outside experts, such as university professors, who offer in-service training to teachers. Parents might ask that schools begin to offer some of these courses for both parents and teachers together or individually. There are some good packaged programs that include books, tapes, and speakers on positive reinforcement, transactional analysis, teacher effectiveness training, and systematic training for effective teaching. (Appendix D contains information on alternatives offered by the National Education Association).

When questioning teachers about discipline, you should ask which method the teacher is using. Teachers rarely have a theoretical base for their actions; if parents are more informed than teachers and administrators, it will create an imbalance that the school will have to correct. If schools employ people to give in-service training in school discipline, they will find very few teachers who will still support the use of corporal punishment.

Using the Media

Any campaign to eliminate corporal punishment will have to depend on a friendly or sympathetic press. My experience has been that reporters and radio and television personnel are frequently sympathetic if issues are presented clearly, concisely, and appear to be newsworthy. The media love stories of violence and gore. They snap up cases of school-related child abuse quickly because these kinds of issues often polarize the community. Each media specialist puts a different angle on what is basically the same story.

Smaller local community newspapers are dependent on cooperative sentiment, however, and often will not be helpful in reporting corporal punishment episodes. One study that we conducted at the NCSCPAS was related to editorial opinion written after the Supreme Court decision of *Ingraham v. Wright*. We found that editorial opinion favoring corporal punishment was strongest in the southern states and was correlated with communities that had low per capita income, low per pupil expenditure for education, and a high illiteracy rate. Editors of smaller local newspapers, especially in rural communities, are often part of the establishment. It is naive to think that these people who are part of the establishment will side with parents fighting against tradition. These parents should try to attract coverage by larger newspapers from small cities and other urban areas. Newspapers that are distant tend to be more objective.

Local talk shows will feature debates about corporal punishment. This is especially true of the local affiliates of National Public Broadcasting, on both radio and television. Those who present the anti–corporal punishment side must be articulate and should not be afraid to show emotion. Television producers seek controversy, emotion, and human drama. The issue of beating children is not an academic subject that should always be handled in a decorous, unemotional manner. If you are going to appear on a television show, let the other side have it! Don't hold back, trying to be objective and overly fair to the other side. They are the ones who are defending abuse.

Developing Strategies for Eliminating Psychological Maltreatment

I have added this section on psychological abuse, although most of the strategies to eliminate physical maltreatment apply to psychological maltreatment. Most professionals are just beginning to work in this area, so there is not much experience to call upon in this latest battle against abuse.

Local efforts may be most successful in convincing school personnel to stop the practices that constitute psychological maltreatment. The majority of educators will acknowledge that calling students names, scapegoating, denigration, and humiliation are pedagogically poor practices. These terms, however, may have no substance for individual teachers. What one considers a put-down another may consider a minor bit of humor.

Almost all public schools conduct yearly in-service training programs, and parents have the right to suggest topics that reflect community concerns. A parent who is concerned about a particular teacher, a group of teachers, or a school can suggest to the district that it conduct training to sensitize teachers to the topic. This general approach does not target anyone in particular and therefore may avoid defensiveness.

An approach that can complement in-service training is to

develop guidelines that spell out the dimensions of psychological maltreatment by listing examples of abuse and pointing out the consequences that they have for children. (Information for such material is found throughout this book.) The guidelines should encourage teachers to avoid the use of damaging verbal messages and might even indicate penalties for teachers who regularly maltreat students psychologically. When the guidelines are developed, they can be submitted for approval by the board of education and then become the official policy of the school district. (Specific information may be obtained from the NCSCPAS and the National Committee for the Prevention of Child Abuse.)

Litigation is a remedy that should be considered when the psychological maltreatment has severe consequence for the student. Much of the information provided in the case of corporal punishment applies here. Expanding litigation in this area will go a long way to convince educators to avoid psychological maltreatment.

Conclusion

What is in store? Several trends allow fairly safe predictions. It is obvious that the U.S. Supreme Court will not offer school children constitutional protection from overly severe disciplinarian practices. In fact, the Reagan nominees seem inclined to roll back the constitutional gains that school children accrued in the 1960s and 1970s. Moreover, the conservative Reagan-appointed judges throughout the country cannot be expected to take a liberal stand on issues of school discipline.

I predict an increasing number of tort cases. Parents will litigate in increasing numbers as they begin to understand the long-term effects of overly abusive disciplinary procedures in the schools.

There is increasing pressure in the states to legislate against corporal punishment in the public schools. Parent groups with a wide variety of connections have banded together and have been aided by organizations of professionals including psychologists, social workers, and pediatricians. The pressure will continue. I predict that within five to ten years, corporal punishment will be illegal in the public schools of all states. I suspect that in the Deep

South and other religiously conservative areas, the legislatures will leave the Christian schools alone. Schools owned by various denominations on the religious right will continue to paddle. Parochial schools will abolish corporal punishment on their own.

The issue of psychological maltreatment in the schools will require a sustained public effort that has yet to begin. The movement to deal with emotional abuse in homes and institutions is in its infancy. It will be helped by growing awareness of the importance of self-esteem in educating children. Many policymakers are aware of this issue, yet the two movements need to be linked. I hope this book will help to push in the right direction and that by the turn of the century, all the schools in America will be physically and psychologically safe for all children.

This last chapter has been a call to battle. There are a number of levels at which we can attack this insidious problem, which contributes to the violence in society. There are a number of areas in which we must work. I hope this book will help to galvanize people in each state where corporal punishment and psychological maltreatment are particularly severe problems. I have tried to present all of the scientific and educational data currently available. Readers will have a sophisticated knowledge of the issues and will be equipped to counter any arguments to support corporal punishment or psychological assaults. Readers will not naively assume that the judiciary, prosecutors, the police, and other officials are sympathetic to the plight of children abused in schools. The issues are clear for the struggle that lies ahead. If you have read this book and you want to do something, get angry, become informed, and join the struggle. I look forward to meeting you on the battlefield.

Appendix A

Countries, States, Some Major Cities, and Organizations against Corporal Punishment

Countries

The following countries do not allow teachers to hit school children:

				Dates unknown:
1783	Poland	1949	China	
1820	Netherlands	1950	Portugal	Iceland
1845	Luxembourg	1958	Sweden	Japan
1860	Italy	1967	Spain	Ecuador
1867	Belgium	1967	Denmark	Jordan
1870	Austria	1967	Cyprus	Qatar
1881	France	1970	Germany	Mauritius
1890	Finland	1970	Switzerland	Israel
1917	Soviet Union	1982	Ireland	Philippines

Compiled by Adah Maurer of End-Violence against the Next Generation, the National Coalition to Abolish Corporal Punishment in Schools, and the National Association of School Psychologists.

1823	Turkey	1986	United	Communist
1936	Norway		Kingdom	bloc
1946	Rumania			countries

Countries still permitting school corporal punishment include the United States, Iran, Uganda, parts of Canada, Australia (banned in 70 percent of schools), and New Zealand.

States

The following states forbid corporal punishment in schools:

New Jersey	1867	Vermont	1984	Alaska	1989
Massachusetts	1971	New York	1985	Minnesota	1989
Hawaii	1973	California	1987	Michigan	1989
Rhode Island	1975	Nebraska	1988	Virginia	1989
Maine	1975	Wisconsin	1988	Connecticut	1989
New Hampshire	1975	Iowa	1989	Oregon	1989
		North Dakota	1989		

The District of Columbia, Puerto Rico, and overseas military bases also forbid it.

Two states have bills pending forbidding corporal punishment: Ohio, and Pennsylvania. And three states have stalled bills scheduled to be reintroduced: Indiana, Kentucky, and Washington. Five states have groups planning such legislation: Florida, Georgia, Oklahoma, South Carolina, Tennessee, and Indiana.

In a large number of states, local efforts are winning individual school districts:

Colorado	(Commerce City and others)
Kansas	(Wichita, Topeka, and others)
Arizona	(Phoenix, Tucson, and others)
Louisiana	(New Orleans)

New Mexico	(Albuquerque, Santa Fe, and others)
Wyoming	(Laramie and others)
Delaware	(Seaford)
Missouri	(St. Louis and others)
Illinois	(Chicago, Rockford, Urbana)
Texas	(Alamo Heights and others)
South Dakota	(Pierre)
Arkansas	(Little Rock)
Florida	(Dade County)
Nevada	(Douglas City)

In other states, there have been changes. Maryland organized a valiant effort and almost won. Half the counties, including about 85 percent of the children, are now protected. West Virginia's supreme court ruled that corporal punishment was legal but that the use of an instrument was cruel and unusual. For a year, swats all but stopped until the legislature rushed to make paddles legal again but with a twenty-four-hour waiting period to let teachers' tempers cool. North Carolina also sent a case to the state supreme court, but the seventeen-year-old honor student who was brutally beaten until she hemorrhaged lost her case with the strong message that among the Tarheels, any punitiveness is justified. In Idaho, corporal punishment is legal but not used.

These major cities, in states that allow corporal punishment, have abolished it (there are many more):

Albuquerque	Dayton	Sault Ste. Marie
Atlanta	Little Rock	San Jose
Baltimore	New Haven	Seattle
Battle Creek	New Orleans	Spokane
Boulder	Ottawa	St. Louis
Columbus, Ohio	Philadelphia	Urbana

Chicago	Phoenix	Walla Walla
Cleveland	Pittsburgh	Washington, D.C.
Cincinnati	Salt Lake City	

Major Organizations

The following organizations favor outlawing corporal punishment:

American Academy of Pediatrics

American Bar Association

American Civil Liberties Union

American Humanist Association

American Medical Association

American Orthopsychiatric Association

American Psychological Association

American Public Health Association

Association of Junior Leagues

Child Welfare League of America

Council for Exceptional Children

National Association for the Advancement of Colored People

National PTA

National Committee for the Prevention of Child Abuse

National Association of School Psychologists

National Association of Social Workers

National Committee for Citizens in Education

National Education Association

National Mental Health Association

Society for Adolescent Medicine

Unitarian Universalist Assembly

U.S. Department of Defense Dependent Schools

U.S. Students Association

Young Democrats in America

Appendix B
Office of Civil Rights Surveys of Corporal Punishment

OFFICE OF CIVIL RIGHTS STATEWIDE SURVEY OF REPORTED INCIDENCE OF
CORPORAL PUNISHMENT IN SCHOOLS: 1976

State	Total Number of Students	Total Number of Students Sampled	Number of Children in Sample Who Received Corporal Punishment	Percentage of Children Who Received Corporal Punishment[a]
United States	43,713,009	43,713,009	1,521,896	3
Alabama	757,619	757,619	53,765	7
Alaska	88,295	88,295	1,233	1
Arizona	491,944	491,944	13,818	3
Arkansas	455,101	455,101	46,719	10
California	4,313,926	4,313,926	30,920	1
Colorado	561,757	561,757	5,377	1
Connecticut	613,123	613,123	699	
Delaware	121,762	121,762	3,186	3
District of Columbia	125,058	125,058	5	
Florida	1,536,830	1,536,830	170,172	11
Georgia	1,068,813	1,068,813	121,256	11
Hawaii	173,692	173,692	2	
Idaho	197,769	197,769	4,192	2
Illinois	2,211,075	2,211,075	76,300	3
Indiana	1,150,020	1,150,020	50,019	4

Iowa	598,955	598,955	3,753	1
Kansas	454,104	454,104	8,929	2
Kentucky	690,121	690,121	46,531	7
Louisiana	834,056	834,056	24,340	3
Maine	238,263	238,263	120	
Maryland	862,103	862,103	4,730	1
Massachusetts	1,061,995	1,061,995	0	
Michigan	2,010,743	2,010,743	25,267	1
Minnesota	857,800	857,800	544	
Mississippi	497,993	497,993	50,758	10
Missouri	904,963	904,963	38,912	4
Montana	178,392	178,392	1,681	1
Nebraska	300,407	300,407	791	
Nevada	140,817	140,817	4,702	3
New Hampshire	171,934	171,934	14	
New Jersey	1,402,010	1,402,010	0	
New Mexico	278,472	278,472	14,512	5
New York	3,270,428	3,270,428	2,320	
North Carolina	1,175,272	1,175,272	50,150	4
North Dakota	126,774	126,774	77	
Ohio	2,189,492	2,189,492	110,072	5
Oklahoma	590,461	590,461	65,651	11
Oregon	470,600	470,600	7,465	2
Pennsylvania	2,151,746	2,151,746	35,712	2
Rhode Island	167,640	167,640	0	

OFFICE OF CIVIL RIGHTS STATEWIDE SURVEY OF REPORTED INCIDENCE OF CORPORAL PUNISHMENT IN SCHOOLS: 1976 *continued*

State	Total Number of Students	Total Number of Students Sampled	Number of Children in Sample Who Received Corporal Punishment	Percentage of Children Who Received Corporal Punishment[a]
South Carolina	640,291	640,291	33,322	5
South Dakota	145,644	145,644	129	
Tennessee	874,039	870,439	77,411	9
Texas	2,827,101	2,827,101	262,663	9
Utah	312,380	312,380	402	
Vermont	102,679	102,679	107	
Virginia	1,097,329	1,097,329	19,921	2
Washington	776,873	776,873	10,067	1
West Virginia	406,179	406,179	18,149	4
Wisconsin	940,072	940,072	808	
Wyoming	89,703	89,703	2,031	2
Totals	87,417,624	87,414,024	3,021,600	158

[a]Empty cell indicates incident rate of less than 1 percent.

OFFICE OF CIVIL RIGHTS STATEWIDE SURVEY OF REPORTED INCIDENCE OF CORPORAL PUNISHMENT IN SCHOOLS: 1984

State	Total Number of Students	Total Number of Students Sampled	Number of Children in Sample Who Received Corporal Punishment	Percentage of Children Who Received Corporal Punishment[a]
United States	39,451,897	0	1,332,317	
Alabama	693,070	410,202	37,383	9
Alaska	110,100	83,883	327	
Arizona	516,613	337,088	6,961	2
Arkansas	477,549	191,392	22,486	12
California	4,405,616	2,286,966	6,971	
Colorado	494,690	336,498	779	
Connecticut	553,773	269,860	353	
Delaware	98,115	80,190	4,234	5
District of Columbia	83,231	82,596	0	
Florida	1,606,364	1,105,122	97,214	9
Georgia	931,928	511,762	30,062	6
Hawaii	170,472	169,171	0	
Idaho	186,437	121,084	597	
Illinois	1,670,740	711,819	6,443	1
Indiana	1,073,575	431,908	16,040	4

OFFICE OF CIVIL RIGHTS STATEWIDE SURVEY OF REPORTED INCIDENCE OF
CORPORAL PUNISHMENT IN SCHOOLS: 1984 *continued*

State	Total Number of Students	Total Number of Students Sampled	Number of Children in Sample Who Received Corporal Punishment	Percentage of Children Who Received Corporal Punishment[a]
Iowa	453,241	157,164	281	1
Kansas	508,918	217,876	1,462	7
Kentucky	577,630	293,291	19,103	5
Louisiana	763,294	523,964	24,064	
Maine	200,454	100,608	4	
Maryland	502,435	438,515	222	
Massachusetts	763,017	276,757	0	
Michigan	1,586,176	510,236	4,448	1
Minnesota	735,185	295,239	53	
Mississippi	385,943	223,349	27,071	12
Missouri	670,000	264,160	4,603	2
Montana	165,731	84,082	332	
Nebraska	314,890	153,367	161	
Nevada	150,838	133,630	1,457	1
New Hampshire	140,812	84,470	0	
New Jersey	1,256,067	481,936	0	
New Mexico	275,386	189,090	6,544	3

New York	2,661,253	1,156,354	23	
North Carolina	1,171,378	615,919	28,790	5
North Dakota	122,405	67,708	23	5
Ohio	1,675,794	513,639	26,238	8
Oklahoma	557,257	241,050	20,384	
Oregon	511,344	251,834	556	
Pennsylvania	1,919,650	537,212	3,246	1
Rhode Island	149,881	107,494	1	
South Carolina	646,112	400,138	23,353	6
South Dakota	126,037	70,522	13	
Tennessee	866,528	461,692	42,197	9
Texas	3,193,934	1,468,395	97,398	7
Utah	437,389	328,974	8	
Vermont	88,541	45,251	0	
Virginia	919,024	608,798	2,779	
Washington	761,597	376,931	4,228	1
West Virginia	316,147	213,983	2,499	1
Wisconsin	711,053	258,216	346	
Wyoming	94,283	70,095	432	1
Totals	79,596,864	19,761,682	1,941,869	134

[a]Empty cell indicates incident rate of less than 1 percent.

OFFICE OF CIVIL RIGHTS STATEWIDE SURVEY OF REPORTED INCIDENCE OF CORPORAL PUNISHMENT IN SCHOOLS: 1986

State	Total Number of Students	Total Number of Students Sampled	Number of Children in Sample Who Received Corporal Punishment	Percentage of Children Who Received Corporal Punishment[a]
Alabama	755,824	445,708	42,770	10
Alaska	98,608	88,078	233	
Arizona	586,583	286,883	5,911	2
Arkansas	470,224	207,965	23,013	11
California	5,028,304	2,825,200	5,103	
Colorado	622,285	413,703	683	
Connecticut	492,025	262,453	89	
Delaware	86,755	85,009	1,204	1
District of Columbia	86,125	84,630	152	
Florida	1,576,212	1,318,229	87,218	7
Georgia	1,191,158	728,704	49,186	7
Hawaii	80,305	178,947	0	
Idaho	206,143	141,416	534	
Illinois	1,713,625	783,709	957	
Indiana	1,144,490	499,159	15,975	3
Iowa	482,448	210,146	269	

Kansas	459,107	222,066	1,167	1
Kentucky	632,985	353,415	14,733	4
Louisiana	786,442	569,399	23,476	4
Maine	199,191	102,608	0	
Maryland	606,441	550,694	552	
Massachusetts	763,174	382,122	0	
Michigan	1,626,732	703,700	4,322	1
Minnesota	738,500	400,640	21	
Mississippi	539,174	313,211	33,463	11
Missouri	900,172	431,065	5,589	1
Montana	180,461	91,588	158	
Nebraska	307,106	143,389	173	
Nevada	160,439	146,490	917	1
New Hampshire	157,002	92,326	0	
New Jersey	1,234,431	607,768	11	
New Mexico	286,055	214,574	6,787	3
New York	3,138,207	1,660,453	23	
North Carolina	1,043,809	634,966	18,300	3
North Dakota	120,080	69,901	5	
Ohio	1,597,848	655,304	19,747	3
Oklahoma	645,918	392,931	26,493	7
Oregon	493,929	264,046	631	
Pennsylvania	1,586,882	588,584	2,424	
Rhode Island	145,399	108,306	1	
South Carolina	560,533	412,683	21,051	5

OFFICE OF CIVIL RIGHTS STATEWIDE SURVEY OF REPORTED INCIDENCE OF
CORPORAL PUNISHMENT IN SCHOOLS: 1986 *continued*

State	Total Number of Students	Total Number of Students Sampled	Number of Children in Sample Who Received Corporal Punishment	Percentage of Children Who Received Corporal Punishment[a]
South Dakota	133,800	78,854	67	
Tennessee	745,538	448,275	42,769	10
Texas	3,342,108	1,945,398	121,862	6
Utah	336,484	293,797	55	
Vermont	76,497	41,063	0	
Virginia	993,976	959,760	3,059	
Washington	783,722	473,414	2,021	
West Virginia	340,379	229,751	2,597	1
Wisconsin	676,248	310,461	101	
Wyoming	96,153	71,422	189	
Totals	41,056,036	23,524,363	586,061	104

[a]Empty cells indicate a rate of less than 1 percent.

Appendix C

Checklist to Determine the Extent of Physical or Psychological Maltreatment in Schools

Students: I want you to think about the one worst thing that ever happened to you in school that was done by a teacher, principal, or other adult. This can be anything that happened from kindergarten until now. Tell me about it [if the child is too young to read] or write it down. Be sure to give all the details. Tell exactly what happened, who was there, what you did first, what the teacher or principal did, and what you did. [Obtain a full description.]

A. I would like you to tell me or write about how many times the teacher [or other educator] did any of these things to you.

	How Many Times
1. Put you down for not doing well	————
2. Made fun of you	————

Adapted from versions of the School Trauma Survey developed by W. Zelikoff, I. Hyman, Barbara Witkowski, Charles Lambert, Loretta Alderman, and Elizabeth Tucker. Copyright the National Center for the Study of Corporal Punishment and Alternatives in the Schools, Temple University, February 1, 1988.

3. Made you feel that you were not as good as everyone else   ————

4. Yelled at you   ————

5. Said they would do something bad to you (made a threat)   ————

6. Called you names because of what you looked like   ————

7. Put you down because of your religion or race (color)   ————

8. Let other children tease you   ————

9. Let other children hit, push, slap, or push you   ————

10. Gave you detention for no reason   ————

11. Suspended you for no reason   ————

12. Expelled you from school for no reason   ————

13. Didn't let you be a part of special subjects or activities, such as music, sports, trips, art   ————

14. Wouldn't let you go to the bathroom as punishment   ————

15. Threw things at you like a book, eraser, or something else   ————

16. Pinched or squeezed you so that it hurt   ————

17. Slapped or punched you   ————

18. Pushed you   ————

19. Grabbed you hard   ————

20. Shook you hard   ————

21. Pulled your ears or hair   ————

22. Hit you with a ruler, paddle, or something else   ————

23. Lied about you so that you got in trouble   ————

24. Ignored you, would not pay attention to you   ————

25. Made you stay alone, away from everybody   ————

26. Made sexual comments that you did not like   ————

27. Touched you sexually but did not force you   ————

28. Touched you sexually and forced you to let it happen   _____

29. Forced you to have sex   _____

30. None of these things ever happened to me   _____

If you marked more than one, go back and circle the very worst one.

B. Now I would like to find out how you felt and what happened to you because of what the teacher or principal did to you. I have a list of the kinds of things that sometimes happen to boys and girls after something bad happens to them. Check off any of the things below that happened to you [or I will read them to you, and you can tell me if it happened to you].

[If the following instructions are too difficult to follow, have the child indicate whether he or she had the symptom. If you want to obtain more information to help the child, it is better to use the whole scale.]

If the sentence describes how you felt or acted after the worst school experience you wrote about, put an **A, B, C, D,** or **E** on each of the three lines below to show:

In **Column 1:** How many times you felt or acted this way
In **Column 2:** How long it lasted
In **Column 3:** How much of a problem this was for you

Use these boxes to find the right letter for each question:

Column 1 How many times	**Column 2** How long it lasted	**Column 3** How much of a problem
A = one time	A = one day	A = none
B = a few times	B = one week	B = a little
C = sometimes	C = one month	C = some
D = many times	D = 1 month to 1 year	D = much
E = all the time	E = more than 1 year	E = a lot

	Column 1	**Column 2**	**Column 3**
1. I worried about how I was doing in my schoolwork.	——	——	——
2. I tried to stay away from the person who did it.	——	——	——
3. I got headaches.	——	——	——
4. Every little thing started to bother me.	——	——	——
5. I had bad dreams about what happened.	——	——	——
6. I thought I was not as good a kid as I used to be.	——	——	——
7. I got angry very fast.	——	——	——
8. I couldn't control how I acted or felt.	——	——	——
9. I was afraid the person would do it to me again.	——	——	——
10. I thought about what happened, though I didn't want to.	——	——	——
11. I didn't do things outside of school as much as I used to (clubs, sports, friends).	——	——	——
12. I did whatever I wanted to do even if other people didn't like it.	——	——	——
13. I couldn't sit still anymore.	——	——	——

14. I got in trouble in class. ___ ___ ___

15. I picked on other kids. ___ ___ ___

16. I thought about things I could do to get back at the person who did it. ___ ___ ___

17. I had nightmares. ___ ___ ___

18. I hated school. ___ ___ ___

19. I got stomachaches. ___ ___ ___

20. I got twitches in a part of my body because I was nervous. ___ ___ ___

21. I had trouble thinking because I kept remembering what happened. ___ ___ ___

22. I cut classes. ___ ___ ___

23. I skipped school. ___ ___ ___

24. Adults started to upset me more than before. ___ ___ ___

25. I "mouthed off" to adults. ___ ___ ___

26. I stayed away from the place where it happened. ___ ___ ___

27. I spent a lot of time by myself. ___ ___ ___

28. I lost my appetite and did not eat. ___ ___ ___

29. I tried to get people to be nice to me. ___ ___ ___

30. I tried to stay away from people who were there when it happened.   ——   ——   ——

31. I couldn't think about things for as long as I used to.   ——   ——   ——

32. When somebody was nasty to me, it got me more upset than it used to.   ——   ——   ——

33. I was more tired than I used to be.   ——   ——   ——

34. I couldn't get as excited about things as before.   ——   ——   ——

35. It was harder to make myself do the things that I had to do.   ——   ——   ——

36. I got bad grades in school.   ——   ——   ——

37. Thinking about school made me cry.   ——   ——   ——

38. I didn't like things that made me think about what happened.   ——   ——   ——

39. I couldn't remember anything about what happened.   ——   ——   ——

40. I had trouble falling or staying asleep.   ——   ——   ——

41. I wanted to stay near my mom or dad.   ——   ——   ——

42. Parts of my body hurt.   ——   ——   ——

43. I was afraid to let anyone touch me. ——— ——— ———

44. I said I was sick so I could stay home. ——— ——— ———

45. I didn't do my homework. ——— ——— ———

46. I tried not to think about what happened. ——— ——— ———

47. I thought that my life would never get better. ——— ——— ———

48. I kept an eye on adults so that I wouldn't get hurt again. ——— ——— ———

49. I wished I was dead. ——— ——— ———

50. I talked about what happened. ——— ——— ———

51. I got nervous about things. ——— ——— ———

52. I was jumpy when something surprised me. ——— ——— ———

53. I stuttered. ——— ——— ———

54. I had a hard time re-membering things about school. ——— ——— ———

55. I didn't trust adults. ——— ——— ———

56. I threw up when I thought about school. ——— ——— ———

57. I sucked my thumb. ——— ——— ———

58. I went to the bath-room in my pants. ——— ——— ———

59. I went to the bath-
room in my sleep. ———— ———— ————

60. I was not as happy as
I used to be. ———— ———— ————

61. Pictures of what hap-
pened popped into
my mind. ———— ———— ————

62. I was afraid to go to
bed by myself. ———— ———— ————

63. I bit my nails. ———— ———— ————

64. I thought that I was
the one who was
wrong about what
happened. ———— ———— ————

65. I stayed away from
my family. ———— ———— ————

66. I stayed away from
my friends. ———— ———— ————

67. I ignored my family. ———— ———— ————

68. I ignored my friends. ———— ———— ————

69. I couldn't talk about
what happened. ———— ———— ————

70. I was afraid of any
adult who was like
the one who did it to
me. ———— ———— ————

71. I felt like fighting all
the time. ———— ———— ————

72. I wished that I was a
little kid again. ———— ———— ————

When the student completes this form you will have a good idea of the results of his or her worst school experience. In the ideal situation, your child should have had no experience bad enough to result in stress-related symptoms. This is probably true for around half of all school children. Some schools have low rates of maltreatment, and some have very high rates.

If your child does indicate one of the "worst school experiences" and you wish to discover how badly he or she is affected, you can score the scale. In order to score the scale, convert each letter under the headings how many times, how long It lasted, and how much of a problem to a numerical value as follows: $A = 1$; $B = 2$; $C = 3$; $D = 4$; and $E = 5$. Add each column; you will then have three total scores. Now add the three total scores. scores.

The average total score from our first sample is 65 (Lambert 1990). This means that the respondent with a score of 65 has or has had symptoms equal to the average for students who have been maltreated. This does not mean the child is average, and you need not worry. (For instance, let us assume you obtained an average for the length of bone fractures of all students who fractured their bones playing football. If the average was 65 millimeters, you would not say that a player with a fracture of only 20 millimeters didn't have a problem. Only you and your child can determine if a low score is not significant. Even if the score is low, you might want to see a psychologist if the problem is significant for your child. Higher scores, however, do suggest problems that definitely need attention.)

A score of 115 places the student in the upper 15 percent; 139 places the student in the upper 10 percent, and 164 in the upper 4 percent. While we have not yet developed norms to show which students have EIPTSD, it is clear from our research that the students in the upper 15 percent are similar to the students whom I have evaluated and diagnosed as suffering from EIPTSD. If you are worried about post-traumatic stress disorder, take this form to a school or child psychologist or psychiatrist who is independent of the school district where the event occurred so that you can develop a plan for help.

Appendix D

Some Alternatives to the Use of Physical Punishment

Short-Range Solutions

The first step to take is to eliminate the use of punishment as a means of maintaining discipline. Then the following ideas can be used as temporary measures to maintain discipline while longer-range programs are being put into effect.

- Quiet places (corners, small rooms, retreats).
- Student-teacher agreement on immediate alternatives.
- Teaming of adults—teachers, administrators, aides, and volunteers (parents and others)—to take students aside when they are disruptive and listen to them, talk to them, and counsel them until the instability subsides.
- Similar services for educators whose stamina is exhausted.
- Social workers, psychologists, and psychiatrists to work on a one-to-one basis with disruptive students or distraught teachers.
- Provision of alternative experiences for students who are bored, turned off, or otherwise unreceptive to particular educational experiences. They include independent projects, listening and viewing experiences with technological learning devices, library research, student-teacher human rela-

From National Education Association (1972), with additions from NCSCPAS.

tions retreats and outings, and teacher (or other staff) student-parent conferences.

- In-service programs to help teachers and other school staff learn a variety of techniques for building better interpersonal relations between themselves and students and among students. These include class meetings, role playing, case study, student-teacher human relations retreats and outings, and teacher (or other staff) conferences with students and parents.

- Class discussion of natural consequences of good and bad behavior (not threats or promises), of what behavior is right, of what behavior achieves desired results, and of causes of a "bad day" for the class.

- Privileges to bestow or withdraw.

- Approval or disapproval.

- Other staff members to work with a class whose teacher needs a break.

Intermediate-Range Solutions

- Staff-student jointly developed discipline policy and procedures.
- Staff-student committee to implement discipline policy.
- Parent education programs in interpersonal relations.
- Staff in-service program on interpersonal relations, on understanding emotions, and on dealing with children when they are disruptive.
- Student human relations councils and grievance procedure.
- Training for students and teachers in crisis intervention.
- Training for teachers in dealing with fear of physical violence.
- Training for students in student advocacy.
- Regular opportunities for principals to experience classroom situations.

Long-Range Solutions in Schools

- Full involvement of students in the decision-making process in the school.
- Curriculum content revision and expansion by students and staff to motivate student interest.
- Teacher in-service programs on new teaching strategies to maintain student interest.
- Alternate programs for students.
- Work-study programs.
- Drop-out, drop-back-in programs.
- Alternative schools within the public school system.
- Early entrance to college.
- Alternatives to formal program during last two years of high school.
- Few enough students per staff member that staff can get to know students.
- Adequate professional specialists: psychiatrists, psychologists, and social workers.
- Aides and technicians to carry out paraprofessional, clerical, and technical duties so that professional staff are free to work directly with students more of the time.
- A wide variety of learning materials and technological devices.
- Full implementation of the *Code of Student Rights.*
- Full implementation of National Education Association Resolution 71-12, Student Involvement:

The National Education Association believes that genuine student involvement requires responsible student action which is possible if students are guaranteed certain basic rights, among which are the following: the right to free inquiry and expression; the right to due process; the right to freedom of association; the right to freedom of peaceful assembly and petition;

the right to participate in the governance of the school, college, and university; the right to freedom from discrimination; and the right to equal educational opportunity.

Long-Range Solutions with Other Agencies

- Staff help from local and regional mental health and human relations agencies.
- More consultant staff to work with individual problem students.
- Mass media presentations directed to both the public and the profession on the place of children in contemporary American society.
- Long-range intensive in-service programs to prepare all staff to act as counselors.
- Some educational experiences relocated to business, industry, and social agencies.
- Increased human relations training in preservice teacher education and specific preparation in constructive disciplinary procedures.

Additional Solutions

- A clearly presented and unambiguous definition of the schools' and/or particular classrooms' conduct codes, curriculum, administrative procedures for dealing with disciplinary problems, grading system, and procedures for requesting and availability of special services.
- Structuring the classroom in a way to minimize oppositional or negative behavior. Three major areas in this regard are emphasizing the students' concern about who they are (identify), how they relate to others (relationship), and how they can influence what happens to them (power). When these concerns are ignored, students are likely to become hostile or tune out. Strategies recommended include the following:

- Have group discussions of problem situations.

- Provide opportunities for students to interact with each other, share in decision making, and experience ways of learning that accommodate different styles of learning.

- Classrooms structured in a compartmentalized learning center format and what Kopple refers to as the "problems, plans, and sharing" format (a time set aside for students to air concerns, help plan for individual or group work, and so forth).

- Help to facilitate a teacher's awareness and understanding of his or her own feelings as they relate to students, individual needs, motivations, and other areas.

- "One door to the right": A child who gets beyond the tolerance level for a teacher is sent to the classroom next door. The change in group and place is sometimes enough to help the child at the moment.

- Attempt to recognize the feelings of the child and then follow through with a clear statement regarding the inappropriateness of the particular behavior. Followed by clarifying limits, boundaries, and alternatives for the behavior.

- Self-disclosure, "messages," and other similar techniques.

- Life Space interview technique. First, listen; try to find out the child's psychological perception of the event. Ask the child what he or she thinks should be done about the situation. Highlight the reality of the situation for the child. Explore the child's motivation for change and explore alternatives. Develop a plan or contract.

- Journal entries reflecting both positive and negative aspects of a student's behavior.

- Peer pressure in the form of competition between class teams to earn points for being good. (Use with caution to avoid bullying.)

- Keep chart for progress in the desired behavior direction. No matter how slight, when progress is noticed, reinforce it verbally or through other positive means.

- Carpets in the classroom. Carpeting can help calm young

children who are often easily overstimulated by environmental noise.

- Peer counseling in secondary schools.
- Knowledge and understanding of the development and growth patterns of students allow the teacher to realize whether certain behaviors and trends are characteristic of a child's level of maturity. deFafra (1968) suggests a variety of practical management techniques for the classroom, among them:
- Provide adequate instruction at the appropriate instructional level for each pupil.
- Be aware of each pupil's background and previous experience.
- Avoid punishing the entire group as a result of misbehavior by a few individuals.
- Convey rejection of a behavior, not an individual.
- Never give additional homework as a punishment.
- Recognize that much of unacceptable behavior is a symptom of a possible need for attention, affection, expression of fear, resentment, insecurity, or something else.
- Make the punishment for the individual, not necessarily the offense.
- Avoid punishing in the heat of your own anger.
- A visit by teacher to the home of a student with child and parents present can be both revealing and helpful.
- Avoid personally or publicly humiliating an individual.
- Do not take taunting, provocative, or aggressive behaviors as a personal affront. Be aware you are an authority figure in the eyes of most of your students.
- Use seating arrangements as a tool to achieve good discipline.
- If consequences for misbehavior are not always carried out by the teacher, the resultant inconsistency may result in children disregarding requests for control, work, and attentiveness.

- A child who exhibits low frustration tolerance and poor impulse control may respond enthusiastically to a simple behavior modification program. After obtaining a measure or estimate of the child's specific undesirable behavior, present him or her with a daily or weekly chart and a set of positive reinforcements (free time, "homework passes," candy, fruit, nuts, stars, extra credit). Explain the behavior shaping program to the child. Make initial goals easily attainable. Reward generously at first for the desired and attained behavior. Be absolutely consistent. Avoid punishing relapses; just reinforce the positive developments. Discuss the program with the appropriate administrator and parents before it begins. Pair the tangible reinforcers with praise. Over time gradually work toward withdrawing the reinforcement. Eventually give just verbal approval.

Appendix E

Laws Governing Corporal Punishment

Information was compiled by Jacqueline Clarke, 1985 for NCSCPAS.

State	Standard for Civil Tort Liability		Does State Law Authorize School Personnel to Corporally Punish Children	
	Punishment Must Be Reasonable	Punishment Must Be Without Malice/Cannot Cause Permanent Injury	Authorizes Teachers and/or Principals	Authorizes Teachers, Principals, and Others
Alabama				
Alaska				
Arizona	●			
Arkansas	●			
California				
Colorado				
Connecticut	●			
Delaware			●	
District of Columbia				
Florida	●			●
Georgia	●			
Hawaii				
Idaho				
Illinois		●		
Indiana	●			●
Iowa	●			
Kansas				
Kentucky	●		●	
Louisiana	●			
Maine	●			
Maryland				

Does State Law Authorize School Personnel to Corporally Punish Children		Standards for Criminal Liability		
Authorizes School District	Expressly Forbids Corporal Punishment	Corporal Punishment Must Be Reasonable	Corporal Punishment Must Be Without Malice or Not Cause Permanent Injury	State Has a Justification Statute
	•			
	•			
		•		•
		•		•
	•			
	•			
				•
	•			
				•
•				•
	•			•
	•			
		•	•	
	•			
		•		
				•
	•			•
•				

Laws Governing Corporal Punishment continued

State	Standard for Civil Tort Liability		Does State Law Authorize School Personnel to Corporally Punish Children	
	Punishment Must Be Reasonable	Punishment Must Be Without Malice/Cannot Cause Permanent Injury	Authorizes Teachers and/or Principals	Authorizes Teachers, Principals, and Others
Massachusetts	●			
Michigan				
Minnesota				
Mississippi				
Missouri	●			
Montana			●	
Nebraska				
Nevada				
New Hampshire	●			
New Jersey				
New Mexico				
New York			●	
North Carolina		●	●	
North Dakota				
Ohio	●			●
Oklahoma			●	
Oregon				
Pennsylvania	●		●	

| Does State Law Authorize School Personnel to Corporally Punish Children | | Standards for Criminal Liability | | |
Authorizes School District	Expressly Forbids Corporal Punishment	Corporal Punishment Must Be Reasonable	Corporal Punishment Must Be Without Malice or Not Cause Permanent Injury	State Has a Justification Statute
	●			
	●			
	●			
		●		
				●
	●			
●				
	●			
	●			
	●			
			●	
	●			
			●	
				●
	●			
			●	

Laws Governing Corporal Punishment continued

| | Standard for Civil Tort Liability | | Does State Law Authorize School Personnel to Corporally Punish Children | |
| | Punishment Must Be Reasonable | Punishment Must Be Without Malice/Cannot Cause Permanent Injury | Authorizes Teachers and/or Principals | Authorizes Teachers, Principals, and Others |
State				
Puerto Rico				
Rhode Island				
South Carolina				
South Dakota				●
Tennessee	●			
Texas	●			
Utah				
Vermont	●			●
Virginia			●	
Washington				
West Virginia				
Wisconsin				
Wyoming				

Does State Law Authorize School Personnel to Corporally Punish Children		Standards for Criminal Liability		
Authorizes School District	Expressly Forbids Corporal Punishment	Corporal Punishment Must Be Reasonable	Corporal Punishment Must Be Without Malice or Not Cause Permanent Injury	State Has a Justification Statute
•	•			
	•			
•				
				•
		•		
		•		•
				•
	•			
				•
				•

Nineteen states and fifty-nine major American cities ban the use of corporal punishment.

In *Massachusetts,* corporal punishment has been illegal for about ten years. This law was recently amended to permit school personnel to use reasonable force to protect themselves or others from bodily harm. Each school district is allowed to establish its own disciplinary code(s).

In 1867, *New Jersey* passed a law banning the use of corporal punishment, thus making it the first state to have such a statute. This state prohibits physical punishment in all schools, public and nonpublic. The statute includes a clause that allows the use of reasonable force to prevent harm to oneself and/or others.

Maine has prohibited corporal punishment for about twelve years. The law states that physical force should be used only to restrain someone from hurting another or themselves.

Hawaii passed a regulation in 1982 that prohibited the use of corporal punishment.

In 1984, *Vermont* passed a ban on the use of corporal punishment but reserved the right to implement the reasonable and necessary clause in case of emergency.

In *Rhode Island,* neither state law nor school board regulation denies educators the right to use corporal punishment. Each of the twenty-seven local school boards has individually developed its own anti–corporal punishment policy. Although there is no law in Rhode Island regarding corporal punishment, a regulation of the state board of education governs its use. It states that it may be allowed only in cases of self-defense or under "very exceptional circumstances." It is not felt to be a "desirable method" of discipline.

In *Illinois* and *Pennsylvania* parents may request that corporal punishment not be used on their child.

In *Michigan* and *Texas,* the local school districts must adopt their own policies.

In *Louisiana, Oklahoma, Pennsylvania,* and *West Virginia,* laws place the educators in loco parentis.

Laws in *North Carolina* do not allow school boards to deny administrators and teachers the right to hit children.

The commonwealth of *Puerto Rico* has laws prohibiting its use.

References

American Psychiatric Association (1980). *Diagnostic and statistical manual of mental disorders*. 3d ed. Washington, D.C.: American Psychiatric Association.

———— (1987). *Diagnostic and statistical manual of mental disorders*. 3d ed. Washington, D.C.: American Psychiatric Association.

Babcock, A. (1977). A cross cultural examination of corporal punishment: An initial theoretical conceptualization. In J. Wise (ed.), *Proceedings: Conference on corporal punishment in schools*. Washington, D.C.: National Institute of Education.

Bacon, G., and Hyman, I. (1979). Brief of the American psychological association task force on the rights of children and youth as amicus curiae in support of petitioners in the case of *Ingraham v. Wright*. In I. Hyman and J. Wise (eds.), *Corporal punishment in American education*. Philadelphia: Temple University Press.

Baily, T., and Baily, W. (1986). *Operational definitions of child emotional maltreatment*. Augusta: Bureau of Social Services, Main Department of Human Services.

Bandura, A. (1973). *Aggression: A social learning analysis*. Englewood Cliffs, N.J.: Prentice-Hall.

Bandura, A., and Huston, A. (1961). Identification as a process of incidental learning. *Journal of Abnormal and Experimental Psychology 63*, 311–318.

Bandura, A., and Walters, R. (1963). *Social learning and personality development*. New York: Holt, Rinehart & Winston.

Bellak, L., and Antell, M. (1979). An intercultural study of aggressive behavior on children's playgrounds. In I. Hyman and J. Wise (eds.), *Corporal punishment in American education*. Philadelphia: Temple University Press.

Bogacki, D. (1981). Attitudes toward corporal punishment: Authoritarian personality and pupil control ideology of school personnel. Ph.D. dissertation, Temple University.

Bongiovanni, A. (1979). An analysis of research on punishment and its relation to the use of corporal punishment in the schools. In I. Hyman and J. Wise (eds.), *Corporal punishment in American education*. Philadelphia: Temple University Press.

Brassard, M.; Germain, R.; and Hart, S. (eds.) (1987). *Psychological maltreatment of children and youth*. New York: Pergamon.

Breznitz, S. (ed.) (1983). *Stress in Israel*. New York: Van Nostrand Reinhold.

Brown, G. W. (1977). School: Child advocate or adversary? *Clinical Pediatrics 16* (5), 439–446.

Butterfield, K. (May 19, 1983). Bartonville police studying charges of physical abuse. *Peoria Journal Star* (ILL).

Caplan, G. (1970). *The theory and practice of mental health consultation.* New York: Basic Books.

Carmen, E.; Reiker, P.; and Mills, T. (1984). Victims of violence and psychiatric illness. *American Journal of Psychiatry 141,* 378–383.

Cassie, K. (1979). Discipline in Soviet schools. In I. Hyman and J. Wise (eds.), *Corporal punishment in American education.* Philadelphia: Temple University Press.

Chandler, L.A., and Shermis, M.D. (1985). The use of the stress response scale in diagnostic assessment with children. *Journal of Psychoeducational Assessment 3*(1), 15–29.

Clarke, J. (1986). Some effects of corporal punishment and psychological abuse on school students and their parents. Ph.D. dissertation, Temple University.

Clarke, J.; Erdlen, R.; and Hyman, I.A. (1984). Analysis of recent corporal punishment cases reported in national newspapers. Paper presented at the annual convention of the National Association of School Psychologists, Philadelphia, April.

Clarke, J.; Liberman-Lascoe, R.; and Hyman, I.A. (1982). Corporal punishment as reported in nationwide newspapers. *Child and Youth Services 4* (1, 2), 47–56.

Collins, D. (1963). *Dickens and Education.* London: McMillan and Co.

Cordes, C. (1984). Researchers flunk Reagan on discipline theme. *A.P.A. Monitor,* March 12.

Cosby, W. (1986). *Fatherhood.* Garden City, N.Y.: Doubleday.

Cunningham v. Beavers. 858 F.2d 269 (5th Cir. 1988).

Danieli, Y. (1985). The treatment and prevention of long-term effects and intergenerational transmission of victimization: A lesson from Holocaust survivors and their children. In C. Figley (ed.), *Trauma and its wake.* New York: Brunner/Mazel.

deFafra, C. (1968). *Sixty-two suggestions to improve classroom discipline.* West Orange, N.J.: Economics Press.

Dempster, F. (1988). The spacing effect: A case study of the failure to apply the results of psychological research. *American Psychologist, 43*(8):627–634.

Dennison, E. (1984). Elementary school principals' knowledge, attitude, and use of corporal punishment. Unpublished thesis, West Virginia College of Graduate Studies.

Deykin, E.Y.; Alpert, J.J.; and McNamara, J.J. (1985). A pilot study of the effect of exposure to child abuse or neglect on adolescent suicidal behavior. *American Journal of Psychiatry 142*(11), 1299–1303.

Downey, B. (1973). Soviet discipline. In G. Lane (ed.), *Impressions of Soviet Education.* Washington: George Washington University Press.

Ehrenreich, B., and Nasaw, D. (1983). Kids as consumers and commodities. *Nation, 236* (May 14):597–599.

Elam, S. (1989). The second annual Gallup/Phi Delta Kappa poll of teachers' attitudes toward the public schools. *Phi Delta Kappan 70* (10), 785–798.

Eron, L.; Walder, L.; and Lefkowitz, M. (1971). *Learning aggression in children.* Boston: Little, Brown.

Eyre, R. (1984). Teacher firing. *Dallas Times Herald,* April 29.

Farley, A. (1983). National survey of the use and non-use of corporal punishment as a disciplinary technique in U.S. public schools. Ph.D. dissertation, Temple University.

Farber, E.D., and Joseph, J.A. (1985). The maltreated adolescent: Patterns of physical abuse. Special issue: C. Henry Kempe memorial research issue. *Child Abuse and Neglect 9*(2), 201–206.

Figley, C.R. (1985). *Trauma and its wake.* New York: Brunner/Mazel.

Finkelhor, D., and Browne, A. (1985). The traumatic impact of child sexual abuse: A conceptualization. *American Journal of Orthopsychiatry 55*(4), 530–541.

Fraser, M. (1973). *Children in conflict.* London: Harmondsworth.

Frederick, C. (1986). Human induced violence. Paper presented at the Second Annual Meeting of the Society for Traumatic Stress Studies, Denver, September 26.

Freeman, C. (1979). The children's petition of 1669 and its sequel. In I. Hyman and J. Wise (eds.), *Corporal punishment in American education.* Philadelphia: Temple University Press.

Freeman, T., and Weir, D. (1983). Polluting the most vulnerable. *Nation,* May 14, 600–604.

Garbarino, J., and Yondra, J. (1983). Psychological maltreatment of children and youth. In S. Hart, M. Brassard, and B. Germain (eds.), *Proceedings of the International Conference on Psychological Abuse of Children and Youth.* Indianapolis: Center for the Study of the Psychological Rights of the Child, University of Indiana–Indianapolis.

Garbarino, J.; Guttman, E.; and Seeley, J. (1986). *The psychologically battered child.* San Francisco: Jossey-Bass.

Garcia v. Miera, 817 F.2d 650 (10th Cir. 1987).

Garmezy, N. (1982). Children under severe stress: Critique and commentary. *Journal of the American Academy of Child Psychiatry 25*(3), 384–392.

Gasphersohn v. Harnett County Board of Education, 75 N.C. App. 23, 28, 330 S.E.2d. 489, 493 (1985), appeal denied, 314 N.C. 539 (1985).

Gelles, R., and Strauss, M. (1979). Violence in the American family. *Journal of Social Issues 35,* 15–39.

Gibson, I. (1978). *The English vice.* London: Duckworth.

Gil, D. (1970). *Violence against children.* Boston: Harvard University Press.

Glackman, T.; Berv, V.; Martin, R.; McDowell, E.; Spino, R.; and Hyman, I.A. (1978). The relation between corporal punishment, suspensions and discrimination. *Inequality in Education 23,* 61–65.

Gold, H. (1978). Children's rights and child abuse. *Day Care and Early Education* (Spring), 25–27.

Greven, P. (1977). *The Protestant temperament.* New York: Alfred Knopf.

Handford, H.A.; Mayes, S.D.; Mattison, R.E.; Humphrey, F.J.; Bagnato, S.; Bixler, E.D.; and Kales, J.D. (1986). Child and parent reaction to the Three Mile Island nuclear accident. *Journal of the American Academy of Child Psychiatry 25*(3), 346–356.

Harbison, J., and Harbison, J. (1980). *A society under stress: Children and young people of Northern Ireland.* Somerset, England: Open Books.

Hart, S. (1987). Psychological maltreatment in schooling. *School Psychology Review 16* (2), 169–180.

Hart, S.; Brassard, M.; and Germaine, B. (eds.) (1983). *Proceedings of the International Conference on Psychological Abuse of Children and Youth.* Indianapolis: Center for the Study of the Psychological Rights of the Child, University of Indiana–Indianapolis.

Hewitt, J. (1981). Corporal punishment: The tip of the authoritarian iceberg. Ph.D. dissertation, University of Toronto.

Hughes, H., and Barad, S. (1983). Psychological functioning of children in a battered women's shelter: Preliminary investigation. *American Journal of Orthopsychiatry 53*, 525–531.

Hyman, I. (1970). Democracy, mental health and achievement: A modern educational mythology. In *Annual yearbook of New Jersey Association of Secondary School Teachers.* East Orange, New Jersey.

——— (1978). A social science review of evidence cited in litigation on corporal punishment in schools. *Journal of Child Clinical Psychology 7*, 195–200.

——— (1985). Psychological abuse in the schools: A school psychologist's perspective. Paper presented at the meeting of the American Psychological Association, Los Angeles.

——— (1987). Psychological correlates of corporal punishment and physical abuse. In M. Brassard, S. Hart, and B. Germaine (eds.), *Psychological maltreatment of children and youth.* Elmsford, N.Y.: Pergamon Press.

——— (1988a). Corporal punishment in the schools. In *Encyclopedia of school administration and supervision.* Phoenix, Ariz.: Oryx Press.

——— (1988b). Eliminating corporal punishment in schools: Moving from advocacy research to policy implementation. Paper presented at the Ninety-sixth Annual Convention of the American Psychological Association, Atlanta, Georgia, August 13.

——— (1988c). School psychology: A retreat from excellence. *Education Week,* Sept. 21, p. 40.

——— (1989a). Advocacy research to change public policy: A case study. Paper presented at the Annual Convention of the American Psychological Association, New Orleans.

——— (1989b). The make-believe world of *Lean on Me. Education Week,* 27 (April 26).

Hyman, I.A.; Bilus, F.; Dennehy, M.N.; Feldman, G.; Flannagan, D.; Maital, S.; and McDowell, E. (1979). Discipline in American education. *Journal of Education 7*(2), 51–70.

Hyman, I.; Clarke, J.; and Erdlen, R. (1987). An analysis of physical abuse in American schools. *Aggressive Behavior 13*, 1–7.

Hyman, I.A., and D'Allesandro, J. (1984). Good old-fashioned discipline: The politics of punitiveness. *Phi Delta Kappan 66* (1), 39–45.

Hyman, I., and Fina, A. (1983). National Center for the Study of Corporal Punishment and Alternatives in the Schools: Moving from policy formation to implementation. *Journal of Clinical Child Psychology 12* (Winter), 257–260.

Hyman, I.A.; Fudell, R.; Johnson, R.; and Clarke, J. (1985). Child abuse in the schools: Community and judicial attitudes. Paper presented at the meeting of the American Orthopsychiatric Association, New York, April.

Hyman, I., and Lally, D. (1982). The effectiveness of staff development programs to improve school discipline. *Urban Review 14* (3), 181–196.

Hyman, I., and Schreiber, K. (1975). Selected concepts and practices of child advocacy in school psychology. *Psychology in the Schools 12*(1), 50–58.

Hyman, I.A., and Wise, J. (1979). *Corporal punishment in American education.* Philadelphia: Temple University Press.

Hyman, I.; Zelikoff, W.; and Clarke, J. (1988). Psychological and physical abuse in schools: A paradigm for understanding posttraumatic stress disorder in children. *Journal of Traumatic Stress 1*(2), 243–267.

Ingraham v. Wright, 45 U.S.L.W. 4364 (4/19/77).

Jaffe, P.; Wolfe, D.; Wilson, S.; and Zack, L. (1986). Similarities in behavioral and social maladjustment among child victims and witnesses to family violence. *American Journal of Orthopsychiatry 56*(1), 142–146.

Janus, M.; McCormack, A.; and Burgess, A. (1986). Symptomatology associated with post traumatic stress disorder. In *Running for their lives: Youth in turmoil.* Lexington, Mass.: Lexington Books.

Kija, J.; Oropallo, C.; and Hyman, I. (1988). Can attitudes towards corporal punishment be changed in the Deep South? Paper presented at the Annual Meeting of the National Association of School Psychologists, Chicago, April 8.

King, P. (1989). Evidence for a moral tradition. *Psychology Today, 23*(1), 72–73.

Kopple, H. (1975). Alternatives to corporal punishment. Paper presented to the American Psychological Association, September 1.

Kounin, J. (1977). *Discipline and group management.* New York: Holt, Rinehart & Winston.

Kreutter, K. (1982). Student and teacher attitudes toward disciplinary practices in a junior high setting. Ph.D. dissertation, Temple University.

Krugman, R.D., and Krugman, M.K. (1984). Emotional abuse in the classroom. *American Journal of Disease of Children 138* (March), 284–286.

Lambert, C. (1990). A factorial structure of a scale measuring stress responses of students as a result of maltreatment in school. Unpublished dissertation, Temple University.

Lambert, C.; Witkowski, B.; Hyman, I.; Alderman, L.; and Tucker, E. (1988). Psychological and physical abuse in the schools: A survey of students. Paper presented at the Annual Meeting of the National Association of School Psychologists, Chicago.

Lamberth, R. (1979). The effects of punishment on academic achievement: A review of recent research. In I. Hyman and J. Wise (eds.), *Corporal punishment in American education.* Philadelphia: Temple University Press.

Lamphear, V.S. (1985). The impact of maltreatment on children's psychosocial adjustment: A review of the research. Special issue: C. Henry Kempe memorial research issue. *Child Abuse and Neglect 9*(2), 251–263.

Laury, G.V., and Meerloo, J.A. (1967). Mental cruelty and child abuse. *Psychiatric Quarterly 41*(2), 203–254.

Lifton, R.J. (1967). *Death in life: Survivors of Hiroshima.* New York: Random House.

Lifton, R.J., and Olson, E. (1976). The human meaning of total disaster: The Buffalo Creek experience. *Psychiatry 39*, 1–18.

Lindy, J.D., and Tichener, J. (1983). Acts of God and man: Long-term character change in survivors of disasters and the law. *Behavioral Sciences and the Law 1*(3), 85–96.

Lennox, N. (1982). Teacher use of corporal punishment as a function of modeling behavior. Ph.D. dissertation, Temple University.

Logan, J. (1989). Educators evaluate Joe Clark's methods. *Philadelphia Inquirer,* March 17, 1989. 1D–8D.

McCord, J. (1988). Parental aggressiveness and physical punishment in long-term perspective. In G. Hotaling, D. Finkelhor, J. Kilpatrick, and M. Straus (eds.), *Family abuse and its consequences.* Newbury Park, Calif.: Sage Publications.

McDowell, E., and Friedman, R. (1979). An analysis of editorial opinions regarding corporal punishment: Some dynamics of regional differences. In I.A. Hyman and J. Wise (eds.), *Corporal punishment in American education.* Philadelphia: Temple University Press.

Manning, J. (1979). Discipline in the good old days. In I. Hyman and J. Wise (eds.), *Corporal punishment in American education.* Philadelphia: Temple University Press.

Milgram, R.M., and Milgram, N.A. (1976). The effects of the Yom Kippur War on anxiety levels in Israeli children. *Journal of Professional Psychology 94,* 107–113.

Miller, A. (1980). *For your own good.* New York: Farrar, Straus & Giroux.

Minor, M. and Hyman, I. (1988). Psychological types of secondary teachers and their ratings of the seriousness of student misbehaviors. *Journal of Psychological Type, 14,* 25–31.

Mishkin, A. (1987). Corporal punishment: Why some parents use less severe discipline practices than they experienced as children. Ph.D. dissertation, Temple University.

Montague, A. (1983). Review of For Your Own Good. *Psychology Today,* May: 80–81.

Moskovitz, S. (1983). *Love despite hate: Child survivors of the Holocaust and their adult lives.* New York: Schocken Books.

National Center for the Study of Corporal Punishment and Alternatives in the Schools (1989). *Publication List.* Philadelphia: Temple University.

National Education Association (1972). *Report of the Task Force on Corporal Punishment.* Washington, D.C.: National Education Association.

Oates, R.K.; Forrest, D.; and Peacock, A. (1985). Self-esteem of abused children. Special issue: C. Henry Kempe memorial research issue. *Child Abuse and Neglect 9*(2), 159–163.

Oliner, P. (1988). *The altruistic personality: Rescuers of Jews in Europe.* New York: Free Press.

Pennsylvania State Education Association v. Commonwealth of Pennsylvania Department of Public Welfare, et al. Respondents (1982). *School Law Information Exchange 19* (74). Harrisburg, Pa.: Pennsylvania School Board Solicitors Association.

Player's punishment reported by witnesses (1978). *Virginia Tribune,* March 27.

Pokalo, M. (1986). Caregivers' attitudes toward the severity of punishment for forty-four misbehaviors in mental retardation institutions. Ph.D. dissertation, Temple University.

Polier, J.W. (1975). Professional abuse of children: Responsibility for the delivery of services. *American Journal of Orthopsychiatry 45* (3), 357–362.

Porter, B., and O'Leary, K. (1980). Marital discord and childhood behavior problems. *Journal of Abnormal Child Psychology 80,* 287–295.

Psychologist criticizes "closet" punishment (1983). *News American* (Baltimore), November 8.

Pynoos, R., and Eth, S. (1985). Developmental perspectives on psychic trauma. In C.R. Figley (ed.), *Trauma and its wake.* New York: Brunner/Mazel.

Radbill, S. (1974). A history of child abuse and infanticide. In R. Helford and C. Kempe (eds.), *The battered child.* Chicago: University of Chicago Press.

Raifman, L.J. (1983). Problems of diagnosis and legal causation in courtroom use of post-traumatic stress disorder. *Behavioral Sciences and the Law 1* (3), 115–130.

Richardson, L. (1981). The lost day of Stephanie Halbert. *Times Herald* (Texas), October 1.

Risinger, C. (1989). Texas public school principals and corporal punishment: the relationship between their legal awareness of it and their attitude toward its use. Unpublished dissertation, University of North Texas.

Roland, B.C.; Zelhart, P.F.; Cochran, S.W.; and Funderburk, V.W. (1985). MMPI correlates of clinical women who report early sexual abuse. *Journal of Clinical Psychology 41*(6), 763–766.

Rose, T. (1984). Current uses of corporal punishment in American public schools. *Journal of Educational Psychology 76,* (3), 427–441.

Rosenbaum, A., and O'Leary, K. (1981). Children: The unintended victims of marital violence. *American Journal of Orthopsychiatry 51,* 692–699.

Rossi, F. (1987). The toughest principal in America. *Philadelphia Inquirer Magazine,* March 22, 16–23.

Rounds, J. (1988). Jury finds Douglass guilty. *Hershey Chronicle* (Pennsylvania), September 28, 1–2.

Russell, W. (1988). Analysis of OCR data from 1978–1986. Unpublished paper. Philadelphia: NCSCPAS, Temple University.

——— (1989). The OCR data on corporal punishment: What does it really mean. Paper presented at the Third National Conference on Abolishing Corporal Punishment in the Schools, Chicago.

Rust, J., and Kinnard, K. (1983). Personality characteristics of the users of corporal punishment. *Journal of School Psychology 21* (2), 91–95.

Sack, W.H.; Angell, R.H.; Kinzie, J.D.; and Rath, B. (1986). The psychiatric effects of massive trauma on Cambodian children: II. The family, the home, and the school. *Journal of the American Academy of Child Psychiatry 25*(3), 370–376.

School shooting spree (1978). *St. Joseph* (Missouri) *Gazette*, October 18.

Silver, S.M., and Iacono, C.U. (1984). Factor-analytic support for DSM III's post-traumatic stress disorder in Vietnam veterans. *Journal of Clinical Psychology 40*, (1), 115–130.

Sofer, B. (1983). Psychologist's attitudes toward corporal punishment. Ph.D. dissertation, Temple University.

Statistical abstract of the United States (1982). Document 003 024050102. Washington, D.C.: Government Printing Office.

Stein, A. (1986). Children of poverty: Crises in New York. *New York Times Sunday Magazine*, June 8.

Straus, M. (1989). Corporal punishment and crime: A theoretical model and some empirical data. Paper presented at the Department of Criminal Justice, Indiana University.

Straus, M.; Gelles, R.; and Steinmetz, S. (1980). *Behind closed doors: Violence in the American family*. Garden City, N.Y.: Anchor Books of Doubleday Press.

Student hits Idabel principal (1979). *Oklahoma Daily Gazette*, February 15.

Terr, L. (1979). Children of Chowchilla: A study of psychic trauma. *Psychoanalytic Study of Children 34*, 547–623.

—— (1983). Chowchilla revisited: The effects of psychic trauma four years after a school bus kidnapping. *American Journal of Psychiatry 140* (12), 1543–1550.

Toby, J. (1983). Violence in school. In M. Torry and N. Morris (eds.), *Crime and justice: An annual review of research*, vol. 4. Chicago: University of Chicago Press.

Walberg, H. (1986). Synthesis of research on teaching. In M. Wittrock (ed.), *Handbook of research on teaching*. 3d ed. New York: Macmillan.

West Virginia Department of Human Services v. Janet Boley and the Fayette County Board of Education (1985). Civil Action 84-C-52, February 21.

Wiehe, V. (1989). Religious influence of parental attitudes toward the use of corporal punishment. Unpublished manuscript, Department of Social Work, University of Kentucky, Lexington.

Zelikoff, W. (1986). Evidence for a new diagnostic construct: Educator-induced post traumatic stress disorder. Unpublished manuscript. Philadelphia: Temple University.

Zvi, A., and Israeli, R. (1973). Effects of bombardment on the manifest anxiety level of children living in kibbutzim. *Journal of Consulting and Clinical Psychology 40*, 187–291.

Index

About the Author

D R. IRWIN HYMAN is a professor of school psychology and director of the National Center for the Study of Corporal Punishment and Alternatives in the Schools at Temple University, where he has been on the faculty since 1968. His career in education and psychology began in 1957 when he taught for four years in a small, rural elementary school. He has received international recognition and numerous awards for child advocacy. He is a prolific writer and the preeminent researcher in the area of corporal punishment and psychological abuse in schools. A frequent speaker at professional conferences and a presenter of workshops on school discipline and parenting, Dr. Hyman has served as a consultant to many schools, state and national legislatures, and professional and citizen groups. He also has been a guest on many radio and television news shows and has been quoted by all of the major newspapers in the United States. He is a licensed psychologist, with extensive experience as a psychotherapist, with a wide range of clients.